CHURCH RENEWAL

A Handbook for Christian Leaders

DAVID KORNFIELD

Exeter, U.K.
THE PATERNOSTER PRESS

BAKER BOOK HOUSE
Grand Rapids, U.S.A.

AUSTRALIA:
Bookhouse Australia Ltd.,
P.O. Box 115, Flemington Markets, NSW 2129

SOUTH AFRICA:
Oxford University Press,
P.O. Box 1141, Cape Town

British Library Cataloguing in Publication Data

Kornfield, David
  Church renewal : a handbook for christian leaders.
  1. Christian church. Renewal
  I. Title
  262.0017

ISBN 0-85364-445-4

Photoset in Great Britain by
Photoprint, Torquay, Devon,
and printed for The Paternoster Press,
Paternoster House, 3 Mount Radford Crescent, Exeter, Devon,
and Baker Book House, P.O. Box 6287,
Grand Rapids, MI. 49516–6287, U.S.A.
by The Guernsey Press Co. Ltd., Guernsey, Channel Islands.

Dedicated to

DEBRA

Without whom this manual would never have been written

'Many daughters have done nobly,
But you excel them all.'
Prov. 31:29

CONTENTS

v

NOTE

This book has been written in a way which we hope will render it useful to churches of many different types. But inevitably the writer's own doctrinal positions and interpretations of Scripture are involved, and there may be some points at which some Christians will register mild disagreement with the author's position. David Kornfield does not insist that you share his distinctives in order to benefit from his book; he does not even insist that by the time you read it these will be his views any more! (Nor should everything in this book be taken to reflect the position of the publishers, World Evangelical Fellowship, since W.E.F. exists to bring together evangelical Christians of the most widely varying views.) We hope that readers will be able to make whatever minor adjustments are necessary to accommodate their own thinking, without losing any of the value of what we are sure they will find a most important and helpful book.

PREFACE

I have written this manual as a member of the World Evangelical Fellowship's Commission on Church Renewal. The Commission's intention — and that of the manual — is to assist churches around the world which are pursuing renewal. Renewal is truly a work of the Holy Spirit. No human effort alone can accomplish it. But experience, study, and observation do yield certain lessons and insights. These we want to share with our brothers and sisters worldwide. My personal experience has been largely in Latin America, but I have sought the counsel of people of all continents in preparing the manual. I have tried to make this manual simple without being simplistic, cross-culturally sensitive, and succinct so as to be easily reproducible and economical.

The manual is a tool to be used rather than a book to be read. After reading the introductory section, the user will normally select the chapter about the area of church life in which he or she feels his church needs renewal. The chapters are not designed to teach *about* renewal. Frankly, they do not make good reading! Rather they are are written to lead a church actually *into* renewal in a given aspect of church life. Thus each chapter is full of reflection questions, exercises, inductive Bible studies and aids for the planning and implementing of renewal.

Once church leaders have worked through a particular chapter together, they will not normally go on to any other chapter until a significant measure of renewal has been realized in that area of church life. Months later, as the Spirit prompts attention to a new area of church experience, the manual can be used again. In this way, it may be years before a church makes full use of the manual. Indeed, any given church may be so sufficiently mature in some areas that she will never need certain chapters.

It is difficult to be free of theological bias. My aim is biblical orthodoxy. I have no wish to endorse any particular denomination or movement rather than another.

Church renewal takes many different forms. And so it is difficult to be cross-culturally relevant in describing church renewal. In fact, culturally tuned forms of expressing Christ's life together are vital to renewal. I have attempted to focus here on functions and principles which can be tailored to any cultural setting. I deeply regret that due to time constraints the Resources sections reflect largely North American or British sources. The scoring system suggested in the diagnostic survey at the end of Chapter 1 may not be acceptable to everyone. Please adapt the manual to make it as usable as possible in your own cultural context!

Church renewal is never a 'finished product.' Rather it is a continual process. It is a seeking, a pilgrimage. I invite you to joint me in the pilgrimage. I would welcome any suggestions for how to refine the manual, especially to make it more fully cross/cultural. If the manual is useful, I anticipate a second edition, refined through the field of testing this one. In that edition we will expand the Resources (with the help of your contributions!) to represent the work of God in all continents. Please write to me, c/o the publishers, if you have insights to suggest. Also, if you would like to interact with Commission members regarding some dimension regarding church renewal, we would be glad to respond or refer you to someone who may be able to serve you.

David E. Kornfield
Commission on Church Renewal
World Evangelical Fellowship

April, 1988

SECTION 1

READ THIS FIRST

This section will help you understand how to use the rest of the book. Read it carefully and refer back to it whenever necessary.

HOW TO USE THIS HANDBOOK

The Reformation's cry was *'Semper reformata, semper reformanda!'* ('Always reformed, always reforming!'). It is a ringing call to be responding always in fresh obedience to Christ. As we do, he will re-form our thoughts, attitudes, actions and structures (Rom. 12:1,2). To be authentically re-formed has consequences. We become agents of re-formation in the context in which we live (II Cor. 5: 16–20).

This handbook is intended to help churches desiring reformation or renewal in any of thirteen areas of church life. **Chapters One and Two** provide some guidelines and principles for pursuing renewal in any area of church life. **The remaining thirteen chapters** each focus on one specific dimension of our church practice. These chapters are organized into three sections:

(1) renewing our relationship with God
(2) renewing our relationship with God's people
(3) renewing our relationship with the world.

This handbook will in some ways be a tool for personal renewal as well as corporate renewal. The two are inseparable. At the same time, the manual's usefulness depends in great measure on your walk with God as you work through it. The manual can in no way substitute for a close personal walk with God. It can, however, help to translate that close personal walk into a close corporate walk.

What brings renewal in our lives? There are two dimensions — the **dream** and the **journey**. The dream comes from God. As we tune our hearts to his, our vision of his desires becomes clearer. The journey is the living out of the dream — putting into practice the vision God gives us. The manual is meant to help clarify our vision, and then offer practical ways of living it out in the context of the local church.

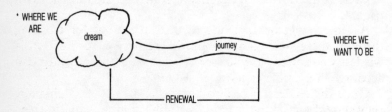

HOW TO DO IT

God's Kingdom is corporate — the journey is meant to be shared. This manual is intended to be used in a group context, initially by the core group of four to six people who are the principal leaders of the church. The leadership group can use the diagnostic survey at the end of this chapter to help identify the area of church life in which to focus renewal first. Once an area is selected, they should next turn to the appropriate chapter in the manual and follow the guidelines there.

(In some cases the leadership group might want church members particularly gifted in the area under study to join

1. Reflecting on your present vision, both personal and corporate. (*Where have you come in your journey thus far?*)
2. Seeking God's vision through inductive Bible study. (*What is the dream God wants you to pursue?*)
3. Clarifying in summary fashion your theological understanding of this aspect of church life. (*What is next? Why is it important? How can it be expressed in your context?*)
4. Developing your action plan for renewing the church's vision and practice in this area (*Identifying needs, desired outcomes, methods of achieving those outcomes, and resources available for your journey*).

them. Or the leadership might choose a study group to go through a chapter, and present their recommendations — as a tentative action plan — to the full leadership group for their consideration.)

Each of the thirteen focal chapters include the four steps on page 4.

A retreat together provides the ideal setting for working through these four steps. You will want to seek the Lord's wisdom continually as you work together. Only the Spirit can accomplish genuine renewal!

Once the leadership group has worked through a chapter, they should not share the *results* with the church body. Rather, they should consider how to involve the congregation in a similar pilgrimage to the one they have just travelled. A shared pilgrimage results in a shared dream. A shared dream motivates people to share the journey.

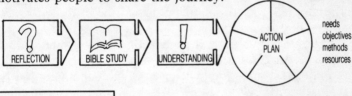

WHERE TO BEGIN

While the Spirit will guide you in which area to focus upon first, some chapters logically precede others. You may want to begin with Chapter One, on a vision for the Kingdom of God. This vision provides the framework for everything God intends his Church to be. Chapter Six, on discipling and pastoral care, might follow as a second foundational chapter. By building up your pastoral resources, you give people a means of encouragement, counsel and accountability while they grow in other areas of church life. Most of us know much more about what our Christian lives should be than we are presently practising. Discipling or pastoral care can help us live out what we have been taught.

In a sense, our relationship with God is our first priority. Attention to it must precede the second priority, of our relationship with one another as his Body. Our walk with him empowers us to live and function as a body. Similarly, our focus on this second priority must preceded the priority of reaching out to the world. Our love and unity are our most powerful witnesses. We do not want to win people to Christ, only to have them come into a sick or lethargic Body.

In practice, however, all three priorities must be pursued together. Congregations which focus determinedly on working everything through in the first two areas, before getting on with outreach, tend to become ingrown and stagnant. They become real candidates for in-fighting, politicking and even division. The energy that should be going to win the world is turned inward on the Body. We must seek the Spirit afresh at each turning point in the life of the church in order to maintain healthy balance and perspective.

A journey is an adventure, seldom smooth and predictable! We hope this manual can provide some landmarks for your pursuit of the dream.

You may feel that we have overlooked some important area of church life. If so, the simple pattern used in these chapters should enable you to design an approach for renewal for that area. The survey on the last page of this chapter intentionally includes a fourteenth area for you to specify if the Spirit guides you to focus on something we have not included here. (*By the way, if you do develop a chapter on an area not included in this book, we would most appreciate your sharing it with us!*)

EXAMINE YOURSELVES . . .

The survey below may help you to assess in a general fashion how well you are doing as a church. You may want to copy the survey to make it reusable. Each person in the leadership group should fill it out individually first, then share his conclusions with the group. Ask the Lord for his wisdom to help you see each area of church life as he sees it.

The principal areas of church life are listed on the left below. After thinking about each area, write in a figure between 0 and 100 in each of the columns on the right.

■ In column 'A' estimate the percentage of regular attenders who take initiative in each of the thirteen areas listed on the left side of the page.

How many adults and youth regularly attend your church? AREAS OF CHURCH LIFE	COLUMN A % of reg. attenders regularly expressing	COLUMN B Quality of church life in this area	TOTAL
1. Vision for the Kingdom of God			
2. Prayer and an active devotional life			
3. Corporate worship			
4. Stewardship			
5. Teaching and study of the Word			
6. Discipling and pastoral care			
7. Christian community life			
8. Ministry and spiritual gifts			
9. Family life			
10. Witness to people around us			
11. Mission involvement (beyond your city)			
12. Social action (involvement in your city)			
13. Victory in spiritual warfare			
14. Other (specify)			

YOU MIGHT LIKE TO END YOUR TIME TOGETHER BY SINGING A HYMN WHICH REMINDS YOU OF THE AIM OF YOUR WORK.

■ In column 'B' assess the quality of that area of church life, assigning a figure on a scale from 0 (= 'non-existent') to 100 (= 'the ideal Spirit-led fruitful consistent expression'). To make the scoring simpler, you might wish to use '10' for 'very weak', '25' for 'weak', '40' for 'somewhat good', '60' for 'good', '80' for 'unusually good' and '90' for 'excellent'.

■ When you have filled out both columns individually, add them together. Then compare your assessment with that of other church leaders. Together, seek to reach a group consensus. By no means, however, should this tool dictate your choice of the area of church life on which to focus. Let the Spirit guide you, using this tool as one means to help you identify where to concentrate in the coming months.

GUIDELINES FOR PURSUING RENEWAL IN ANY AREA OF CHURCH LIFE

A vision without a plan is really just a *wish*! Unrealized visions bring frustration, discouragement, and even sometimes a sense of hopelessness. This chapter will show you how to turn a *vision* into *reality* through Spirit-filled planning.

There are two main sections in this chapter. First we look at the *basic principles* which should guide the planning process. Then, based on these principles, we suggest an *action plan* to bring about renewal, in the form of a step-by-step guide. You can use the action plan for any of the thirteen dimensions of renewal discussed in this manual.

You need to read through this chapter right now, before beginning to tackle the chapters in Section 2, which deal with specific areas such as Worship, Prayer, Stewardship, and so on. BUT you will need to return to this chapter many times in the course of the book. After you have finished reading any of the Section Two chapters, TURN BACK TO THE ACTION PLAN DETAILED HERE — and it will show you how to turn the *vision* you have developed into practical action.

THE KEY PRINCIPLES OF PLANNING

There are seven vital principles which need to underlie all our planning.

A. Worship Worship is offering all that we know of ourselves in response to all that we know of God. Planning begins in worship, flows from it and ends in it! As we come into God's presence through worship, we have access to his thoughts and desires (Rom, 12:1, 2 talks about this). Our attitudes and relationships can be refocused to honour the Lord more fully. Use hymns and Scriptures which you know and can readily call to mind, to enhance the quality of your worship — whether you are worshipping individually or in a group.

B. Confession We *confess* when we realize that we have fallen short, and commit ourselves to a change of life. God's forgiveness (and my brother's, if appropriate) frees me from my past misdeeds so that I can grow. We do not need to be imprisoned by our past — either as individuals or as a church (read Mt. 3:2,3; 4:17). There is a revealing example of corporate church repentance in Rev. 3:19,20.

C. Demonstration The church leaders should seek to demonstrate renewal in their own lives as they lead the church into renewal. Paul said, 'Join in following my example' (Phil. 3:17), not as if he had already become perfect (3:12,13), but rather because he was pressing on in his growth (3:13,14). Church members will be encouraged to grow in a given area of church life as they see their leaders' own pursuit of renewal.

D. Regular training meetings The pastor will need to have regular training meetings (preferably weekly) with the people who bear most responsibility for helping to lead the church into growth. As the pastor equips his leaders, they will minister to the church.

E. Participative learning Where people can be increasingly involved in choosing *what they will learn* and *how they will learn it*, growth will happen much more quickly. This is true at every level of church life! Church leaders and teachers might profit from reading a good book on how adults learn, or perhaps on dynamics. (Several titles are suggested as resources for Chapter 7.)

F. Obedience-oriented discipleship   Our goal is not simply
to learn information, but to see our lives change. We want to
understand the Bible so that we may obey it (James 1:22–25).
Only when we practise what we have learned are we ready to
learn more! Teaching people, *without* insisting on obedience in
action, only reinforces the passive mentality of listening and
not doing. Mt. 7:24–27 shows what Jesus thought about that.

G. Structural renewal   We may preach, teach, study and
commit ourselves to renewal in a given area – and do it all with
the best of intentions; but if there is no *structure* in place to
encourage the expression of that commitment, *it will not last.*
Renewal may require the revision of present church structures, the realigning of priorities, the resetting of programmes
and budget allocations. If we are not ready for this challenge,
we are not ready for renewal. The specific changes which will
be necessary in your case should suggest themselves naturally
in the course of the total renewal process.

So, to sum up the *basic principles*:

Planning for renewal requires seven things:

- A pervading atmosphere of *worship*, to open us up to God's
  thoughts and desires:
- A willingness to confess past mistakes and leave them
  behind us;
- A commitment by the leaders to lead by personal example;
- A system of regular, delegated training — the pastor to the
  leaders, the leaders to the people;
- A scheme of learning which allows people to participate in
  their own learning process;
- An emphasis on practical obedience in action as the result of
  the teaching;
- A readiness to face the challenge of changing our structures.

With this background, let us now look at a six step
planning process for renewal . . .

THE SIX-STEP PLANNING PROCESS

Here are the six steps involved in planning towards renewal.

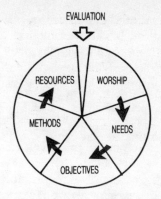

A. **Worship**........................	(getting in step with God).
B. **Assessing the needs**	(explaining *why* we want to do something)
C. **Naming our objectives**.....	(explaining *what* we want to do).
D. **Selecting our methods**.....	(explaining *how* we will try to do it).
E. **Finding the resources**	(explaining *with whom* and *with what* we will do it).
F. **Evaluating our progress** ...	(checking whether the plan can be improved).

Let's have a look at each of them . . .

A. Worship

As we shall see in Chapter 4, *worship* is to be the environment in which Christians live. The planning process needs to begin with worship. Thereby we can align ourselves with our Lord, both individually and as a group, submitting our agenda to him. In planning something such as a six-month church focus on one area of renewal, it might be appropriate to spend an hour in worship first. The worship time might include:

1. 'Songs of ascent' (by which I mean joyful songs to gather us together)

2. Confession (reflecting and cleansing, allowing the Spirit to speak and work freely in us)
3. A short devotional or homily looking at our immediate context and relating our situation to what we know of the greatness of God.
4. Adoration (songs and prayers of thanksgiving)
5. The Lord's Supper (affirming our unity with Christ and with each other)
6. Intercession (asking for the Spirit's infilling, Christ's mind, and Christ's continued presence throughout the planning process)
7. Listening to God (asking him to speak to us, having a time of silence, and then sharing what we feel he may want us to hear)
8. A hug or greeting of peace (blessing one another, thus making an encouraging transition to the next stage of the planning work)

This should be a good way to start planning. But at many points in the rest of the planning process it will be appropriate to stop and pray again, seeking the Lord's wisdom and guidance.

PUTTING IT TO WORK
Begin the planning process by spending time in worship. Turn to the resource section (page 286) for helpful ideas. After sensing that you have truly come into the King's presence, you could ask him to give you insight into key elements of your plan even while you are in prayer.

B. Assessing the Needs

In the church there are at least three types of needs:

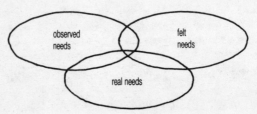

■ **Observed needs** are what we observe the church to need.
■ **Felt needs** are what the church members feel they need.
■ **Real needs** are what God knows the Church needs!

We want to recognize and respond to real needs, which will change as the church changes. Thus we walk in continual dependence on God for perception and wisdom. A particular plan may serve well for a while, but need to be modified or replaced as the situation changes. Our faith rests not on human plans, but on God's power to renew us.

But we need to remember that people's *felt needs* are what motivate them. Lasting motivation is *internal* motivation — which can be aroused through raising a person's consciousness of his situation, and of the alternatives available to him. Reflecting on the gap between *our present situation* and *what God intends for us* can provide the motivation for change.

Most people are motivated by moderate challenges — not small or large ones. A small challenge is dismissed as unimportant. A large challenge may be dismissed as impossible.

---

1. **Real needs** give us God's agenda. You should try to list these in the context of worship and the experience of God's presence. Commonly the list will not be long, since God's Spirit tends to give us only what we can handle!

2. **Observed needs** are what we as church leaders believe the church members need. You should list these in the context of the *real needs* you have identified. The observed needs may spell out more specifically the various dimensions of each of the real needs.

3. **Felt needs** are the starting point for motivating people. Only church members themselves can identify their felt needs. So it is good to involve them in some way, to see how their perspective corresponds to yours. Do the church members confirm the focus that the leaders feel God is giving them? A key to whether planning will be resisted or be fruitful is your ability to involve in the planning process *the people who will be most affected by the plan.*

The challenge needs to be in proportion to the means the people have of reaching it.

However, the resources we have available include the Holy Spirit! This means that we can actually challenge people with God's mind to reach for what would normally seem much too great a challenge. Once again we are dependent on God. It is *his* mind and an awareness of *his* resources that will free us from our present situation, to pursue renewal effectively.

Let us summarize and make all of this practical. Once we have clearly grasped the needs of the church — and not until then! — we can go on to thinking about objectives for action.

PUTTING IT TO WORK

* The general need you want to address was already clear in your mind when you chose the chapter you have just been working on! Turn to the resource section (page 201) and you will find one possible way of expressing it. Modify it if you would like to. Then list the key ways in which this need is evident in your church: 'Our church needs to . . . as indicated by: . . .' Working individually, each member of the group should make a list of three of the main *indicators* of the need, as he sees it.

* Still working individually, you should each put your three indicators into an order of priority, numbering them from one to three to indicate which are the most urgent areas on which the church should be focusing.

* As a group, write down together your definition of the basic need which you are addressing. Make sure you add the words 'as indicated by:'. Then each member of the group should share what in his opinion is the main indicator of this need. When you have everyone's contribution, it will give you an idea of the areas where your plan for renewal will have to be focused. If you end up with a long list, you might want to prioritize it too, and indicate the three main areas on which you want to focus.

C. Naming our Objectives

Our ultimate goal is to honour the Lord in the way we live out the many dimensions of church life (and there are more than the thirteen discussed in this manual!). As we focus on any one area, it is useful to specify concrete *objectives* based on the *needs* we have already identified. Good objectives have four key characteristics.

1. **Objectives should state clearly how the church members should change**. We are not aiming at the growth of a pastor or a programme. The key people in whom growth and change must happen are the church members. And so a well-written objective will begin with words such as '*The church members will . . .*'

2. **Objectives should be measurable**. A well-written objective clarifies how we can measure when the fulfilment has been reached. This involves stating clearly (a) the degree of growth expected, and (b) the time allotted to it.

We are aiming to see *internal* change — attitudes, know-ledge, beliefs — expressed externally. We do not want behavioural change without inner renewal. That would be simply conformism, rather than conviction and growth. But any attempt to measure internal motivations, attitudes and values will be very frustrating unless it is based on our observation of external actions. So the objective must specify *observable behaviour* as the indicator of whether the need has been met.

3. **Objectives should be realistic**. A good objective takes into account what the people are really like. It does not expect magic results. What obstacles need to be overcome in achieving your objective? Take these obstacles into account and work at making your objectives realistic. At the same time, take into account the reality of God, and set objectives that stretch your faith a bit — do not settle for something that could be achieved without him!

4. **Objectives correspond to the needs you have already identified**. A well-written objective is practically just the *need* rewritten in a positive form. The need alerts us to the *lack* of something; the objective tells us *what will fill that lack*. For example, one need might be described like this: 'The church

members lack committed Christian community life in the following areas:' (This would be followed by a list of half a dozen indicators of the church's present situation.) Then the objective might read: 'Over the next twelve months, a majority of church members will demonstrate committed Christian community life in the following areas . . .' And this might be followed by half a dozen positive indicators of Christian community life. If the need you are addressing is clear, you will be able to identify your desired objective. If you find you are having difficulty in writing your objective, you may need to clarify further the need you are addressing.

PUTTING IT TO WORK
* To arrive at your general objective, simply state the *need* as a *goal*. An example of how to do this appears in the resource section (page 202) under the heading 'TURNING NEEDS INTO OBJECTIVES'. Once again, make sure you add the phrase 'as indicated by:'. Each person should then try on his own to write down realistic and measurable *indicators* which will show that you have accomplished this objective. Remember that 'measurable indicators' normally require some specific numbers to be stated — including the amount of time you think it should take to accomplish that indicator. (The indicators you choose could bear some relationship to the chief indicators of *need*, on which you have just been working.)
* Still working on your own, put the indicators into an order of importance, numbering the most vital as Number One.
* Get back together as a group. Write down together the *general objective* and include the phrase 'as indicated by:'. Then ask each person to share what he feels could be a main indicator of accomplishing this objective. Once everything that seems important is listed, put the list into an order of importance and urgency once again. Identify the main two or three areas on which you want to focus. You may find that most of the other areas on your list fall broadly under the heading of one of these main areas.

Remember that all change — even change which is welcomed — brings stress! Too many changes too quickly will make people feel insecure and threatened by the loss of too many familiar landmarks. It is important to be extremely sensitive to the feelings of people involved in the change process, and to stay on the look-out for any signals of distress. We may be impatient to see the changes completed, but we have to remember that God is rarely in as much of a hurry as we are! On the other hand, it is important not to be held back by the undue caution of a few diehards. Lyle Schaller's book The Change Agent *(for details see page 21) contains a lot of good advice about how to read the situation correctly and advance wisely. Biblical material giving some clues about how to defuse possible problems and accommodate change successfully can be found in Acts 15, the story of the Council of Jerusalem.*

D. Selecting our Methods

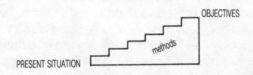

Methods are the activities necessary for accomplishing your objectives. It may help to visualize them as the successive steps in a stairway from one floor (our present situation) to another floor (the objective, where we would like to be). The following guidelines may be helpful in discovering effective methods.

1. **List the methods**. Begin by listing all the possible methods you can think of which could help you accomplish the objective. All suggestions are welcome; none of them should be judged good or bad at this stage, no matter how crazy it may sound!

2. **Work out your priorities**. Now is the time to identify those methods which you feel will *most effectively* help you reach your target. Look for 'developmental' methods, which will help the church members mature. The characteristics of developmental methods include:

■ That they are likely to be accepted and adopted by the people. They are easily reproduced, so that everyone will be able to use them — not just the highly skilled people!

■ That they depend on resources found within the church community, and do not require dependence on outside help.

■ That they do not replace people, but rather make them more effective. The time of church members is one of the church's greatest resources. Good methods do not create 'church unemployment'!

■ That they are simple and modest enough to be methods for reaching a greater end, rather than becoming ends in themselves.

■ That they help maximize the resources, knowledge and abilities available to the church community.

3. **Put your chosen methods in order**. Once you have worked out your priorities and identified the methods you want to employ, they need to be put in sequence much like the steps in a staircase. Which comes first? Which second? And so on.

4. **Choose a coordinator for each activity involved**. One specific individual needs to bear responsibility for each of the activities you will be undertaking. In some cases it will help if

We may enter the planning process with fairly definite ideas about the time some activities should take. But we need to be sensitive to the possibility that what God really wants to do will not take nearly as long . . . or, on the other hand, may take a good deal more time! Indeed, as we implement the plan, we are likely to find that we will need to adjust our timetable at least once!

At the end of this chapter are two planning charts that may help the church leaders with all these steps. If you decide to use them, make copies for everyone in the leadership group, and for the coordinators of the specific activities.

PUTTING IT TO WORK

★ Decide together whether your *main indicators* are so different that they should really each be treated as *objectives* with a separate plan for each. If they are quite similar, you can work on one joint plan. If they are sufficiently different, you may want to break into sub-groups to produce an initial listing of methods for accomplishing each one.

★ For each objective,

   a. List all the possible methods you can imagine. At this initial point, *do not pass judgement* on any method suggested. Let your imagination flow! When you are ready for some further input on possible methods, check the action steps suggested in the resource section (page 203) and incorporate any ideas that seem helpful.

   b. Once you have listed everything you can think of, select those methods which you think will most effectively accomplish the objective.

   c. Finally, put your selected methods in chronological order, if any need to be tackled before others. Once you have done this, estimate the total time it may take to accomplish the objective. Using a copy of the chart on page 24 might be helpful at this point.

★ If you have been working in sub-groups on several plans, share them together to see how they might fit in with each other. Do not get bogged down in details. Have someone note which items will need further attention. But these plans are really only a first draft; someone can be asked to refine them, and present an amended version to the group at a later date.

★ Earlier you estimated how much time it would take to accomplish the general objective. Now that you have done some work on spelling out the specific methods to be used, you may need to modify this time estimate somewhat.

the coordinator has several assistants; but nonetheless it should always be clear who is responsible. As the Haitians say, 'The goat with many masters dies in the sun.' These coordinators will be accountable to whoever is overseeing the entire renewal venture. They should meet with the overall supervisor as often as they need to.

5. **Establish a timetable and name dates**. Until dates and places for the activities are defined, your project is nothing more than a dream. The timetable needs to include not only the time when a given event will take place, but also the amount of preparation time allotted beforehand and the follow-up needed afterwards (if this particular activity requires follow-up). In many activities, the visible programme is only about ten percent of the total work needed to bring it about. Establishing a timetable will help you bring reality to bear on your ambitions!

E. Finding the Resources

Our most important resource is the Holy Spirit! But earthly resources available include PEOPLE, TIME, MONEY, FACILITIES, and the church community's POSSESSIONS. The second planning chart at the end of this chapter is designed to help in planning the resources needed for each method.

Keep in mind also that there are many types of instructional resources: print (reading materials), audiovisuals (films, television, cassettes, radio, videotapes, slides, posters), experts, demonstrations (living case studies or examples), information centres (seminaries, national associations, libraries, computer information bases). There is much more available in some countries than in others, of course. But there is usually more help available to us than we at first realise — whatever country we are in!

Below are listed some resources in the general area of management and planning.

1. Books on adult education and group dynamics (see the resource section at the end of Chapter Seven)

2. Blanchard, Kenneth; and Johnson, Spencer; *The One Minute*

Manager, Berkley Books, New York, NY 10016, USA, 1981, 106 pages. Available in Great Britain from Wyvern Business Library, 3 Short Rd., Stretham, Ely, Cambs., CB6 3NE. Very well written in story form, simple, possibly the best book for its size on managing people effectively. How to give yourself and others 'the gift' of getting greater results in less time. Key concepts are one minute goals, one minute praisings and one minute reprimands; also, to encourage people, speak the truth, laugh, work and enjoy!

3. Engstrom, Ted W.; and Dayton, Edward R.; *The Christian Leader's 60-Second Management Guide*, Word Book Publ., Waco, Texas, 1984, 143 pages. Practical Christian insights on 30 everyday management issues. (Books by Engstrom and Dayton are available in Britain through MARC Europe, Cosmos House, 6 Homesdale Rd., Bromley, Kent BR2 9EX.)

4. *Evaluation Sourcebook for Private and Voluntary Organizations*, published by 'Approaches to Evaluation', ACVAFS, 200 Park Avenue South, New York, NY 10003, USA, 274 pages. It discusses 12 key questions for planning effective evaluation. Some of them are: Why evaluate? Who wants it? For what decisions? What are the key issues? What specific questions should we ask? What methods do we use? Who participates? Similar aids are available in Great Britain through the National Council for Voluntary Organizations, 26 Bedford Square, London WC1, and National Youth Bureau, 17–23 Albion St., Leicester LE1 6GD. World Action Ministries, 205 Lichfield Rd., Four Oaks, Sutton Coldfield, B74 2XB, offers a ministry of administration designed to organise or assist in the running of events or societies.

5. Schaller, Lyle; *The Change Agent (The Strategy of Innovative Leadership)*, Abingdon Press, Nashville, TN, 1972, 207 pages. Easy to read; a classic in the field of change management. Chapters include: How to Cut Your Own Throat, The Nature of Change, The Process of Planned Change, Questions for the Change Agent, The Use of Power and Social Change, Anticipating and Managing Conflict, and Organizational Change. Footnotes and Index.

6. World Relief (International headquarters at PO Box WRC, Wheaton, IL 60189, USA; phone: 312/665–0235) and World Vision (International headquarters at 919 W. Huntington Drive, Monrovia, CA 91016, USA; phone: 818?357–7979) have excellent practical training courses and manuals on project planning.

While these focus on community development, the principles of community development can well be applied to church development. This training is available in many countries around the world. (In Britain, World Vision's address is Dychurch House, 8 Abington St., Northampton NN1 2AJ.)

PUTTING IT TO WORK

* Use a copy of the chart on page 23 to help you identify the resources needed for each *objective* and *set of methods* you have identified above. If you were using sub-groups earlier, you could go into them again at this point. Consider as resources key people, books, programmes, and model churches (or movements) that are examples of what you are aiming at.

* If you work in sub-groups, share your results. Again give one another feedback and make sure the plans you have evolved do not over-use the same resources!

* Mark down any of the resources listed in the resource section (pages 199–295) which seem to you to be possible sources of help.

* Finally, end the whole process in worship. Prayers which you may find useful are suggested in the resource section (page 286).

FINALLY, EVALUATE YOUR RESULTS

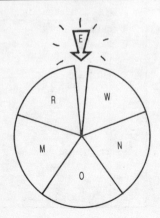

RESOURCE PLANNING SHEET

OBJECTIVE:

METHODS	RESOURCES				
	People	Money	Time	Facilities	Materials
1.					
2.					
3.					
4.					
5.					
6.					

The above plan was prepared by: ....   The person responsible for its over-all implementation: ....

MAKING SURE YOU ACT AS YOU HAVE PLANNED

MAJOR OBJECTIVE (Specify):

ACTIVITIES OR METHODS	PERSON RESPONSIBLE	SCHEDULE		Date Completed

1. If greater detail is needed than the space here permits, use a separate page.
2. The columns under 'Schedule' can correspond to days, weeks or months according to the duration of the activities. The schedule gives the *anticipated* time it will take to accomplish an activity. The last column 'Date Completed' gives the *actual* time of completion.

Evaluation can happen at several levels. Both church leaders *and* church members should assess progress from time to time. It helps to have established agreed indicators *en route* to the objective, as evidence that needs are being met.

The degree of cooperation and unity among the people should also be assessed periodically. You can do this by working out how many people you would like to see involved in a certain activity by a given date, and how much they should be contributing to the overall plan.

Evaluation cannot be done unless we know two things. First, the precise situation at the time the programme was begun; and second, the measurable objectives which the programme is aiming to reach. And do not simply focus on long-range goals; include short-term goals in your evaluation, too, for the encouragement of your members! People derive a great deal of satisfaction from realizing immediate goals!

(If ever you plan to carry out a rigorous evaluation of your church, the *Evaluation Sourcebook* mentioned in the resources listed above is an excellent tool — or in Britain, the Bible Society's course *Is Your Church Worth Joining?*.)

SECTION 2

THIRTEEN DIMENSIONS
OF RENEWAL

To understand how to use this section, first read
SECTION 1 (pp. 1–25)

1

RENEWING OUR VISION
FOR THE KINGDOM OF GOD

McDonald's fast food restaurant chain did not exist before 1955. But when Ray Kroc began to build his empire from small beginnings in Chicago, it suddenly started to grow like a gigantic mushroom. By 1981 there were 6,739 outlets in America, and McDonald's was the fiftieth largest retailing company in the USA.

Today it is difficult to find a major city anywhere in the world where McDonald's have not set up a branch. The familiar red-and-yellow striped awnings are everywhere . . . Paris, Rome, Singapore, Mexico, Bangkok. In its first thirty years of existence, McDonald's has conquered the world.

The same is true of Coca-Cola. It is hard to find a sport on the earth's surface where Coca-Cola cannot be bought. (In countries where it is unavailable — such as Poland — it is only because its rival Pepsi-Cola has conquered the market!) Observers describe the aggressive conquering techniques of Coca-Cola chiefs as 'Coca-Colanisation'. Country after country has succumbed to the massive, ambitious, forward-looking campaigns of the Coca-Cola corporation. The dynamism and dedication of their men has even been satirized in a popular movie, *The Coca-Cola Kid*.

What is it that has enabled Coca-Cola to sell over six billion dollars' worth of its products annually? How is it that Mexicans, for example, consume so much of the drink that on average every member of the population of Mexico drinks five bottles a week? The only answer is that the promoters of Coca-Cola are dedicated to their task of winning the world. They have a compelling vision which they are determined not to compromise.

Often firms like these have begun with very few resources and very limited staff. The secret of their success has been their ability to fire the imagination, create a sense of dedication and send their people into effective, meaningful action. Avis Rent-a-Car was a struggling organisation until they decided to set themselves a simple objective.

> We want to become the fastest growing company, with the highest profit margin, in the business of renting and leasing vehicles without drivers.

Ray Ortlund describes what happened next:

> They put it up everywhere — in all the offices, on all the desks. Immediately it became obvious that they'd have to get rid of some branches of the company that didn't fit: 'We're going to get rid of everything that doesn't fulfil this. We're going to put blinders on our eyes to everything else.' (Ray Ortlund, *Lord, Make My Life a Miracle*, Gospel Light)

The result was enormous success. Their single-minded dedication, their willingness to do practically anything to see their cause established, brought immediately results.

In telling the story, Ray Ortlund comments, 'I have a strong hunch that less than one per cent of all Christians have ever sat down with pencil and paper and said, "I'm going to define my life's objective!"' (Ortlund, op. cit.) We tend not to think in such a purposeful, dynamic way . . .

Yet what is our cause? Unless we Christians have a cause that is just as compelling, and much more worthwhile than simply selling hamburgers or soft drinks, *we might as well give up*. Douglas Hurd, a Communist leader who became a Christian, suggests that we may have some things to learn from the Communists too. They seem to be better than most Christians at instilling dedication and developing leadership. In his book *Dedication and Leadership*, Hyde says that if someone has grown up in Christian circles he will know that Christianity, like Communism, demands the whole man and that Christians were intended, and are expected, to change the world. That they, too, should be active; that membership of a church is not like membership of a club. That in theory, at least, the Christian should be relating his Christianity to his whole life and to the whole world about him, all the time, everywhere. Yet in practice, although Christianity has taught him that total dedication is something to be admired and something to which one should aspire in one's own life, a Communist may be the first totally dedicated person he has met. Or, if that is putting it too harshly, *the Communist may be the first dedicated person he has met who is not wrapped up in his own salvation but is devoting himself to the transformation of society and to changing the world* (University of Notre Dame Press, Notre Dame, IND, USA, 1966: 37).

Do we as Christians have a cause in this world? Or are we too wrapped up in our pursuit of personal peace, prosperity and happiness? Is religion just the 'opiate of the people'? Lost somewhere in the shuffle of the last 2000 years, conveniently hidden under the dust of church history volumes and martyrs' lives, carefully exegeted away so as not to make us uncomfortable, *there is such a cause*! Listen to the piercing cry of the King's herald ringing through the Judean wilderness) Mt. 3: 1–3). Listen to the message the King proclaimed from the beginning of His earthly ministry (Mt. 4: 17,23; Lk. 4: 42,43). Listen to Christ's prayer (Mt. 6: 9,10) and the heart of the Sermon on the Mount (Mt. 6: 33).

Christ's cause is greater far than that of the Communists, worth living for, worth dying for — worth radically changing our lives for! In the course of this chapter, we will examine that cause, with the prayer that Christ's vision will become our vision as well.

What lies ahead in this chapter? The chapter has four sections, designed for church leaders to work through together in ten to twelve hours. A retreat setting would be ideal. If this seems too large a time commitment, take into account that in this time you are: a) opening your lives to a life-changing

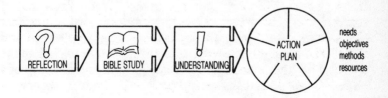

understanding and commitment to the Kingdom of God;
b) deepening team relationships among yourselves as leaders;
c) laying foundations for the church's future; and, d) outlining
the church's specific course for the next four to twelve
months. The four sections, with the approximate time each
might require, follow below.

---

1. Reflecting on your **personal and corporate vision** (*1 hour*).
2. Looking at Christ's vision for the Kingdom of God through an **inductive Bible study** (*3 hours*).
3. Clarifying in summary fashion your understanding of the Kingdom of God (the **what, why and how** of the Kingdom of God) (*1½ hours*).
4. Developing your *action plan* for renewing the church's vision and practice of the Kingdom of God.
   A. Identifying **your church's needs** in this area (*1 hour*).
   B. Identifying **desired objectives** for the coming months (*1 hour*).
   C. Identifying **methods** for reaching those objectives (*2 hours*).
   D. Identifying **resources** for helping accomplish those objectives (*1 hour*).

Throughout the above process you will need to enter regularly
into the Lord's presence in prayer and worship so that his
Spirit can freely teach you. No structure, no human teacher,
no manual will adequately communicate the truths of God
apart from the Spirit's work! In fact before going any further,
please stop and spend some time in prayer lifting all of this to
the Lord. Appropriate prayers could include:

* confession of your need for him to teach you in this area as
  only he can do.
* praise for all he is going to do in and through you in the
  coming weeks and months.

* intercession for the church members, that the Lord will be preparing their hearts for where he wants to lead them in the coming months.
* prayer for his wisdom to modify all that follows in this chapter to suit your context well.

| 1 REFLECTION ON YOUR PERSONAL |
| AND CORPORATE VISION |

Reflect on your Church's vision as you answer the questions below. Do this individually first, writing your responses in a notebook. Later you will discuss some responses as a group. Continue to use your notebook to keep track of all you are learning about the Kingdom of God.

A. Reflecting on your vision.
   ■ How *clearly* do you think most members of the church could express the church's vision? (*Very clearly, quite, somewhat, poorly, hardly at all*).
   ■ How *convincingly* could most members of the church express the church's vision? 'Convincingly' means motivating oneself and others to give sacrificially of their time, money, energy and gifts with an understanding of the reasons why. Could they do this *very convincingly, quite convincingly, somewhat convincingly, poorly,* or *hardly at all*?
   ■ What is your vision for your church? Summarize it in one or two paragraphs.
   ■ What is your vision for the Kingdom of God? Summarize it in one or two paragraphs.
   ■ How similar or different are your answers to the above two questions? What insights come to you in comparing them?

B. *What* do you understand the Kingdom of God to be? Try defining the concept 'Kingdom of God' in twenty-five words or less.

C. *Why* is the Kingdom of God important? List at least three reasons why pursuit of the King and his kingdom could be more important to you than anything else in life.

D. *How* is the Kingdom of God experienced in this present age? List three methods by which the Kingdom of God is being or could be) visibly expressed in and around you.

E. As a group discuss your answers to the questions in section A above before going on together to the inductive study below. By comparing your answers as leaders you will get further insight into how clearly and how convincingly your members may be able to present the church's vision.

> **2. INDUCTIVE BIBLE STUDY ON THE KINGDOM OF GOD**

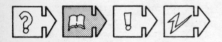

The group leader should now guide the group in inductive Bible study which you will find in the Resource section (turn to page 220). Rather than talking a lot, he will seek to help others in expressing their insights. His main task is repeatedly to ask the following question: *'What does this passage tell us about the Kingdom of God?'* The leader's task is simple (though it may not be easy!). Advance study will help him in asking the group pertinent questions to draw out the essence of the passages. Everyone should take notes in his workbook on anything he may want to remember or review later. This kind of inductive study works well in groups ranging from four to twenty or even twenty-five. The Bible study outline will require two sessions of approximately one and a half hours apiece. The leader may want to choose certain passages in advance that he might skip if there is insufficient time. Similarly, he may choose to substitute other passages.

While everyone will be responding to the same general question underlined above, each person will also have a secondary question to keep in mind. Each person should be assigned to take notes to contribute later to a discussion of one of these three questions:

1. *What* is the Kingdom of God?
2. *Why* is the Kingdom of God so important?
3. *How* is the Kingdom of God expressed in the here and now? (If you have a large group, ask most of the people to focus on this area.)

NOW TURN TO THE BIBLE STUDY ON PAGE 220.

Two limited views of the Kingdom of God need to be briefly mentioned in an introductory fashion. Both of these views have hindered a biblical understanding of the Kingdom of God. If you hold either of them, please ask God for an open mind as you approach the biblical reflection section below. The conservative bias has been a tendency to project the Kingdom of God as something that will *only* be made present when Christ returns at some time *in the future*. The liberal bias has been a humanistic tendency toward believing that we Christians are 'bringing in the Kingdom' *in the present* and therefore have no need to look to Christ's return for the Kingdom to become fully present.

The biblical perspective is surely that the Kingdom of God is past, present *and* future. Evangelicals have long held that our salvation has all three time dimensions. We have been saved (II Tim. 1:9); we are being saved (I Pet. 3:21); we will be saved (Rom. 5:9). Similarly, the Kingdom of God has come, it is in the process of coming and it will fully come only when Christ returns. As you work on your definitions, keep this in mind. Since we have little or no responsibility regarding its future culmination, and much responsibility for its present expression, *you might want to focus your thinking in this area.*

---
3. DESCRIPTION OF WHAT THE
KINGDOM OF GOD LOOKS LIKE

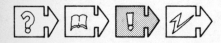

A. Clarifying your perspective on the Kingdom of God

Divide into your three sub-groups regarding the what, why and how of the Kingdom of God. Take about fifteen minutes to develop a short presentation for the larger group. The presentation should both stimulate the larger group to consider your question further and present the sub-group's thinking. The following group process guidelines may be helpful:

1. **What** is the Kingdom of God? (Group one)
   a. Share your definitions or thoughts and come to agreement on a single definition.
   b. Write your definition where everyone can see it. In presenting this, you might ask the larger group to go back to their individual definitions written at the beginning of the study. They could compare and contrast them with your work. Encourage the larger group to note whether anything critical has been left out of your definition.
   c. As a large group reach consensus on a working definition. This is not set in concrete. We are all constantly learning. It is simply the group's working definition to use until the Spirit shows them something further.
2. **Why** is the Kingdom of God important? (Group two)
   a. Seek to come up with a few truly compelling reasons. Our reasons should surpass those of the Communists or any other ideology.
   b. In presenting this, you might ask the large group for its ideas and list them on a flip chart sheet or blackboard. Affirm each idea before adding any of your ideas that the larger group overlooked.
3. **How** is the Kingdom of God expressed now? (Group three)
   a. As a group develop two lists: 1) the church's strengths

in expressing and extending the Kingdom of God; and,
2) the church's weaknesses in expressing and extending
the Kingdom of God.
  b. In presenting this to the larger group, you might ask for
  their ideas as you present each list. Using a separate flip
  chart sheet for each list, once you have a number of
  ideas from the large group, add from the list your sub-
  group developed.

NOTES FOR THE GROUP LEADER: While everyone
should be taking his own notes, you might assign one
person to take formal notes of the three groups'
presentations. These can later be typed up and distributed to all the participants. This will be a working
theology of the Kingdom of God. It forms the biblical
base for the action plan that will be developed by the end
of this chapter. Read the comments below regarding the
what, why and how of the Kingdom ahead of time. Insert
them at appropriate moments in the group's discussion,
but not until the group has first done some significant
thinking on each question for itself.

B. Some further thoughts on the what, why and how of the Kingdom of God

1. **What** is the Kingdom of God? A possible working
definition might include the following elements: The
Kingdom of God is the ever-expanding and redemptive
sphere in which Christ's government is recognized, obeyed
and enjoyed. (*If the group's definition is fairly short and
catchy, people will remember it more easily. You may want to
have the group recall it every so often in the ongoing discussion
until they have it down well.*)
2. **Why** is the Kingdom of God important?
  a. It frees us *from* temporal and eternal bondage. Bondage
  to selfishness, alienation, sin, Satan and death has been
  overcome (cf. Col. 1:13)!
  b. It frees us *to* live as we were created to live — in right
  relationship with God, with ourselves, with God's
  people, with the world and with his creation.

   c. The biblical concept of Lordship is inherent in the Kingdom of God. However, we sometimes water down 'Lordship'. The term Kingdom of God can help restore its original intent. We may view Lordship as simply 1) spiritual, 2) private (between God and me) and 3) individual. The Kingdom of God helps restore 1) a holistic understanding (embracing all of life), 2) an understanding of the Christian life as submitted and accountable, and, 3) a corporate identity.

3. **How** is the Kingdom of God to be expressed in the here and now?

   a. The Kingdom of God can be visualized in ever larger circles. It begins in the inner circle of my life and flows out consecutively through my family, my core group at church, my church as a whole, my job, my neighbourhood and society. His reign makes itself visible starting from the inner circle and working out. Individually bringing our heart, our kind, our emotions and our body under Christ's rule is the starting point of the Kingdom of God. As his power and life manifest themselves in our individual lives, we can extend his Kingdom to the next sphere over which we have the most responsibility and influence our family. As our family comes to model in miniature the worship, fellowship and outreach of the church, we are in a good position to see God's Kingdom extended into and through the core group of Christians with whom we experience Christ's life. As these brothers and sisters come to be an effective extended family, a support group and a ministry group, we together can contribute toward seeing our church as a whole better express and extend the Kingdom of God. As the church expresses Christian community, God's power and life, we have the base from which to penetrate meaningfully other spheres of our lives: our jobs, neighbourhoods and society. In actuality, these spheres overlap and inter-relate. Growth in any sphere will commonly produce growth in other spheres. A block in any given sphere, if unremoved, will hinder growth in other spheres. The inner spheres are, however, foundational to the outer spheres. In terms of prioritizing our energy, we should move from the inside, out.

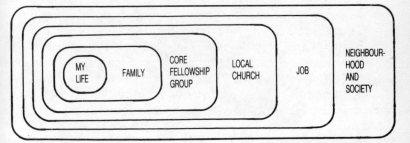

b. The loving government of the Kingdom of God becomes practical and real through a spiritual director, discipler, or pastoral leader. Too few Christians today have someone who is committed to encourage, guide and hold them accountable in living a Kingdom life. All of us have good intentions that are never accomplished for lack of support and guidance. The gap between our ideals and our reality can be greatly diminished through a spiritual mentor (Chapter 6 develops this further).

c. While the Kingdom of God will not be revealed in its fulness until Christ returns, the church is to be the central corporate expression of his Kingdom in this age. The Kingdom is broader than the church, but the church is a foretaste of his coming Kingdom, a present expression of what that Kingdom will be like. Each of the remaining twelve emphases in this manual is to enable the church to demonstrate visibly the Kingdom of God for everyone to see.

> **NOW IT IS TIME TO DEVELOP YOUR *ACTION PLAN*. TURN BACK TO PAGE 9 FOR INSTRUCTIONS ON HOW TO DO SO. YOU WILL ALSO FIND OUT HOW TO USE THE RESOURCE MATERIAL IN SECTION 3.**

2

RENEWING OUR PRAYER
AND DEVOTIONAL LIFE

'A prayerless ministry is the undertaker for all God's truth and
for God's Church. He may have the most costly casket and the
most beautiful flowers, but it is a funeral, notwithstanding the
charmful array.' (E.M. Bounds, *Power Through Prayer*,
1962:74).

What would your church notice if the gift of prayer were
withdrawn from the world? What kind of change might
it make? Significant, but not overwhelming? Devastating?
Prayerless ministry is powerless ministry. What kind of power
is evident in your church? What kind of praying is evident?

Prayer has never been an easy exercise, and great Christians
of the past have struggled with the temptation to neglect it.
Many years ago, one wise Christian wrote these words:

Spiritual work is taxing work, and men are loath to do it.
Praying, true praying, costs an outlay of serious attention and
of time, which flesh and blood do not relish. Few persons are
made of such strong fibre that they will make a costly outlay
when surface work will pass as well in the market. We can
habituate ourselves to our beggarly praying until it looks well
to us, at least it keeps up a decent form and quiets conscience
— the deadliest of opiates! We can slight our praying, and not
realize the peril till the foundations are gone. Hurried
devotions make weak faith, feeble convictions, questionable
piety. To be little with God is to be little for God. To cut short
the praying makes the whole religious character short, scrimp,
niggardly, and slovenly (*Ibid*, p.k 81).

In contrast to stunted spiritual life stand the great movements
of revival and renewal. Renewed churches are praying

churches. Do just a few faithful pray? or just the pastor(s)? Hardly! In Korea the largest and the fastest growing churches are those that have mobilized in prayer. People pray — from 4 a.m. to 7 a.m. — hundreds gathering from a single church — every day! How can that kind of church help but grow?

Our relationship with God can be assessed by the quality of our prayer life — be it at the individual level or the corporate level. This chapter focuses on strengthening a church's corporate communication with God. As in every area of renewal there is a reciprocal relationship between individual renewal and corporate renewal. While the focus here is not the individual's prayer life, concentrating on corporate prayer renewal will surely change our individual prayer lives. And, as our individual prayer lives are strengthened, our corporate prayer life will also be stronger!

Prayer encompasses several areas that are dealt with in depth in other chapters. Worship, including confession and thanksgiving, is covered in chapter three. Spiritual warfare is covered in chapter thirteen. Thus this chapter will focus specifically on our intercessor prayer life and hearing from God, even though these areas of prayer cannot truly be divorced from the others.

What lies ahead in this chapter? The chapter has four sections, designed for church leaders to work through together in ten to twelve hours. A retreat setting would be ideal. If this seems too large a time commitment, take into account that in this time you are: a) opening your lives to a life-changing understanding and commitment to corporate prayer; b) deepening team relationships among yourselves as leaders; c) laying foundations for the church's future; and, d) outlining the church's specific course for the next four to twelve months. The four sections, with the approximate time each might require, follow below.

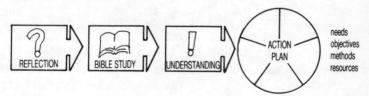

1. Reflecting on the **corporate prayer life of your church** (*1 hour*).
2. Looking at God's vision for His people's prayer life through an **inductive Bible Study** (*3 hours*).
3. Clarifying in summary fashion your understanding of corporate prayer (the **what, why and how** of corporate prayer) (*1½ hours*).
4. Developing your **action plan** for renewing the church's vision and practice of corporate prayer.
   A. Identifying **your church's needs** in this area (*1 hour*).
   B. Identifying **desired objectives** for the coming months (*1 hour*).
   C. Identifying **methods** for reaching those objectives (*2 hours*).
   D. Identifying **resources** for helping accomplish those objectives (*1 hour*).

Throughout the above process you will need to enter regularly into the Lord's presence in prayer and worship so that his Spirit can freely teach you. No structure, no human teacher, no manual will adequately communicate the truths of God apart from the Spirit's work! In fact before going any further, please stop and spend some time in prayer lifting all of this to the Lord. Appropriate prayers could include:

* confession of your need for him to teach you in this area as only he can do.
* praise for all he is going to do in and through you in the coming weeks and months.
* intercession for the church members, that the Lord will be preparing their hearts for where he wants to lead them in the coming months.
* prayer for his wisdom to modify all that follows in this chapter to suit your context well.

---
1. REFLECTION ON THE CORPORATE
PRAYER LIFE OF YOUR CHURCH

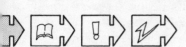

Reflect on your church's practice of corporate prayer as you answer the questions below. Do this individually first, writing your responses in a notebook. Later you will discuss some responses as a group. Continue to use your notebook to keep track of all you are learning about corporate prayer.

A. Reflecting on your church's corporate prayer life.
- What impact have your church's corporate prayers had over the last three months? the last year?
- How eagerly do you think the average church member anticipates items of corporate prayer? (Very eagerly, quite eagerly, somewhat, not too much, hardly at all!)
- What forms or moulds church members' attitudes toward corporate prayer?
- What is your vision for the corporate prayer life of your church? Summarize it in one or two paragraphs.
- What is your church's present experience of corporate prayer? Summarize it in one or two paragraphs.
- How similar or different are your answers to the above two questions? What insights come to you in comparing them?

B. *What* do you understand corporate prayer to be? Try defining the concept 'corporate prayer' in twenty-five words or less.

C. *Why* is corporate prayer important? List at least three reasons why the church's corporate prayer life is key for your growth in the Lord.

D. *How* should people be taught to pray together? List three activities which could result in corporate prayer changing your life.

E. As a group discuss your answers to the questions in Section A above before going on together to the inductive study below.

2. INDUCTIVE BIBLE STUDY ON CORPORATE PRAYER

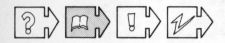

The group leader should now guide the group in the inductive Bible study which you will find in the Resource section (turn to page 224). Rather than talking a lot, he will seek to help others in expressing their insights. His main task is to repeatedly ask the following question: '*What does this passage tell us about corporate prayer?*' The leader's task is simple (though it may not be easy!). Advance study will help him in asking the group pertinent questions to draw out the essence of the Bible passages. Everyone should take notes in his workbook on anything he may want to remember or review later. This kind of inductive study works well in groups ranging from four to twenty or even twenty-five. The Bible study outline will require two sessions of approximately one and a half hours apiece. The leader may want to choose certain passages in advance that he might skip if there is insufficient time. Similarly, he may choose to substitute other passages.

While everyone will be responding to the same general question underlined above, each person will also have a secondary question to keep in mind. Each person should be assigned to take notes on one of these three questions to contribute to a discussion later on:

1. *What* is corporate prayer?
2. *Why* is corporate prayer important?
3. *How* can we most meaningfully and effectively pray together? (If you have a large group, most of the people might focus on this area.)

NOW TURN TO THE BIBLE STUDY ON PAGE 224.

3. DESCRIPTION OF WHAT
CORPORATE PRAYER LOOKS LIKE

A. Clarifying your perspective on corporate prayer

Divide into your three sub-groups regarding the what, why and how of corporate prayer. Take about fifteen minutes to develop a short presentation for the larger group. The presentation should both stimulate the larger group to consider your question further and present the sub-group's thinking. The following group process guidelines may be helpful.

1. **What** is corporate prayer? (Group one)
   a. Share your definitions or thoughts and come to agreement on a single definition.
   b. Write your definition where everyone can see it. In presenting this, you might ask the larger group to go back to their individual definitions written at the beginning of the study. They could compare and contrast them with your work. Encourage the larger group to note whether anything critical has been left out of your definition.
   c. As a large group reach consensus on a working definition. This is not set in concrete. We all are constantly learning. It is simply the group's working definition to use until the Spirit shows you something further.
2. **Why** is corporate prayer important? (Group two)
   a. Seek to come up with a few truly compelling reasons. Real conviction is more important than a long list of reasons!
   b. In presenting this, you might ask the large group for its ideas and list them on a flip chart sheet or blackboard. Affirm each idea before adding any of your own that the larger group overlooked.
3. **How** can we most meaningfully and effectively pray together? (Group three)
   a. As a group develop two lists: 1) the church's strengths in

praying meaningfully and effectively together; and, 2) the church's weaknesses in corporate prayer.

b. In presenting this to the group, you might ask for their ideas as you present each list. Using a separate flip chart sheet for each list, once you have a number of ideas from the large group, add from the list your sub-group developed.

NOTES FOR THE GROUP LEADER: While everyone should be taking his own notes, you might assign one person to take formal notes of the three groups' presentations. These can later be typed up and distributed to all the participants. This will be a working theology of corporate prayer. It forms the biblical base for the action plan that will be developed by the end of this chapter. Read the comments below regarding the what, why and how of corporate prayer ahead of time. Insert them at appropriate moments in the group's discussion, but not until the group has first done some significant thinking on each question for itself.

B. Some further thoughts on the what, why and how of corporate prayer

1. **What** is corporate prayer? A possible working definition might include the following elements: corporate prayer is a dialogue expressing the church's unity with God and activating the covenant partnership he has made with us. (*If the group's definition is short and catchy, people will remember it more easily. You may want to have the group recall it every so often in the ongoing discussion until they have it down well.*)

2. **Why** is corporate prayer important? Only through corporate prayer can God give us the following as a church:

   a. *Joy* in his companionship. He made us to glorify and enjoy him forever. In the midst of all we want to do for him, or want him to do for us, let us not forget the wonder of being sons of God! We will lose this joy if we do not spend time with our Father.

   b. *Confidence* of being under his direction. When we need

guidance either individually or corporately, God can speak to us through times of corporate prayer, making his will known to all.

c. *Wisdom,* having an accurate picture of God and of ourselves. Without prayer, we easily overestimate or underestimate the significance of problems and situations we encounter.

d. *Power* to effect change supernaturally. Again and again prayer changes people and circumstances. Praying with the laying on of hands in Scripture commonly brought supernatural empowering or manifestations.

In short, **through prayer we enjoy God and we partner with him to see his Kingdom come in and around us**.

3. **How** can we meaningfully and effectively pray together? Worship and spiritual warfare are so important they are covered in depth in chapters three and thirteen respectively. Here we will focus briefly on three areas: hearing from God, intercessory prayer, and times when God seems silent or distant.

a. *Hearing from God.* This requires confidence that God still speaks today. We need to avoid two extremes: 1) thinking he wants to tell us how to handle every detail of our lives; and 2) thinking he intends to further guidance for us than common sense and his written Word. Our underlying vision is to do only what we see the Father doing (John 5:19). When we feel a need to hear from God, the following guidelines may help:

1) *Have the right heart.* Attitudes important to hearing from God include:

A) Purity. Sin blinds, making it hard to hear from God (Rom. 1:21).

B) Submission or surrender . . . laying down our preferences (Prov. 3:4,5), being willing to obey whatever he says.

C) Being filled with the Spirit. The Holy Spirit gives us the mind of Christ (II Cor. 2:10–16).

D) Worship, drawing close to him. When we seek him first, he can easily direct us (Mt. 6:33; Phil. 4:4–6).

E) Humility. Asking for his wisdom (Is. 55:6; James 1:2–8).

Church Renewal

2) *Listen!* 'Be still and know that I am God' (Ps. 46:10). The school of silence brings a quieting of the mind, a quickening of the soul, release from the world, and heart to heart communication. Here lies the key to creative power. Probably the better half of our conversations with God will be when we listen! (I Kings 19:11–13; Eccl. 5:1–3; Is. 30:15,16; Lam. 3:25,26).

3) *Confirm his message*, once we believe we have heard from him (cf. I Cor. 14:29–33). The message may come in many forms such as illumination of a particular Scripture, a prophecy, a vision, or a divine 'coincidence'. In a corporate process, the Spirit often speaks a similar message to or through several people. If the message comes in a spoken form, it is helpful to have someone write it down. Normally any such direction from God will be in harmony with a) the Scriptures, b) our conscience, and c) godly authority.

b. *Intercession*

1) Definition: 'to intervene between parties with a view to reconciling differences. Synonym: mediate' — Webster's. Intercession is love on its knees, working with God.

2) Why intercede?

A) Because God has chosen to accomplish his work on earth in response to intercessors.

B) Because God is using intercessory work to refine and mature us in preparation for the positions of responsibility we will hold in the future — both here and in eternity.

3) Biblical examples

A) Moses in Num. 14:1–45, and again in Ex. 32:1–33:6, is a clear example of listening to the people, speaking to God for the people, listening to God, and speaking to the people for God.

B) Abraham in Genesis 18 and 19.

C) The need for a person (or people) to stand in the gap: Ps. 106:23,28,29; Is. 59:15,16; 63:4,5; Exek. 13:5; 22:30,31.

D) The Christian's call to reconciliation: Mt. 5:21–24; II Cor. 5:17–21.

4) Guidelines for intercessory prayer
   A) Make sure that your heart is clean before God by having given the Holy Spirit time to convict, should there be any unconfessed sin (Ps. 66:18; 139: 23–24).
   B) Acknowledge that you cannot really pray without the direction and energy of the Holy Spirit (Rom. 8:26).
   C) Die to your own imagination, desires and burdens for what you feel you should pray (Prov. 3:5,6; 28:26; Is. 55:8).
   D) Ask God to control you utterly by his Spirit (Eph. 5:18), then thank him for doing so (Heb. 11:6).
   E) Praise him now in faith for the remarkable prayer encounter you are going to have. He is a remarkable God and will do something consistent with his character.
   F) Deal aggressively with the enemy. Come against him in the all-powerful Name of Jesus Christ and with the 'Sword of the Spirit' — the Word of God (James 4:7).
   G) Wait in silent expectation. Then, in obedience and faith, utter what God brings to your mind believing (John 10:27). Be sure not to move on to the next subject until you have given God sufficient time to discharge all he wants to say to you regarding this particular burden; especially in corporate prayer.
   H) Always have your Bible with you, in case God should give you direction or confirmation from it (Ps. 119:105).
   I) Sometimes certain intercession may take days or weeks or longer. Hold on to God until a victory is won in the heavenlies. This is sometimes called 'soaking prayer'. Moses interceded two separate times for forty days (Deut. 9:17–20; 9:23–26); Daniel took three weeks (Dan. 10:12–14,21). Other illustrations abound (Gen. 32:24–28; Lk. 11:5–10; 18:1–8).
   J) When God ceases to bring things to your mind for

prayer, finish by praising and thanking him for what he has done. Remind yourself that 'from him and through him and to him are all things. To him be the glory forever' (Rom. 11:36).

c. *When God seems silent or distant.*

If my heart is right and I am following the kinds of guidelines mentioned above, what can I do when I feel my prayers are going nowhere? What do I do when I am in the middle of a dry period in my life? The following principles apply both individually and corporately.

1) Tell God about it. Many of the Psalms are expressions of frustration, discouragement, or dryness. Rereading the Psalms and writing some letters to God or psalms of your own would be very worthwhile. Expressing our feelings is often the water that primes the pump.

2) 'Confess your faults (needs, struggles, sins) to one another and pray for each other that you may be healed' (James 5:16). Two dynamics emerge here: the dynamic of admitting and sharing our struggles and the dynamic of coming to the throneroom with others. The first is critical to avoid falling into Satan's traps of isolation and alienation — easy pickings for his additional traps and deceptions. The second is equally important and can take a number of forms. One is simply to receive prayer ministry through the laying on of hands as your needs are raised to the Lord and as the group listens with you for anything the Lord might want to say to you. A second is having a prayer partner who will meet regularly with you and continue to walk faithfully with you in prayer (Eccl. 4:9–12).

3) Worship and give thanks. God does not change, regardless of how we feel. We need to remind ourselves that our feelings can not guide our lives. Living according to God's Word, even when we do not feel like it, will help bring our feelings in line with who God is. Participating in times of worship and singing helps us to focus our minds and hearts on the Lord. Ask God to renew your vision of his love.

Ask God to release you from the sense of relating to him out of duty or discipline. Open your ears daily to hear his love song.

4) Change your environment. This can be in small daily ways, such as going for a walk while you pray, instead of praying wherever you are accustomed to doing it. This can also be done in more major ways by taking several days off work, and getting out in nature somewhere where the majesty and beauty of God is revealed. If your life is too hectic and you do not have a regular time for prayer, it will help to reorganize your life to have a stable regular time for meeting with God. If you have not used a good devotional book, the structure of doing so is sometimes very helpful. If your life is too routine, it will help to do some new things, take some risks, get adventurous! If you have not been involved in meaningful ways of serving others, find some. Few things so undermine our love relationship with the Lord as the lack of outlets for expressing that love to others.

5) Get good physical exercise and take care of your body. Our spirits are affected by our bodies. If our bodies are run down, overweight, or under chronic stress, this will affect our prayer life. Physical lethargy and heaviness commonly translate into spiritual lethargy and heaviness.

NOW IT IS TIME TO DEVELOP YOUR *ACTION PLAN*. TURN BACK TO PAGE 9 FOR INSTRUCTIONS ON HOW TO DO SO. YOU WILL ALSO FIND OUT HOW TO USE THE RESOURCE MATERIAL IN SECTION 3.

3

RENEWING OUR CORPORATE WORSHIP

We're here to be worshippers first and workers only second.
We take a convert and immediately make a worker out of him.
God never meant it to be so. God meant that a convert should
learn to be a worshipper, and after that he can learn to be a
worker.
   Jesus said, 'Go ye into all the world, and preach the Gospel.'
Peter wanted to go at once but Christ said, 'Don't go yet. Wait
until you are endued with power.' Power for service? Yes, but
that's only half of it; maybe that's only one-tenth of it. The
other nine-tenths are that the Holy Ghost may restore to us
again the spirit of worship. Out of enraptured, admiring,
adoring, worshipping souls, then, God does his work. The
work done by a worshipper will have eternity in it (A.W.
Tozer, *Worship: The Missing Jewel in the Evangelical Church*,
Christian Publ. Inc. 25 South Tenth Street, Harrisburg,
PA 17101, USA, 1961: 14).

In his book *Sit, Walk, Stand*, Watchman Nee insists that the
Christian life has an inherent order of priority. Until we have
sat in the presence of God, we cannot walk in the Christian life
or stand in spiritual warfare (Eph. 2:6; 4:1; 6:10–12). When
we worship, we put our roots down into the rich soil of God's
life. We are nourished, strengthened, revitalized. An environment that draws us close to our Lord produces naturally the
fruit of spiritual service and victory.
   What is your church's worship like? Rich and revitalizing?
A sweet offering to gladden the heart of God? A deep
communion that overflows in joyful, effective service?
   At the heart of many quickly growing renewal churches and
movements is active and participative worship. Our worship
expresses the reality of our life with God. In every area of

church life there is a reciprocal relationship between individual renewal and corporate renewal. While our focus in this chapter is renewal in corporate worship, renewal of our individual worship will both strengthen and grow from the Body at worship together.

Our life of worship encompasses several areas that are deal with in depth in other chapters. Prayer, particularly intercession and hearing from God, is addressed in chapter two. Spiritual warfare is the subject of chapter thirteen. This chapter will focus specifically on preparation for and participation in corporate celebrations of worship, including the Lord's Supper.

What lies ahead in this chapter? The chapter has four sections, designed for church leaders to work through together in ten to twelve hours. A retreat setting would be ideal. If this seems too large a time commitment, take into account that in this time you are: a) opening your lives to a life-changing understanding and commitment to corporate worship; b) deepening team relationships among yourselves as leaders; c) laying foundations for the church's future; and, d) outlining the church's specific course for the next four to twelve

1. Reflecting on the **corporate worship life** of your church (*1 hour*).
2. Looking at God's vision for his people's worship through **an inductive Bible study** (*3 hours*).
3. Clarifying in summary fashion your understanding of corporate worship (the **what, why and how** of corporate worship) (*1½ hours*).
4. Developing your **action plan** for renewing the church's vision and practice of corporate worship.
   A. Identifying **your church's needs** in this area (*1 hour*).
   B. Identifying **desired objectives** for the coming months (*1 hour*).
   C. Identifying **methods** for reaching those objectives (*2 hours*).
   D. Identifying **resources** for helping accomplish those objectives (*1 hour*).

months. The four sections, with the approximate time each might require, are shown on page 53.

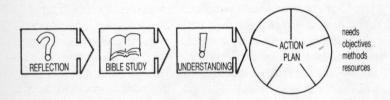

Throughout the above process you will need to enter regularly into the Lord's presence in prayer and worship so that his Spirit can freely teach you. No structure, no human teacher, no manual will adequately communicate the truths of God apart from the Spirit's work! In fact before going any further, please stop and spend some time in prayer lifting all of this to the Lord. Appropriate prayers could include:

* confession of your need for him to teach you in this area as only he can do.
* praise for all he is going to do in and through you in the coming weeks and months.
* intercession for the church members, that the Lord will be preparing their hearts for where he wants to lead them in the coming months.
* prayer for his wisdom to modify all that follows in this chapter to suit your context well.

---

1. REFLECTION ON THE CORPORATE WORSHIP OF YOUR CHURCH

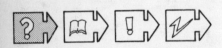

Reflect on your church's practice of corporate worship as you answer the questions below. Do this individually first, writing your responses in a notebook. Later you will discuss some responses as a group. Continue to use your notebook to keep track of all you are learning about worship.

A. Reflecting on your church's corporate worship.
   ■ What is one of the best corporate worship experiences you have had?
     List three or four elements that made it so good.
   ■ What is one of the worst corporate worship experiences you have had?
     List three of four elements that made it so poor.
   ■ What are some blocks to worship?
   ■ What is your vision for the corporate worship life of your church?
     Summarize it in one or two paragraphs.
   ■ What is your church's present experience of corporate worship?
     Summarize it in one or two paragraphs.
   ■ How similar or different are your answers to the above two questions?
     What insights come to you in comparing them?
B. *What* do you understand corporate worship to be? Some people feel it is synonymous with a liturgy or the Sunday morning service; others see it as encompassing all of life. Some people limit it to the church building; others do not. Try defining the concept 'corporate worship' in twenty-five words or less.
C. *Why* is corporate worship important? List at least three reasons why the church's worship together as a Body is key for your growth in the Lord.
D. *How* should people worship together? List three worship activities which are (or could be) a regular source of strength for your life.
E. As a group discuss your answers to the questions in Section A above before going on together to the inductive study below.

> 2. INDUCTIVE BIBLE STUDY
> ON CORPORATE WORSHIP

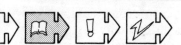

The group leader should now guide the group in the inductive Bible study which you will find in the Resource section (turn to page 227). Rather than talking a lot, he will seek to help others in expressing their insights. His main task is repeatedly to ask the following question: '*What does this passage tell us about corporate worship*' The leader's task is simple (though it may not be easy!). Advance study will help him in asking the group pertinent questions to draw out the essence of the Bible passages. Everyone should take notes in his workbook on anything he may want to remember or review later. This kind of inductive study works well in groups ranging from four to twenty or even twenty-five. The Bible study outline will require two sessions of approximately one and a half hours apiece. The leader may want to choose certain passages in advance that he might skip if there is insufficient time. Similarly, he may choose to substitute other passages.

While everyone will be responding to the same general question underlined above, each person will also have a secondary question to keep in mind. Each person should be assigned to take notes on one of these three questions to contribute to a discussion later on:

1. *What* is corporate worship?
2. *Why* is corporate worship important?
3. *How* can we most meaningfully worship together? (If you have a large group, most of the people might focus on this area.)

NOW TURN TO THE BIBLE STUDY ON PAGE 227.

3. DESCRIPTION OF WHAT CORPORATE WORSHIP LOOKS LIKE

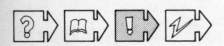

A. Clarifying your perspective on corporate worship

Divide into your three sub-groups regarding the what, why

and how of corporate worship. Take about fifteen minutes to develop a short presentation for the larger group. The presentation should both stimulate the larger group to consider your question further and present the sub-group's thinking. The following group process guidelines may be helpful.

1. **What** is corporate worship? (Group one)
   a. Share your definitions or thoughts and come to agreement on a single definition.
   b. Write your definition where everyone can see it. In presenting this, you might ask the larger group to go back to their individual definitions written at the beginning of the study. They could compare and contrast them with your work. Encourage the larger group to note whether anything critical has been left out of your definition.
   c. As a large group reach consensus on a working definition. This is not set in concrete. We are all constantly learning. It is simply the group's working definition to use until the Spirit shows you something further.
2. **Why** is corporate worship important? (Group two)
   a. Seek to come up with a few truly compelling reasons. Real conviction is more important than a long list of reasons!
   b. In presenting this, you might ask the large group for its ideas and list them on a flip chart sheet or blackboard. Affirm each idea before adding any of your own that the larger group overlooked.
3. **How** can we most meaningfully worship together? (Group three)
   a. As a group develop two lists: 1) the church's strengths in corporate worship; and, 2) the church's weaknesses in corporate worship.
   b. In presenting this to the group, you might ask for their ideas as you present each list. Using a separate flip chart sheet for each list, once you have a number of ideas from the large group, add from the list your sub-group developed.

Remember that you are examining an extremely sensitive area. Some people appreciate styles of worship which others find unrewarding; and tradition, nostalgia, cultural preferences, even Scriptural convictions can come into play to reinforce feelings, and make people react angrily when their preferences are attacked. Do not assume that everyone will come up with basically the same list; in fact, you may well find that what features as a 'strength' on one list will feature as a 'weakness' on another! Try to see what it is that makes each of the group feel as they do.

Again, it is possible that you will all feel unitedly about the strengths and weaknesses of your worship patterns. But are your views shared by the rest of the church? If there is a significant body of opinion which you know feels differently, perhaps in drawing up your list you need to interview some of those who do not agree with you, and consider sympathetically whether they have some good reasons for their position. Otherwise, you might fall into the temptation of becoming a pressure group, lobbying for the changes you want, but not managing to be representative of *all* that God is saying to your church.

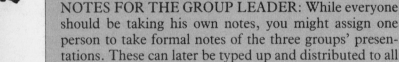

NOTES FOR THE GROUP LEADER: While everyone should be taking his own notes, you might assign one person to take formal notes of the three groups' presentations. These can later be typed up and distributed to all the participants. This will be a working theology of corporate worship. It forms the biblical base for the action plan that will be developed by the end of this chapter. Read the comments below regarding the what, why and how of corporate worship ahead of time. Insert them at appropriate moments in the group's discussion, but not until the group has first done some significant thinking on each question for itself.

B. Some further thoughts on the what, why and how of corporate worship

1. **What** is corporate worship? A possible working definition might include the following elements: 'Corporate worship is offering all we know of ourselves in response to all we know of God.' You may want to distinguish between worship as a lifestyle (akin to abiding in Christ — John 15) and worship as a specific activity or event. The latter, when we set aside everything else to focus only on the Lord can be called adoration. (*If the group's definition is short and catchy, people will remember it more easily. You may want to have the group recall it every so often in the ongoing discussion until they have it down well.*)

2. **Why** is corporate worship important? In corporate worship we express our total devotion to him. We rejoice in his supreme beauty, strength, majesty and holiness. We regain our security in his sovereignty. We sense the heartbeat of his love for us. We know anew that *this* is why we were created and redeemed — to love and enjoy him forever!

   Worship is our natural and only reasonable response to God (Rom. 12:1,2). Worship is due him because he is God and we are his creation! Even if there were no other benefit to us, we would find our highest joy in honouring and glorifying him. However, in his bounty God gives us other rich blessings through corporate worship. These include:

   a. *A fuller understanding of who he is.* We have the privilege of entering directly into the presence of God. The more time we spend with him, the more we know him. As we see him more fully, we are transformed more and more into his likeness. We are constantly becoming like our image of God (I John 3:2,3; II Cor. 3:18; Jer. 2:5; Ps. 135:15,18). In corporate worship our brothers and sisters help us to see God more completely than we could by ourselves.

   b. *A fuller understanding of who we are*
      1) Beloved children. What release, healing and empowerment lies in knowing the awesomeness of God's love (Rom. 5:6–11; Eph. 2:19; 3:14–19). We are cherished and cared for by our Father! In

worship this knowledge moves from our heads to our hearts; from being a general principle to being a personal blessing!

2) God's covenant people — his chosen ones, his priesthood, his temple, indwelt by his Spirit by his spirit (I Cor. 3:16; 6:19; II Cor. 6:16; Eph. 2:20–22; I Pet. 2:5–9; Rev. 1:6). The more we understand our identity as the people of God, the more gratitude will surge within us (Ps. 103: 104; 107: 6–8,32). Ingratitude comes from assuming we *deserve* benefits God extends to us. Thanksgiving and praise befit the language of the Kingdom of God (Eph. 5:4,18–20; Col. 3:15–17).

3) Ministers of reconciliation (II Cor. 5:17–21). To reconcile is to harmonize. We can only harmonize the world to Christ if we are in tune with him as well as with each other (Jn. 17:20–23). We are the harmony to his melody!

c) *Empowerment for victorious living*

1) In overcoming Satan. Satan's main power lies in his words (accusing, lying, deceiving, cursing). Our worship silences him (compare Ps. 8:2 with Mt. 21:16).

2) In overcoming the flesh and the world. Coming before a holy God burns away that which is unworthy of him (Is. 6:1–8). Celebrating the Lord's Supper makes us participants in spiritual mysteries (I Cor. 10:1–4,15–22). It can be a means of grace if we participate rightly or greatly weaken us if we do not (I Cor. 11:27–30).

3) In hearing from God. Worship prepares our hearts to receive God's Word. Then, after hearing a message, worship helps translate that message more fully from our minds into our hearts.

In short, **through corporate worship we honour and enjoy God, we express and establish our identity, we grow into Christlikeness, and we are empowered to be his Body in the world**.

3. **How** can we meaningfully worship together? We will

consider briefly three areas: preparing for worship, participating in worship, and leading worship.

a. *Preparing for corporate worship*

  1) Cultivate a vital individual worship life. The corporate
     worship reflects and climaxes our worship as indivi-
     duals.
  2) Pray for those leading the meeting that they will be
     sensitive to the Lord's direction.
  3) Begin preparing mentally, physically and spiritually
     the previous evening or several hours before the
     service. Ask God for an open heart to receive
     whatever he has to teach or give you. Arrive prepared
     to enter into the meeting with your whole heart.
  4) Ask God if he has anything to give to the Body
     through you (I Cor. 14:26). Be prepared to share if
     there is opportunity.

b. *Participating in corporate worship*

  Corporate worship needs to happen both in large
  gathered celebrations and in small groups like house
  churches of cell groups. Large celebrations affirm our
  identity as a powerful and significant work of God.
  Small group worship allows people to fully express their
  priesthood through active participation and use of their
  gifts. Keys to good corporate worship include:

  1) Time. It takes time for people to leave behind the
     cares of their lives and really enter into worship. Five
     or ten minutes is inadequate for corporate worship. A
     half hour to an hour, apart from time for the sermon,
     might be more fruitful. (Of course, time is a cultural
     concept, so use whatever time frame is appropriate to
     your context!)
  2) Listening. We must listen to one another and to the
     Lord, to blend our worship into a unified expression
     of our homage. The Spirit can wave a theme into
     spontaneous worship that all can contribute to and
     learn from.
  3) Orderliness. All elements of worship are to be carried
     out in a 'fitting and orderly way' with the intent of
     honouring the Lord and strengthening the church (I
     Cor. 14:26–40).

4) Physical expression. Scriptural forms include kneel-
   ing, standing, lifting of hands, clapping and even
   dancing. Sitting may be one of the few postures that
   the Scriptures do not readily identify with worship!
In preparation for worship the leaders' task is to plan the
service to build to a climax, usually either hearing from
God (a sermon or homily) or the Lord's Supper. The early
church used a model of worship that included both of these
high points. If this model is followed, a two hour (or more)
worship period is helpful, with a small break or 'greeting of
peace' between the two hours. The whole experience
carries through one correlated aim and challenges the
whole person — his mind, will, feelings and sense. The
same theme is approached from many angles.

The following model illustrates focusing worship toward
a climax:

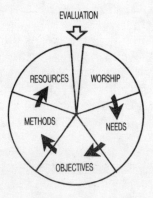

c. *Leading worship*

With all of the above in mind, some practical tips for the
worship leader follow. Most important, the worship
leader needs to move the people's attention from him,
and from the mechanics of worship, to focus on the
Lord himself. The worship leader is truly a leader in
that he guides the people through various phases of
worship. At the same time he is a facilitator setting the
stage for the people to be the principal actors, and
allowing the Spirit to move in and through the royal
priesthood. Some tips for helping to do this include:

1) Have a simple clear structure that allows people to be

comfortable in having a normal order of worship; so that they can *also* be comfortable in the times of spontaneity within that structure.

2) As a general rule, the more the people participate and the less the leader speaks, the better.

3) As a general rule, the more focus *upwards*, and the less *horizontal* instruction or commentary, the better. For instance, an overhead projector with the songs can eliminate the instruction to look up a certain song with the resultant break in simply focusing on the Lord.

4) 'Horizontal'-type songs of rejoicing in each other or songs that challenge or exhort us in some way are best at the beginning of the worship as we warm up and move toward the throneroom. This can be likened to those Psalms which are called 'songs of ascent', sung as people ascended the hill to come to the temple. Once the people are gathered in spirit as well as physically, 'vertical' songs and prayers that focus exclusively on God's character and works make up the heart and centre of a worship service.

5) A test of the priesthood's participation is whether only what is pre-planned happens or whether the Spirit has the liberty to move through the people to introduce a theme or a direction that was not pre-planned. A good worship leader has put some careful thought into how to make the worship experience a real encounter with God. The very fact that we can not direct God means that the leader's plan must include flexibility to move in whatever direction the Spirit may lead.

6) The larger the group, the more difficult it can be to allow free and full participation of the priesthood. Large churches could make a point of having opportunities other than Sunday services for corporate worship in smaller groups.

7) Anointed and gifted musicians make a great different to the worship. The leader of the musicians can also be instrumental in guiding the direction of the worship, if he too is gifted in setting the stage for worship and in following the Spirit's direction in

worship. This requires good coordination and communication with the over-all worship leader.

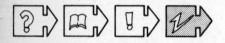

NOW IT IS TIME TO DEVELOP YOUR *ACTION PLAN*. TURN BACK TO PAGE 9 FOR INSTRUCTIONS ON HOW TO DO SO. YOU WILL ALSO FIND OUT HOW TO USE THE RESOURCE MATERIAL IN SECTION 3.

4

RENEWING OUR STEWARDSHIP

Take my life and let it be consecrated, Lord to Thee;
Take my hands and let them move at the impulse of Thy love,
At the impulse of Thy love.

Take my feet and let them be swift and beautiful for Thee;
Take my voice and let me sing always, only, for my King,
Always, only, for my King.

Take my lips and let them be filled with messages for Thee;
Take my silver and my gold, not a mite would I withhold
Not a mite would I withhold.

Take my live, my God, I pour at Thy feet its treasure store;
Take myself and I will be ever, only, all for Thee,
Ever, only, all for Thee.

'The Bible's teaching on wealth is one of the most extensive and clear emphases in all of Scripture . . . In the gospels, Jesus talks more about this issue than almost any other, including heaven and hell, sexual immorality or violence . . . Jesus' concern with the dangers of affluence was not a casual, occasional remark incidental to more important issues of discipleship, but a major emphasis in his teaching. Karl Barth notes that a 'break' with possessions was one of the five 'prominent lines' along which the calling and commanding of Jesus always moved (the other four involved a break with reputation, violence, family and 'religion') . . . Our economic life and our standard of living is not a purely private matter, then, but a critical area of discipleship. Most of us are not aware of the extent to which the five security relationships Barth details, and especially our economic securities, mute our discipleship and blunt its distinctiveness' (Robert Sabbath; 'The Bible and the

Poor', *Seeds of the Kingdom, Sojourners*, Washington D.C., January, 1977:73).

As Christians, we are not called to pursue economic security and wealth, but to be stewards of the resources God puts in our hands. An airplane steward (or stewardess) is in charge of what happens in the airplane. However, he is not there ot eat the best food, sit in the best places, and seek his own pleasure. He is there to serve the passengers in the name of the airline owner.

As stewards we will give an account of how we use each asset the Lord entrusts to us (Mt. 25:14–30; I Cor. 4:2). Stewardship is not optional for Christ's people: we are either good stewards or bad stewards, but we are all stewards.

What kind of stewards does your church have? Responsible and faithful? Generous and sacrificial? Cheerful and thrilled to give for the cause of the Kingdom? Shortage of such stewards can paralyze the growth of the church. A weak vision and practice of stewardship limits the expression and extension of God's Kingdom.

Stewardship intersects several areas that are dealt with in depth in other chapters. Stewardship of our spiritual gifts is discussed in Chapter Eight, while the commitment to share our lives with one another and care for one another is covered more fully in Chapter Seven on Christian community (*koinonia*). Considering how to use our resources and time wisely to extend Christ's Kingdom is considered further in Chapters Ten through Twelve in regard to local evangelism, social responsibility and mission strategy. This chapter focuses on general principles related to managing and sharing the physical resources God gives us: our time, our possessions, and our money.

What lies ahead in this chapter? The chapter has four sections, designed for church leaders to work through together in ten to twelve hours. A retreat setting would be ideal. If this seems too large a time commitment, take into account that in this time you are: a) opening your lives to a life-changing understanding and commitment to stewardship; b) deepening team relationships among yourselves as leaders; c) laying foundations for the church's future; and, d) outlining the church's specific course for the next four to twelve months.

The four sections, with the approximate time each might require, follow below.

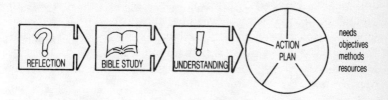

needs
objectives
methods
resources

1. Reflecting on **the stewardship of your church** (*1 hour*).
2. Looking at God's vision regarding stewardship through an **inductive Bible study** (*3 hours*).
3. Clarifying in summary fashion your understanding of stewardship (the **what, why and how** of stewardship) (*1½ hours*).
4. Developing your **action plan** for renewing the church's vision and practice of stewardship.
   A. Identifying **your church's needs** in this area (*1 hour*).
   B. Identifying **desired objectives** for the coming months (*1 hour*).
   C. Identifying **methods** for reaching those objectives (*2 hours*).
   D. Identifying **resources** for helping accomplish those objectives (*1 hour*).

Throughout the above process you will need to enter regularly into the Lord's presence in prayer and worship so that his Spirit can freely teach you. No structure, no human teacher, no manual will adequately communicate the truths of God apart from the Spirit's work! In fact before going any further, please stop and spend some time in prayer lifting all of this to the Lord. Appropriate prayers could include:

* confession of your need for him to teach you in this area as only he can do.

* praise for all he is going to do in and through you in the coming weeks and months.
* intercession for the church members, that the Lord will be preparing their hearts for where he wants to lead them in the coming months.
* prayer for his wisdom to modify all that follows in this chapter to suit your context well.

> ### 1. REFLECTION ON YOUR CHURCH'S STEWARDSHIP

Reflect on your church's stewardship as you answer the questions below. Do this individually first, writing your responses in a notebook. Later you will discuss some responses as a group. Continue to use your notebook to keep track of all you are learning about stewardship.

A. Reflecting on your church's stewardship.
   ■ It would be helpful and insightful to have a copy of the church's budget for the year and a treasurer's report that cover the following kinds of points:
      — how many members give every month, almost every month, half the months of the year, sporadically, and not at all.
      — what percentage of the church's income goes to: 1) buildings, maintenance and upkeep; 2) salaries and benefits; 3) missions; 4) local evangelism; 5) helping the poor; 6) programmes; and 7) other.
      — have there been any significant changes in the church's budget priorities since five years ago?
   ■ What priorities are indicated in the church's budget?
   ■ How well do you think the average church member does in sharing his possessions and house freely with others (Very well, quite well, somewhat well, somewhat poorly, very poorly)?

■ What is your vision for stewardship in your church?
   Summarize it in one or two paragraphs.
■ What is your church's present experience of stewardship? Summarize it in one or two paragraphs.
■ How similar or different are your answers to the above
   two questions? What insights come to you in comparing
   them?

B. *What* do you understand a steward to be? Some people
   equate stewardship with tithing; others see the tithe as the
   most simple and least important part of stewardship. They
   would say that in giving the tithe away, one has relatively
   little responsibility for it; it is the other 90% in which our
   stewardship really comes to bear. Yet others would say
   that money is only one aspect of stewardship. Try defining
   the concept 'Christian steward' in twenty-five words or
   less.

C. *Why* has God made us his stewards? List at least three
   reasons why good stewardship is key for your growth in
   the Lord.

D. *How* can we best steward what God has put in our hands?
   List three stewardship activities which are (or could be) a
   regular source of strength for your life and the life of the
   church.

E. As a group discuss your answers to the questions in
   Section A above before going on together to the inductive
   study below.

---

2. INDUCTIVE BIBLE STUDY ON STEWARDSHIP

The group leader should guide the group in the inductive
Bible study which you will find in the Resource section (turn
to page 230). Rather than talking a lot, he will seek to help
others in expressing their insights. His main task is to ask
repeatedly the following question: *'What does this passage tell us*

about stewardship?' The leader's task is simple (though it may not be easy!). Advance study will help him in asking the group pertinent questions to draw out the essence of the Bible passages. Everyone should take notes in his workbook on anything he may want to remember or review later. This kind of inductive study works well in groups ranging from four to twenty or even twenty-five. The Bible study outline will require two sessions of approximately one and a half hours apiece. The leader may want to choose certain passages in advance that he might skip if there is insufficient time. Similarly, he may choose to substitute other passages.

While everyone will be responding to the same general question underlined above, each person will also have a secondary question to keep in mind. Each person should be assigned to take notes on one of these three questions to contribute to a discussion later on:

1. *What* is a steward?
2. *Why* has God made us his stewards? Why has God shared his assets with us? In his infinite wisdom, could be make better use of them himself? Why has he risked the pollution of his creation, some people living in wasteful affluence while others starve, and people depending on their riches instead of on him? Why has he appointed us his stewards?
3. *How* can we best steward what God has put in our hands? (*If you have a large group, most of the people might focus on this area.*)

 NOW TURN TO THE BIBLE STUDY ON PAGE 230.

3. DESCRIPTION OF WHAT STEWARDSHIP LOOKS LIKE

A. Clarifying your perspective on stewardship

Divide into your three sub-groups regarding the what, why and how of stewardship. Take about fifteen minutes to develop a short presentation for the larger group. The presentation should both stimulate the larger group to consider your question further and present the sub-group's thinking. The following group process guidelines may be helpful.

1. **What** is a steward? (Group one)
   a. Share your definitions or thoughts and come to agreement on a single definition.
   b. Write your definition where everyone can see it. In presenting this, you might ask the larger group to go back to their individual definitions written at the beginning of the study. They could compare and contrast them with your work. Encourage the larger group to note whether anything critical has been left out of your definition.
   c. As a large group reach consensus on a working definition. This is not set in concrete. We are all constantly learning. It is simply the group's working definition to use until the Spirit shows you something further.
2. **Why** has God made us his stewards? (Group two)
   a. Seek to come up with a few truly compelling reasons. Real conviction is more important than a long list of reasons!
   b. In presenting this, you might ask the large group for its ideas and list them on a flip chart sheet or blackboard. Affirm each idea before adding any of your own that the larger group overlooked.
3. **How** can we best steward what God has put in our hands? (Group three)
   a. As a group develop two lists: 1) the church's strengths in stewardship; and, 2) the church's weaknesses in stewardship.
   b. In presenting this to the group, you might ask for their ideas as you present each list. Using a separate flip chart sheet for each list, once you have a number of ideas from the large group, add from the list our sub-group developed.

NOTES FOR THE GROUP LEADER: While everyone should be taking his own notes, you might assign one person to take formal notes of the three groups' presentations. These can later be typed up and distributed to all the participants. This will be a working theology of stewardship. It forms the biblical base for the action plan that will be developed by the end of this chapter. Read the comments below regarding the what, why and how of stewardship ahead of time. Insert them at appropriate moments in the group's discussion, but not until the group has first done some significant thinking on each question for itself.

B. Some further thoughts on the what, why and how of stewardship

1. **What** is a steward? A possible working definition might include the following elements: 'A Christian steward is God's manager of resources temporarily entrusted to him to express and extend God's Kingdom here on earth'. The Greek word for steward, *oikonomos*, means 'to arrange or to be over a house'. (*If the group's definition is short and catchy, people will remember it more easily. You may want to have the group recall it every so often in the ongoing discussion until they have it down well.*)

2. *Why* has God made us his stewards? What are his purposes in delegating responsibility to us to be his managers?

    a. *He wants us to experience the joy of sharing his grace with others.* Having had God's grace poured out on us (Eph. 1:7,8), having been filled with grace, we cannot help but give grace to others (Mt. 10:18; note Mt. 18:21–35). This includes such tangible graces as our homes and possessions. At times we will give these graces outright (a warm meal, money, a birthday present), while at other times we will share the use of some of the graces God has entrusted to us (a car, a bicycle, our time, a house/apartment, a bed, books, music, an interest-free loan, etc.).

    Sometimes this giving calls for real faith on our part,

as it requires of the widow who shared her last flour and oil with Elijah (I Kgs. 17:7–16). God can — and does! — multiply our resources, but first we must offer him what is in our hands, even if it is only five loaves and two fishes to feed five thousand people (Mt. 14:13–21; Lk. 21:1–3; Mal. 3:10–12; I Tim. 6:18; Heb. 13:16).

Grace and forgiveness are stepping stones to responsibility. When our burden is lifted, we are prepared to help lift the burden of others. We can function as good stewards only in those areas of our lives where we know we have received grace. In other areas we unconsciously think we are owners, lords, possessors, and so we have no freedom to give graciously or wisely. When we know we have received freely, we no longer grasp possessively; rather we keep our hands open for God to direct us in the use of his possessions.

b. *He wants us to free others to function as God has called them.* God gives us grace to share what we have so that others can grow into the fullness of ministry that God intends for them (Eph. 4:7,8,12,13). There may be physical resources that will enable people to use their gifts — such as an instrument for a musician, or materials for teaching the children. A pastor, evangelist or missionary who must invest much of his time and energy into providing for his family is not able to give his best service to the church. The Lord's ministry will flourish among us as we support what he ordains.

c. *He wants us to bring glory to his name.* If he administered his assets directly, he could dazzle us all. But how much more glorifying to put his assets in the hands of free agents who *choose* to manage them for him rather than to serve their own ends! Poor choices limit the growth of the Kingdom. Good choices make the spiritual reality of the Kingdom tangible and reveal the King's presence. Where the King is revealed, he will be glorified. Thus the outcome of our stewardship, the outcome of our giving grace to others, is 'that in everything God may receive the glory, through Jesus Christ, since to him alone belong all glory and power forever and ever. Amen' (I Pet. 4:10,11; Note Eph. 1:5,6).

In short, **a good steward enters into the special joy of managing God's resources in order to share, to free others to function more fully as God intends, and to bring glory to God through extending the work of his kingdom**.

3. **How** can we best steward what God has put in our hands? We will consider two areas: *living simply* and *applying financial wisdom.*

   a. *Living simply.* Good stewardship involves living as simply as possible in order to maximize the resources available for the Kingdom. Matthew 6:33 holds the secret of the simple life. If we do not seek the Kingdom of God first, we do not seek it at all. The simple life comes from understanding there is a 'first' and there is an 'all the rest'. While the Gospel does not deny the validity of 'all the rest', no confusion can be allowed between 'all the rest' and seeking first the Kingdom. The simple life is neither austerity nor abundance, but an attitude. All things can be good — very good — *if they are used to support our relationship with God rather than to compete with it.* The simple life involves laying aside every weight that besets us to run the race with total abandon, fixing our eyes on Jesus (Heb. 12:1,2). Called to seek *first* God's Kingdom, we can celebrate this first-ness of the King in at least three ways:

      1. *Celebrating the first day of the week.* Unless we receive grace, we cannot give it. To celebrate God's grace and manage his assets with joy throughout the week, we need one day devoted to restoring our spirit. God renews us through quietness, reflection, rest and relaxation, worship and fellowship, and hearing his Word proclaimed. A careful study of the Old Testament may surprise us with the high value God placed on the Sabbath. This was deepened by Christ's declaring, 'The Son of Man is the Lord of the Sabbath' (Mk. 2:27,28).

      2. *Celebrating the first hour of the day.* While for some people their best hour may not be early in the day, a wise steward gives God his best (or first) hour. Only by walking closely with the King can we be sensitive

to how he wants us to manage his resources. Indeed, such time with him fills us with the most necessary resources he would share with us — his Spirit, his mind and his Word. To accept the deception that we do not have time for this is to be like a soldier rushing off to the battlefield without taking time to collect his weapons or receive his orders.

3. *Celebrating the first fruits of our income.* Giving of the first fruits of our labour is commanded repeatedly in Scripture, and it indicates how we view the whole. 'If the first fruit be holy, the lump is also' (Rom. 11:16). Firstfruits are not left-overs. They are separated out at the beginning of 'the harvest' with the assurance that God's blessings will be on all the rest. The following principles underlie giving and tithing in the Old Testament and the New.

- God is our source and will always meet our needs. Wealth is not our security — God is (Lev. 25:18–22; Prov. 11:28; Jer. 9:23,24; Mt. 6:19–33; II Cor. 9:10,11; Phil. 4:19).
- God wants our giving to be a celebration (Deut. 12:58,12; II Cor. 8:2; 9:7,11–14).
- Our giving is to support God's work and his workers (Num. 18:21?32; I Cor. 9:3–14; Phil. 4:15–19; I Tim. 5:17,18).
- Our giving is to ensure there are no needy people in our midst (II Chron. 31:10,11; Acts 2:44,45; 4:32–37; II Cor. 8,9; Gal. 2:10; Eph. 4:28; I John 3:17).
- Our giving is to be from a joy-filled heart, not begrudgingly or because it is required (I Sam. 15:22; Ps. 51:16,17; II Cor. 8:8,24; 9:7; Gal. 6:7,8; I John 3:16–18).
- Our first fruits (or tithe) are only the starting point of our giving (Deut. 12:6; Acts 4:32–5:11; II Cor. 8,9).
- As in the training of children, when we handle small responsibilities well and faithfully, he will give us larger challenges, both material and spiritual (Lk. 12:42–44; I Cor. 4:2).

b. *Financial wisdom.* God expects us to maximize everything he puts in our hands in order to express and extend his Kingdom as much as possible. Expressing God's Kingdom includes using our money for simple joys and pleasures he delights to give us and have us share with others. Extending God's Kingdom includes conserving our resources in order to have the maximum available for his work. Here now are some principles for a wise use of money. (*In the bibliography, read Burkett for a fuller explanation of these kinds of principles; and read Longacre for some practical money-saving tips.*)

1. People tend to have one of three attitudes toward money: a) buying what they want (using credit to buy beyond their means); b) buying what they can afford (buying according to the money one has); and c) buying what they need (usually less than the money one has). Financially speaking, lifestyle 'a' is unwise and immature; 'b' is better; and 'c' is the wisest and most mature.

2. The maturing process includes our finances. Where there are committed relationships and substantial trust, a person can normally benefit by reviewing his finances with someone who gives him pastoral leadership. The pastoral leader may in turn refer him to one or more other resource people or tools that might be helpful in an area in which he wants to grow further. Sometimes church leaders incorporate such a review process as a part of helping church families economically when they are having financial difficulties. Their rationale is not to treat simply the symptoms by giving them money, but to also treat the causes so that the situation will be less likely to recur. People in financial difficulty are commonly those who do not keep good records of their expenses.

3. Some guidelines for 'plugging the leaks' in your finances include:
   * Regarding your present possessions: if you are not using something, sell it or give it away.
   * Do not buy something from which you will not get full use. Rent or borrow things you use only very

occasionally. Buy top-of-the-line items only when constant use demands them.
* Where possible, fix, paint or patch a used item rather than buying a new one.
* Discuss finances with your spouse, and (when appropriate) with your children. As they become old enough, involve the children in having an income, tithing, saving for future major purchases and helping you in comparison shopping for expensive household purchases.

NOW IT IS TIME TO DEVELOP YOUR *ACTION PLAN.* TURN BACK TO PAGE 9 FOR INSTRUCTIONS ON HOW TO DO SO. YOU WILL ALSO FIND OUT HOW TO USE THE RESOURCE MATERIAL IN SECTION 3.

5

RENEWING OUR TEACHING
AND STUDY OF THE WORD

'That was an interesting lecture,' my nonchristian friend said
to me as we left the church. Surprised, I picked myself up off
the floor. I had never thought of a message as being a lecture!

How many Christian teachers teach or interact with learners
in a way that is noticeably different from nonchristian
teachers? Should there be a difference? Why or why not?
Might there be 'Christian' teaching methods? Certainly there
is 'Christian' content we want to communicate. Certainly we
can limit the power of that content through poor teaching
methods. But beyond this, can we facilitate the Spirit's
teaching work in ways that go beyond good secular teaching
methods?

This chapter attempts to focus on the heart of spiritual
teaching — allowing the Spirit to take a central role in the
teaching process. This chapter is not attempting to outline the
Bible, or cover the basics of homiletics or hermeneutics. The
majority of evangelical church leaders are committed to and
well-established in biblical orthodoxy. This chapter is also not
attempting to focus on the Sunday sermons or on the
believer's individual Bible study, though hopefully insights
gained here will apply to those activities. The focus here is on
getting people involved together in discovering and obeying
what God has to say to them through his Word. The key to
this is giving the Holy Spirit freedom to be our primary
teacher.

What lies ahead in this chapter? The chapter has four
sections, designed for church leaders to work through together
in ten to twelve years. A retreat setting would be ideal. If this
seems too large a time commitment, take into account that in

this time you are: a) opening your lives to a life-changing understanding and commitment to the Spirit's teaching work; b) deepening team relationships among yourselves as leaders; c) laying foundations for the church's future; and, d) outlining the church's specific course for the next four to twelve months. The four sections, with the approximate time each might require, follow below.

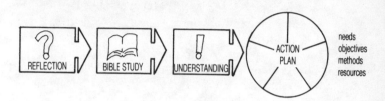

1. Reflecting on the **teaching of the Word in your church** (*1 hour*).
2. Looking at God's vision for the teaching of his Word through an **inductive Bible study** (*3 hours*).
3. Clarifying in summary fashion your understanding of how the Word should be taught (the **what, why and how** of the Spirit's role in Bible teaching) (*1½ hours*).
4. Developing your **action plan** for renewing the church's vision and practice of Bible teaching.
A. Identifying **your church's needs** in this area (*1 hour*).
B. Identifying **desired objectives** for the coming months (*1 hour*).
C. Identifying **methods** for reaching those objectives (*2 hours*).
D. Identifying **resources** for helping accomplish those objectives (*1 hour*).

Throughout the above process you will need to enter regularly into the Lord's presence in prayer and worship so that his Spirit can freely teach you. No structure, no human teacher, no manual will adequately communicate the truths of God apart from the Spirit's work! In fact before going any further, please stop and spend some time in prayer lifting all of this to the Lord. Appropriate prayers could include:

* confession of your need for him to teach you in this area as only he can do.
* praise for all he is going to do in and through you in the coming weeks and months.
* intercession for the church members, that the Lord will be preparing their hearts for where he wants to lead them in the coming months.
* prayer for his wisdom to modify all that follows in this chapter to suit your context well.

---

1. REFLECTION ON THE TEACHING OF THE WORD IN YOUR CHURCH

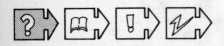

Reflect on your church's practice of teaching the Word as you answer the questions below. Do this individually first, writing your responses in a notebook. Later you will discuss some responses as a group. Continue to use your notebook to keep track of all you are learning about teaching the Word.

A. Reflecting on your church's teaching of the Word.
   ■ Has the Bible been taught in recent years in such a way that it has resulted in some noticeable common changes in most of the church members? If so, what changes have there been in the past two years?
   ■ What do most church members do with the Sunday sermon?
   ■ How regularly do you think the average church member spends ten minutes or more alone in the Word? (*Daily? Almost daily? About every other day? Occasionally? Very rarely?*) How regularly does the average church member

study, discuss and apply the Word in a small group? (*Once or more a week? Biweekly? Monthly? Quarterly? Almost never?*)

■ What is your vision for the Spirit's role in teaching of the Word in your church? Summarize it in one or two paragraphs.

■ What is your church's present experience of the Spirit's role in teaching of the Word? Summarize it in one or two paragraphs.

■ How similar or different are your answers to the above two questions? What insights come to you in comparing them?

B. *What* do you understand 'teaching the Word' to be? Some people feel the Word is adequately taught when it is well expressed. Others feel it is not adequately taught unless it is learned and obeyed. Try defining the concept 'teaching the Word' in twenty-five words or less.

C. *Why* is teaching the Word important? List at least three reasons why the church's teaching of the Word is key for your growth in the Lord.

D. *How* should people be taught the Word? List three teaching activities which are (or could be) changing your life.

E. As a group discuss your answers to the questions in Section A above before going on together to the inductive study below.

---

2. INDUCTIVE BIBLE STUDY ON TEACHING THE WORD

The group leader should now guide the group in the following inductive Bible study which you will find in the Resource section (turn to page 234). Rather than talking a lot, he will seek to help others in expressing their insights. His main task is repeatedly to ask the following question: '*What does this passage tell us about teaching the Word?*' The leader's task is simple (though it may not be easy!). Advance study will help him in asking the group pertinent questions to draw out the essence of the Bible passages. Everyone should take notes in his workbook on anything he may want to remember or review later. This kind of inductive study works well in groups ranging from four to twenty or even twenty-five. The Bible study outline will require two sessions of approximately one and a half hours apiece. The leader may want to choose certain passages in advance that he might skip if there is insufficient time. Similarly, he may choose to substitute other passages.

While everyone will be responding to the same general question underlined above, each person will also have a secondary question to keep in mind. Each person should be assigned to take notes on one of these three questions to contribute to a discussion later on:

1. *What* is teaching the Word?
2. *Why* is teaching the Word important?
3. *How* should we teach the Word so the Spirit can work freely and deeply? (If you have a large group, most of the people might focus on this area.)

NOW TURN TO THE BIBLE STUDY ON PAGE 234.

3. DESCRIPTION OF WHAT
TEACHING THE WORD LOOKS LIKE

A. Clarifying your perspective on teaching the Word

Divide into your three sub-groups regarding the what, why and how of teaching the Word. Take about fifteen minutes to develop a short presentation for the larger group. The presentation should both stimulate the larger group to consider your question further and present the sub-group's thinking. The following group process guidelines may be helpful.

1. **What** is the Spirit's role in teaching the Word? (Group one)
   a. Share your definitions or thoughts and come to an agreement on a single definition, making clear the Spirit's place.
   b. Write your definition where everyone can see it. In presenting this, you might ask the larger group to go back to their individual definitions written at the beginning of the study. They could compare and contrast them with your work. Encourage the larger group to note whether anything critical has been let out of your definition.
   c. As a large group reach consensus on a working definition. This is not set in concrete. We are all constantly learning. It is simply the group's work definition to use until the Spirit shows you something further.
2. **Why** is the Spirit's teaching us through the Word important? (Group two)
   a. Seek to come up with a few truly compelling reasons. Real conviction is more important than a long list of reasons!
   b. In presenting this, you might ask the large group for its ideas and list them on a flip chart sheet or blackboard. Affirm each idea before adding any of your own that the larger group overlooked.
3. **How** do we teach the Word so the Spirit can work freely and deeply? (Group three).
   a. As a group develop two lists: 1) the church's strengths in involving the Spirit in teaching the Word; and, 2) the church's weaknesses in involving the Spirit in teaching the Word.
   b. In presenting this to the group, you might ask for their ideas as you present each list. Using a separate flip chart sheet for each list, once you have a number of ideas from the large group, add from the list your sub-group developed.

NOTES FOR THE GROUP LEADER: While everyone should be taking his own notes, you might assign one person to take formal notes of the three groups' presentations. These can later be typed up and distributed to all the participants. This will be a working theology of teaching the Word. It forms the biblical base for the action plan that will be developed by the end of this chapter. Read the comments below regarding the what, why and how of teaching the Word ahead of time. Insert them at appropriate moments in the group's discussion, but not until the group has first done some significant thinking on each question for itself.

B. Some further thoughts on the what, why and how of teaching the Word

1. **What** is teaching the Word? A possible working definition might include the following elements: Teaching the Word is opening our minds and releasing God's Spirit to communicate his truth in a way that will convict us to obey. (*If the group's definition is short and catchy, people will remember it more easily. You may want to have the group recall it every so often in the ongoing discussion until they have it down well.*)

2. **Why** is the Spirit's teaching us through the Word important? Psalm 19:7–9 gives as many as a dozen reasons why God's Word is important. However, only the Spirit can breathe life into the Scriptures to give us:

   a. *Confidence.* This confidence is not only in the authority of the Word, but also in knowing the living God is speaking to me in my situation now. And he knows what he is talking about!

   b. *Love.* No amount of study *per se* can communicate God's love for us (I Cor. 8:1), but the Spirit can (Eph. 3:14–21). Most Christians today have far more knowledge than they are using, but not nearly as much love as they need to be healthy and strong in the Lord.

   c. *Victory in battle.* God's Word is the sword of the Spirit

(Eph. 6:17). The Word apart from the Spirit will not bring victory over the flesh, the world or the devil.

d. *Changed character*. The Word can help us understand what our lives should be like. However, apart from the Spirit's enabling work such understanding only increases our guilt and the despair of living in Romans 7 instead of Romans 8. Repentance, the key to changing our character, comes from the Spirit's convicting work.

e. *Guidance*. Apart from the Spirit a knowledgeable student of the Word can 'proof text' almost any direction he might want to go. Only the Spirit can enable us to hear God's Word in a way that goes beyond our own preconceptions and desires.

If these five qualities are not the regular result of our teaching and study of the Word, it is likely that the Spirit is not being released or allowed to express himself in our teaching. In short, **the Spirit's role in teaching us God's Word is indispensable in making Christ real to us and giving us grace to live triumphantly in his Kingdom**.

3. **How** do we teach the Word so that the Spirit can work freely and deeply? The ideas below are developed further in the *suggested action steps* in the Resource Section (page 203).

a. *Prepare the soil of people's hearts.*

1) Through worship. Worship is always conducive to hearing from God. Our learning is greatly enhanced if we begin with a time of remembering who God is and who we are. Confession plays an important role here. Sin or broken relationships limit the Spirit's ability to teach and equip us.

2) Through stimulating hunger. We learn in proportion to our hunger (Mt. 5:6; 7:7). Self-sufficiency or self-satisfaction is the greatest hindrance to learning from God.

3) Through meditation and prayer. Meditating is thinking through the Word in God's presence. Prayer is talking with God about it . . . and listening to him! This leads naturally to praise and worship. Such a context puts us all in the role of learners. We lay down the ineffective model of learning something *for*

someone else and join in learning *with* them. No one can really learn something for anyone else; we all need to learn for ourselves. This step is essential in preparing a Bible study or sermon as well as in introducing the learners to the Bible study or sermon.

It is not really worth teaching people something unless they are motivated to learn and apply it. The more the teaching clearly relates to people's felt needs, the better. The first four minutes are commonly where people get motivated or fail to get motivated.

b. *Use small group Bible studies.*
1) For inductive Bible study. Strengths of this approach include:
   ■ Everyone can participate. We develop in proportion to our participation. The Spirit is freed to express himself differently through the gifts and personalities of the different participants. This diversity enriches.
   ■ Personal needs can receive attention.
   ■ Application can be worked through in a supportive environment.
   ■ Application between meetings can be followed up at the next meeting.
   ■ This method can be used in many settings: service/ministry groups, Sunday School classes, caring/discipling groups, etc. An especially valuable application is to have small groups studying the same passage as is being taught on Sunday, thus allowing the Spirit to deepen a specific theme in church members' lives.
   ■ This method does not require professional homiletics or hermeneutics training. It is conducive to a lay-led movement, easily multiplying, but still building depth.
2) To deepen Sunday sermons. People remember only a fraction of what they hear preached. But when they have a chance to thrash out the ideas in open, informal discussion, much more of the value remains.

3) To train new Bible study leaders. The best way of learning how to do it is to participate — and to watch a good leader in action.

c. *Sermon tips.*

1) 'Boy – Book – Boy'. This Christian education slogan simply means we begin with our situation, problems, needs (*Boy*, go on from there to what God says about these issues (*Book*), and conclude with how God's perspective will change the way we live (*Boy*). Other terms for the same basic process are 'contextualization' and 'doing theology'. Any response short of obedient action means the Spirit's teaching has been quenched . . . or at least not yet completed!

2) Ask questions. Get others asking questions. The Bible remains a closed book until we learn to ask questions. A traditional sermon does the work for the people and gives them only the fruit. Often that is good and necessary. Other times we may rob people of the important task of discovering God's truth for themselves. Questions are key. A good question followed by two-minute conversations among church members can do a lot to liven up a sermon. Among the numerous good questions are these simple ones:
   1. What does this passage show me about God?
   2. What does the passage show me about living?
   3. What does this mean for me in my own life here and now?

3) Preach on studying the Bible. Sunday teaching topics can create an awareness of the need for Bible study, and a mastery of some methods of beginning it.

4) Continue on one topic until it is being practised well. It is easy to miss the challenge of one lesson you have learned by skipping on to new material before the lesson has been worked through thoroughly in your lives.

5) Get feedback. You do not know what you have communicated until others tell you what they understood and what they plan to do as a result. The more feedback you can build into or around a message, the better. For instance, some churches have the Sunday

School hour following the morning message so that the morning message can be discussed and applied in small groups immediately.

NOW IT IS TIME TO DEVELOP YOUR *ACTION PLAN.* TURN BACK TO PAGE 9 FOR INSTRUCTIONS ON HOW TO DO SO. YOU WILL ALSO FIND OUT HOW TO USE THE RESOURCE MATERIAL IN SECTION 3.

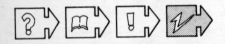

6

RENEWING OUR DISCIPLING AND PASTORAL CARE

> I heard them talking . . . Old bureaucrat, my comrade, it is
> not you who are to blame. No one ever helped you to escape
> . . . Nobody grasped you by the shoulder while there was still
> time. Now the clay of which you were shaped has dried and
> hardened, and naught in you will ever awaken the sleeping
> musician, the poet, the astronomer that possibly inhabited you
> in the beginning. (Antoine de Saint-Exupéry; *Wind, Sand and
> Stars*, Reynal and Hitchcock, New York, 1939:23).

Consider an impoverished peasant, born when art was a
diversion of the wealthy. The world might never have known
the grandeur of the Sistine, the loveliness of the *Pietà*, the
strength of the giant *David*, were it not for the Medici family's
patronage of Michelangelo . . .

Who could have guessed that a brilliant mind was locked
inside the dark and silent imprisonment of a deaf and blind
child? Anne Sullivan's determination to communicate with
Hellen Keller resulted in aid to handicapped people worldwide — as a result of Helen's writing and lecturing!

Would the early church have known or accepted Saul (who
became Paul) were it not for Barnabas' commitment and care?
Would John Mark have ever matured in the Lord and written
the first Gospel without Barnabas' faithful commitment to
him?

Webster's *Dictionary* says that a patron is 'a person chosen,
named or honoured as a special guardian, protector or
supporter.' This is a dimension of a discipling or pastoral
relationship. Other functions include nurture, training and
(often) healing. Always the objective of pastoral care is health,

maturity, and spiritual fruitfulness in the life of the person being discipled.

The terms 'discipling' and 'pastoral care' are used synonymously here. Please use whichever term best fits your situation. Both terms are used here to describe a lay ministry open to every Christian. The ordained pastor's role is to equip the disciplers or pastoral care leaders. These people in turn will equip others. And so not only is the ministry put in the hands of the people, but more and more of the equipping is put in their hands as well!

What lies ahead in this chapter? Four sections, designed for church leaders to work through together in ten to twelve hours. A retreat setting would be ideal. If this seems too large a time commitment, take into account that in this time you are: a) opening your lives to a life-changing understanding and commitment to discipling and pastoral care; b) deepening team relationships among yourselves as leaders; c) laying foundations for the church's future; and d) outlining the church's specific course for the next four to twelve months. The four sections, with the approximate time each might require, follow below.

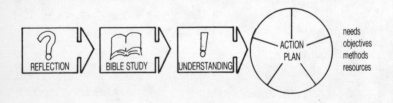

1. Reflecting on *discipling or pastoral care* as it is carried out in your church (*1 hour*).
2. Looking at God's vision for pastoral care through an **inductive Bible study** (*3 hours*).
3. Clarifying in summary fashion your understanding of pastoral care (the **what, why and how** or pastoral care) (*1½ hours*).
4. Developing your **action plan** for renewing the church's vision and practice of pastoral care.
   A. Identifying **your church's needs** in this area (*1 hour*).

B. Identifying **desired objectives** for the coming months (*1 hour*).
C. Identifying **methods** for reaching those objectives (*2 hours*).
D. Identifying **resources** for helping accomplish those objectives (*1 hour*).

Throughout the above process you will need to enter regularly into the Lord's presence in prayer and worship so that his Spirit can freely teach you. No structure, no human teacher, no manual will adequately communicate the truths of God apart from the Spirit's work! In fact, before going any further, please stop and spend some time in prayer lifting all of this to the Lord. Appropriate prayers could include:

* confession of your need for him to teach you in this area as only he can do.

* praise for all he is going to do in and through you in the coming weeks and months.

* intercession for the church members, that the Lord will be preparing their hearts for where he wants to lead them in the coming months.

* prayer for his wisdom to modify all that follows in this chapter to suit your circumstances adequately.

1. REFLECTION ON DISCIPLING
(PASTORAL CARE) IN YOUR CHURCH

Reflect on your church's practice of discipling (pastoral care) as you answer the questions below. Do this individually first, writing your responses in a notebook. Later you will discuss some responses as a group. Continue to use your notebook to keep track of all you are learning about pastoral care.

A. Reflecting on your church's discipling (pastoral care).

■ How many people in your church do you know have been

intentionally discipled by someone else in a healthy way that would be worth reproducing?

■ How many people in your church are presently involved in intentionally discipling someone else in the church?

■ Who are the most mature, Spirit-filled people in the church whom you think would be good to involve as an initial core to receive and then extend pastoral care to others?

■ Who are the most mature, Spirit-filled people in the church whom you think would be good to involve as an initial core to receive and then extend pastoral care to others?

■ What is your vision for pastoral care in your church?

■ What is your church's practice of pastoral care? Summarize it in one or two paragraphs.

■ How similar or different are your answers to the above two questions? What insights come to you in comparing them?

B. *What* do you understand pastoral care to be? Some people consider it to be the general oversight that a pastor gives to a congregation. Others consider it to be a highly structured dependency relationship where all decisions need to be approved by the person over us. Somewhere between these two extremes is healthy discipleship. Considering pastoral care to be synonymous with discipling, try defining the concept in twenty-five words or less.

C. *Why* is pastoral care important? List at least three reasons why pastoral care is vital for your growth in the Lord.

D. *How* should people be discipled personally or cared for pastorally? List three pastoral activities which are (or could be) changing your life.

E. As a group discuss your answers to the questions in Section A above, before going on together to the inductive study below.

---

2. INDUCTIVE BIBLE STUDY ON PASTORAL CARE

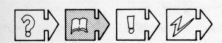

The group leader should now guide the group in the inductive Bible study which you will find in the Resource section (turn to page 237). Rather than talking a lot, he will seek to help others in expressing their insights. His main task is repeatedly to ask the following question: '*What does this passage tell us about pastoral care?*' The leader's task is simple (though it may not be easy!). Advance study will help him in asking the group pertinent questions to draw out the essence of the Bible passages. Everyone should take notes in his workbook on anything he may want to remember or review later. This kind of inductive study works well in groups ranging in size from four to twenty or even twenty-five. The Bible study outline will require two sessions of approximately one and a half hours apiece. The leader may want to choose certain passages in advance that he might skip if there is insufficient time. Similarly, he may choose to substitute other passages.

While everyone will be responding to the same general question underlined above, each person will also have a secondary question to keep in mind. Each person should be assigned to take notes on one of these three questions in order to contribute to a discussion later on:

1. *What* is pastoral care?
2. *Why* is pastoral care important?
3. *How* should pastoral care be expressed? (If you have a large group, ask most of the people to focus on this area).

NOW TURN TO THE BIBLE STUDY ON PAGE 237.

3. DESCRIPTION OF WHAT PASTORAL CARE LOOKS LIKE

A. Clarifying your perspective on pastoral care

Divide into your three sub-groups regarding the what, why

and how of pastoral care. Take about fifteen minutes to develop a short presentation for the larger group. The presentation should both present the sub-group's thinking and also stimulate the larger group to consider your question further. The following group process outlines may be helpful.

1. **What** is pastoral care? (Group one)
   a. Share your definitions or thoughts and come to agreement on a single definition.
   b. Write your definition where everyone can see it. In presenting this, you might ask the larger group to go back to their individual definitions written at the beginning of the study. They could compare and contrast them with your work. Encourage the larger group to note whether anything critical has been left out of your definition.
   c. As a large group reach consensus on a working definition. This is not set in concrete. We are all constantly learning. It is simply the group's working definition to use until the Spirit shows you something further.
2. **Why** is pastoral care important? (Group two)
   a. Seek to come up with a few truly compelling reasons. Real conviction is more important than a long list of reasons!
   b. In presenting this, you might ask the large group for its ideas and list them on a flip chart sheet or blackboard. Affirm each idea before adding any of your own that the larger group overlooked.
3. **How** should pastoral care be expressed? (Group three)
   a. As a group develop two lists: 1) the church's strengths in pastoral care; and 2) the church's weaknesses in pastoral care.
   b. In presenting this to the group, you might ask for their ideas as you present each list. Use a separate flip chart sheet for each list, and, once you have a number of ideas from the large group, add from the list your sub-group developed.

NOTES FOR THE GROUP LEADER: While every-
one should be taking his own notes, you might assign one
person to take formal notes of the three groups' presentations. These can later be typed up and distributed to all
the participants. This will be a working theology of
pastoral care. It forms the biblical base for the action plan
that will be developed by the end of this chapter. Read
the comments below regarding the what, why and how of
pastoral care ahead of time. Insert them at appropriate
moments in the group's discussion, but not until the
group has first done some significant thinking on each
question for itself.

B. Some further thoughts on the what, why and how of pastoral care

1. **What** is pastoral care? A possible working definition might
   include the following elements: Pastoral care is non-
   coercive Spirit-filled leadership called to support, guide
   and nurture others in growing into individual and corporate
   maturity and ministry. (*If the group's definition is short and
   catchy, people will remember it more easily. You may want to
   have the group recall it every so often in the ongoing discussion
   until they have a firm grasp of it.*)
2. **Why** is pastoral care important?
   a. *It equips us* for ministry, affirming and drawing out our
   gifts. As people become more responsible for ministries
   in the church, the pastor is freed further for his
   equipping work.
   b. *It encourages us* in maturing. In bringing each area of our
   lives under Christ's Lordship, we have a 'coach' or
   'mentor' or 'patron' to encourage us. When functioning
   well, pastoral care can free the pastor from 'crisis
   management' and hours of counselling because of the
   preventive help people are receiving.
   c. *It joins us* to the Body, giving us a sense of belonging,
   knowing where and how we fit in the Body of Christ. No
   longer will we go unnoticed or uncared for.

  d. *It protects us.* No longer are we walking uncovered as
     regards attacks or pitfalls of any kind — Satanic or
     human.
  e. *It guides us,* providing encouragement and help in
     difficult situations or important decisions.
  f. *It challenges us,* providing accountability. It helps us
     apply Scripture to our lives in timely and practical ways.
     People without pastoral care may experience a sub-
     stantial gap between their Christian ideals and reality.
     People under pastoral care can go a long way towards
     reducing that gap!
In short, **pastoral care is one of God's primary means of
making Christ's love tangibly real to us and giving us
grace to live triumphantly in His Kingdom**.
3. *How* is pastoral care to be expressed?
  a. *Starting a pastoral care system*
    1. Ideally, the starting point should be that the pastor
       himself is receiving pastoral care (being discipled).
       Being under pastoral care will give him much greater
       confidence in modelling and extending care to others.
       Those under his leadership will also have greater
       confidence and security, knowing they have someone
       to appeal to if problems of any kind develop.
    2. The pastor can care for a core group of four to six
       people. They in turn can pastor others who in turn
       pastor others, and so forth until all church members
       are involved and covered. This pastoral care structure
       can join the whole church together, primarily through
       lay people assuming pastoral care responsibilities.

       Some churches have found this to work best by
       combining what Peter Wagner calls the *church/
       congregation/cell* method. In this structure a church of
       any size might have 'congregations' within it of 40 to
       120 people. Each congregation could have cell groups
       of four to six people. Other churches have found the
       home-church concept helpful — in which groups are
       limited to about 20–25 people by the size of people's
       homes. In this situation, a pastor could pastorally
       care for the leaders of the congregations or home-
       churches. Those leaders would in turn care for the

leaders of the cell groups. Many of the largest churches in the world use some variation of this kind of structure.

3. Pastoral care can be exercised by both men and women, with men commonly leading men and women commonly leading women. The overall pastor could provide pastoral care both for his key men and also for his key women. You may need to modify this model to fit your church situation.

4. Jesus took significant time in choosing those whom he would personally disciple. He got to know them well and prayed at length until He was confident of God's direction. In choosing members of a pastoral care group, you might look for some of the following qualities:

    a. You feel personally drawn to this person.
    b. This person would be enthusiastic about being involved in receiving and giving pastoral care.
    c. This person has or could make the time.
    d. This person has a teachable spirit and is eager to learn.
    e. This person would add a special dimension to the caring group.
    f. This person is someone others naturally follow — and may even be presently leading a small group of some kind.
    g. This person is faithful, able to teach others (II Tim 2:2), and capable of leading a caring group without too much further training.

b. *Elements of a pastoral care meeting*

    1. Frequency and type of meetings: Meetings would normally be in a small group context, weekly at first. Once the group has a solid base and is functioning well, meetings could become biweekly and even later perhaps monthly as the group's maturity warrants. The leader might meet one-on-one with the members of his group once a month.

    Simply meeting in very small cell groups has certain disadvantages. Some churches have found it helpful to alternate small cell groups with home-

church type meetings. Thus the home-churches
might meet every first and third week of the month
and the cell groups every second and fourth week.
All the meetings could be at the same house, thus
facilitating husbands and wives coming together. On
the cell group nights, they would then separate into
different rooms of the house. Once every three
months a given month will have five meeting nights
instead of four. The extra night could be used for a
fun social evening as a change of pace.

2. Format: Meetings could be one and a half to two
   hours long, beginning with a good time of worship.
   The first month could be getting to know each other
   better. Each person could share their story and the
   evening could close with a time of prayer ministry for
   the person who shared. Once people know each other
   well and trust each other, each person in the group
   could decide upon a growth goal that the group
   would encourage him in achieving. As goals are
   reached, new ones could be identified.

3. Content: The content of the meetings could be
   derived from foundational teachings on how to live
   the Christian life. These could be given periodically
   as the Body was ready for them. They could be
   taught as part of the normal meetings of the church
   or as a special course of 6–8 sessions outside the
   normal meetings of the church. As they were offered,
   they could be worked through practically into the
   people's lives in the small group meetings. Some
   such areas could include: life in the Spirit; devotional
   life; Christian personal relationships; marriage (or
   singleness) and the family; fruit of the Spirit;
   emotions in the Christian life; service (spiritual gifts);
   and living in Christian community. Each of these
   courses or series could be taught over perhaps three
   years and then repeated for those who have come into
   the church since it was last offered. Taping the series
   would allow someone an alternative to waiting until
   the next time it was offered.

c. *Decision-making by agreement.*

Over time, people involved in pastoral care should come to understand that their lives are significantly involved in and affecting the lives of others. And so important decisions, especially those which will affect the lives of others to whom one is committed, come to be shared in some fashion. Interdependent decision-making comes to replace dependent and independent styles. As major decisions are being considered, they can be discussed with one's pastoral leader and counsel can be sought. The final responsibility *always* rests in the individual's hands; but the ideal is to sense together that a certain direction is the wisest, the best, or the leading of the Lord. Where agreement is not forthcoming immediately, unless time constraints require a decision, it is best to continue seeking the Lord together to allow him to give further light and bring agreement.

> **NOW IT IS TIME TO DEVELOP YOUR *ACTION PLAN.* TURN BACK TO PAGE 9 FOR INSTRUCTIONS ON HOW TO DO SO. YOU WILL ALSO FIND OUT HOW TO USE THE RESOURCE MATERIAL IN SECTION 3.**

7

RENEWING OUR CHRISTIAN COMMUNITY LIFE

A little shark and a little crab used to meet every morning to play together. The best of friends, they got along famously. One day the shark realized that his friend suffered from a handicap. The little crab walked sideways. The shark knew the many virtues of walking forward and took it upon himself to help his little friend overcome his handicap.

The first few days were slow. In fact one day it looked like the two might even lose their friendship over this issue. But as the little shark persevered, the crab made progress. Every day he could walk forward longer and further. The shark was beginning to feel pleased with his friend's progress. Then he realized that at the beginning of each day, he had to start over again in teaching his friend how to walk. At the beginning of the day the crab walked sideways; by evening he was walking forward — but by the next morning, again he would be walking sideways! The little shark realized something was happening to the crab between the time he left his friend at the end of the day and when he met him again the next morning. He resolved to go home with his friend; there he found, to his surprise and dismay, that *all* crabs walk sideways!

What the shark was trying to do was to influence his friend to live in a thoroughly unnatural way! To the shark, it seemed the right to walk, the normal means of proceeding for everybody. But for a crab it was abnormal.

Under the shark's influence, the crab became influenced by ideas which were strange and alien. And as Christians living in a non-Christian world, it is easy for us to become influenced by the way of living and walking through life which comes naturally to those around us. But for a Christian to live in a sub-Christian way is to deny our new, redeemed nature. It is an unnatural, unhappy compromise . . .

What was it that kept the crab walking in accordance with his true basic nature? It was the fact that every evening he went home to a community of crabs whose example and companionship straightened him out. On his own in the world, he was a prey to the persuasive ideas of well-meaning but uncomprehending people around him; but back in the community, he could discover himself again and act as he ought to.

Can we as Christians overcome the influence of the world, the well-established way in which everyone around us walks? It depends on which way of life is truly dominant for us.

> The greatest influence on a person's life will be that institution or set of institutions on which the person feels most dependent for survival and support. As long as most Christians are more dependent upon the powers and principalities of the world for their survival and security than they are upon the Christian community, the church cannot do anything other than conform to the world — The community of the local church must become the most important and central corporate reality of our lives, the daily environment out of which our lives are lived, the fellowship of people that sustains and supports us. The church must represent a body of people who have committed their lives to one another in Christ, a communion of faith and trust . . . and a corporate sign of the transforming power of the gospel of the kingdom in this world. (Jim Wallis, 'Seeds of the Kingdom,' *Sojourners*, January, 1977).

What kind of community life does your church experience? Is it the 'central corporate reality of church members' lives? Is it a Boyd, committed to one another whether scattered or gathered? Does it have a structure for in-depth personal sharing and fellowship? Christian community is critical for the survival and health of the church. *If we do not practise significant Christian community, we have to ask whether the church or the world is really the primary influence on our lives.*

The subject of Christian community intersects several areas that are dealt with in depth in other chapters. This chapter focuses on reciprocal relationships (the 'one-anothers' of the

New Testament) and authentic meaningful membership in the local church. Chapter Four spells out some of the implications of community relationships in terms of stewardship of our time, money and possessions. Chapter Eight develops the dimension of our spiritual gifts and ministries (and so the study of certain key passages such as Rom. 12, Eph. 4 and I Cor. 12–14 is taken up there).

What lies ahead in this chapter? The chapter has four sections, designed for church leaders to work through together in ten to twelve hours. A retreat setting would be ideal. If this seems too large a time commitment, take into account that in this time you are: a) opening your lives to a life-changing understanding and commitment to Christian community;

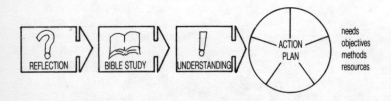

1. Reflecting on **the community life of your church** (*1 hour*).
2. Looking at God's vision regarding Christian community, through an **inductive Bible study** (*3 hours*).
3. Clarifying in summary fashion your understanding of the Body or of community (the **what, why and how** of Christian community) (*1½ hours*).
4. Developing your **action plan** for renewing the church's vision and practice of Christian community.
   A. Identifying **your church's needs** in this area (*1 hour*).
   B. Identifying **desired objectives** for the coming months (*1 hour*).
   C. Identifying **methods** for reaching those objectives (*2 hours*).
   D. Identifying **resources** for helping accomplish those objectives (*1 hour*).

b) deepening team relationships among yourselves as leaders; c) laying foundations for the church's future; and, d) outlining the church's specific course for the next four to twelve months. The four sections, with the approximate time each might require, are shown on page 102.

---

1. REFLECT ON YOUR CHURCH'S EXPERIENCE OF COMMUNITY

Reflect on your church's experience of community as you answer the questions below. Do this individually first, writing your responses in a notebook. Later you will discuss some responses as a group. Continue to use your notebook to keep track of all you are learning about Christian community.

A. Reflecting on your church's Christian community.
- How many people in your church view the church as their first priority after God and their family? That is to say, how many put their church life as a higher priority than their job, recreation or other social groups?
- How many small groups (6–20 people) that meet weekly does your church have? How many people in your church are actively involved and committed to one of these weekly small groups?
- How easy is it to become a member of one of these groups? Are the groups constantly taking in new members or do they tend to be stable?
- What is your vision for Christian community in your church? Summarize it in one or two paragraphs.
- What is your church's present experience of community? Summarize it in one or two paragraphs.
- How similar or different are your answers to the above two questions? What insights come to you in comparing them?

B. *What* do you understand Christian community life to be? Different people think it might be synonymous with coming to church, with being a church member, or with communal living. What do you think? Try defining the concept 'Christian community' in twenty-five words or less.
C. *Why* is Christian community important? List at least three reasons why Christian community is key for your growth in the Lord.
D. *How* can we best experience meaningful community in the church? List three fellowship activities which are (or could be) a regular source of strength for your life and the life of the church.
E. As a group discuss your answers to the questions in Section A above before going on together to the inductive study below.

> **2. INDUCTIVE BIBLE STUDY ON CHRISTIAN COMMUNITY**

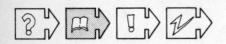

The group leader should now guide the group in the following inductive Bible study which you will find in the Resource Section (turn to page 240). Rather than talking a lot, he will seek to help others in expressing their insights. His main task is repeatedly to ask the following question: '*What does this passage tell us about Christian community?*' The leader's task is simple (though it may not be easy!). Advance study will help him in asking the group pertinent questions to draw out the essence of the Bible passages. Everyone should take notes in his workbook on anything he may want to remember or review later. This kind of inductive study works well in groups ranging from four to twenty or even twenty-five. The Bible study outline will require two sessions of approximately one and a half hours apiece. The leader may want to choose certain passages in advance that he might skip if there is insufficient time. Similarly, he may choose to substitute other passages.

While everyone will be responding to the same general question underlined above, each person will also have a secondary question to keep in mind. Each person should be assigned to take notes on one of these three questions to contribute to a discussion later on:

1. *What* is (Christian) community?
2. *Why* has God called us to be a community? Why has he not purposed for us simply to follow him as individuals?
3. *How* can we best experience meaningful community life? (*If you have a large group, most of the people might focus on this area.*)

NOW TURN TO THE BIBLE STUDY ON PAGE 240.

3. DESCRIPTION OF WHAT CHRISTIAN COMMUNITY LOOKS LIKE

A. Clarifying your perspective on Christian community

Divide into your three sub-groups regarding the what, why and how of Christian community. Take about fifteen minutes to develop a short presentation for the larger group. The presentation should both stimulate the larger group to consider your question further and present the sub-group's thinking. The following group process guidelines may be helpful.

1. **What** is (Christian) community? (Group one)
   a. Share your definitions or thoughts and come to agreement on a single definition.

b. Write your definition where everyone can see it. In
presenting this, you might ask the larger group to go
back to their individual definitions written at the
beginning of the study. They could compare and
contrast them with your work. Encourage the larger
group to note whether anything critical has been left out
of your definition.

c. As a large group reach consensus on a working
definition. This is not set in concrete. We are all
constantly learning. It is simply the group's working
definition to use until the Spirit shows you something
further.

2. **Why** has God called us to be his community? (Group two)

a. Seek to come up with a few truly compelling reasons.
Real conviction is more important than a long list of
reasons!

b. In presenting this, you might ask the large group for its
ideas and list them on a flip chart sheet or blackboard.
Affirm each idea before adding any of your own that the
larger group overlooked.

3. **How** can we best experience meaningful community
life? (Group three)

a. As a group develop two lists: 1) the church's strengths in
Christian community; and, 2) the church's weaknesses
in Christian community.

NOTES FOR THE GROUP LEADER: While every-
one should be taking his own notes, you might assign one
person to take formal notes of the three groups'
presentations. These can later be typed up and distributed
to all the participants. This will be a working theology of
Christian community. It forms the biblical base for the
action plan that will be developed by the end of this
chapter. Read the comments below regarding the what,
why and how of Christian community ahead of time.
Insert them at appropriate moments in the group's
discussion, but not until the group has first done some
significant thinking on each question for itself.

b. In presenting this to the group, you might ask for their ideas as you present each list. Using a separate flip chart sheet for each list, once you have a number of ideas from the large group, add from the list your sub-group developed.

B. Some further thoughts on the what, why and how of Christian community

1. **What** is Christian community? A possible working definition might include the following elements: 'Christian community is the redeemed people of God bound together by Christ's Spirit to care for all aspects of one another's lives'. The Greek word for fellowship or community, *koinonia*, also embodies concepts of partnership, sharing and communion. (*If the group's definition is short and catchy, people will remember it more easily. You may want to have the group recall it every so often in the ongoing discussion until they have it down well!*)

2. **Why** has God called us to be his community? What are his purposes in giving us such a calling?

   a. *God makes himself real to us through his Body.* We are flesh and blood creatures who need flesh and blood expressions of God's holiness, love, grace and forgiveness. God became incarnate 2000 years ago and continues to be incarnate today through his Body. Someone has said, 'I sought my soul, but my soul failed to see. I sought my God, but my God eluded me. I sought my brother, and I found all three.' We need each other to experience the fulness of God.

   b. *Only together can we become all God intends us to be.* We are God's image-bearers, called to corporate life as we reflect his very triune nature. God desires that our unity be like his (John 17:20–23). None of us is complete alone (Gen. 1:26; 2:18). We need the Body to grow into maturity (Eph. 4:11–16). In Christian community, many of our needs can be met, deep-seated problems solved, and healing received. 'Walking closely with people very different from ourselves is hard for the flesh, but good for the spirit. We may have right views, but God is giving us an opportunity to display a right attitude; we may believe aright, but he is testing us to see if we love aright' (Watchman Nee, *A Table in the Wilderness*, Daily Meditations, December 22, Victory Press, London, 1965). God's life is more 'caught' than taught. Association with holy and strong souls builds holiness and strength.

c. *Our unity and our love are perhaps the two greatest proofs to nonchristians of the Good News of Jesus Christ* (John 13:35; 17:20–23). We are the presence of God in this world, revealing him. In a world faced with overwhelming problems, a community of healthy, growing, joyful people living peacefully together will be a tremendous witness to the power and love of God!

d. *The normal Christian needs a Christian environment* if he is going to live out his Christianity in a vital way. We are strongly influenced by the people we interact with on a daily basis. What a privilege to be able to observe firsthand healthy marriage and family life, effective problem-solving, positive communication, unconditional love, and dependable, trusting relationships! These types of models are not common in the world — we need them to help us understand how Kingdom living really works.

e. *He wants us to enter into the joy and benefits of shared lives.* Some of these include:

  1) Sharing in the resources and blessings God has given our brothers and sisters (I Cor. 3:22,23).

  2) Receiving grace so that we can in turn give grace to others (Mt. 10:8).

  3) Stable relationships with others who share our basic values and goals.

  4) Close friends who both help us handle the problems and stresses in our lives and celebrate our joys.

  5) A supportive context in which to discover and use our gifts and vocations or callings.

  6) Effective spiritual warfare against the attacks of the enemy.

In short, **through community life we know God tangibly through seeing Christ in our brothers and sisters, we become more like him, and we make Kingdom ways known to the world.**

3. **How** can we best experience meaningful community life?
The following elements are helpful, if not imperative.

   a. *The leadership team as a model.* As the leadership team of
the church develops a growing measure of community,
the people will be able to follow with confidence.
Modelling community together allows you to test
principles and forms of community life. Your leadership
will ring with authenticity, not calling for anything of
others that you yourselves are not living.

   b. *Consensus decision-making.* As leaders, move as one or
not at all. This can remove defensiveness and politicking
since each leader knows his opinion alone can halt any
action. This breeds a high sense of responsibility. If
there is not agreement, the issue is tabled for further
prayer and study until the next meeting. The Spirit will
commonly give new insight to someone or to the whole
group to help them move forward in unity. One person,
probably the pastor, should be recognized to have the
final say should it be impossible to postpone a decision
and should consensus not be forthcoming. The con-
sensual model is not easy. It requires a radical openness
on the part of the leaders (1) to God in prayer, (2) to
each other, recognizing the gifting and wisdom of each
one, and (3) to the whole Body. Some necessary insights
— words of real prophetic significance — will come to
the leaders from the church members. One caution: to
bring a decision to the Body on which the leaders are
divided is to invite the spirit of division to enter the
church. Only when leaders are in agreement among
themselves should they bring issues to the Body, though
still open to the Spirit modifying their perspective
through the Body's input.

   c. *Small groups.* To practice community well requires small
groups: they are basic to church structure if people are
to share their lives in depth. An operational definition of
'community' is those to whom we turn when we have
needs or problems — people need small groups if they
are to share their lives in depth. In small groups we learn
to put aside our masks of self deception and defensiveness to enter into the abundant life God intends for us.

    In the large Jerusalem church, there was considerable

small group activity in the homes (Acts 2:46). Indeed, house churches were common in the New Testament (Rom. 16:5,23; I Cor. 16:19; Col. 4:16; Philemon 1:2).

d. *Different types of groups*. A key to success with small groups is to encourage a number of different kinds of groups. Seeking to make all groups the same will stifle creativity and gifts and will not allow for certain important functions of the Body to surface. Kevin Springer outlines the following types of groups in *Pastoral Renewal* (September, 1986). (The magazine is available from PO Box 8617, Ann Arbor, MI 48107, USA.)

e. *Trained small group leaders*. Fire can destroy or warm. A knife can kill or heal. So small groups are a powerful tool which need appropriate guidance to be life-giving rather than divisive. It is wise to start small with one good group that includes the pastor and let it multiply as its life and health becomes evident. Attempting to set up a large structure quickly is likely to result in a collapse due to inadequate foundations and leadership formation. For every advantage of small groups one could list a parallel danger that could potentially develop. For instance:

1) *Being close* may deteriorate into being a clique — unless the closeness is outward focused in service and regularly adding new members (which requires multiplying after a certain point).

2) *Being loyal* to the leader can become competitive with loyalty to the overall pastor or leader — unless the group leader is loyal and tied in to the pastor. The pastor and his leadership team need to provide the over-all leadership. Unless the pastor is particularly gifted in small group leadership, he should ask the Lord to give him someone who is gifted in that way to train the leaders of the small groups.

3) *Being supported* can undermine a person's basic support in God — unless the group is constantly drawing each member close to God in worship, intercession and prayer ministry.

4) *Being interdependent* in sharing lives and decisions can

become bondage — unless diversity and individuality is strongly affirmed.

5) *Receiving individualized care* can become dependency under authoritarianism if the group leaders are not in turn under mature interdependent leadership which is itself relating healthily to mature interdependent leadership.

f. *Meaningful relationship.* People are often membered theologically, but not practically. Tools that different churches use to help develop meaningful membership include:

1) Having a careful membering process. Becoming a church member in the second and third centuries commonly took three years! Churches and groups committed to committed or covenant relationships are finding that such a time period is not unreasonable. Individualism is so deeply ingrained in Western culture that the church has to develop intentionally a counter-culture to overcome it. This does not happen in a few months. In much the same way as a couple will develop a healthy friendship and courtship before marriage, so committed or covenant relationships cannot be rushed or forced. They need time to develop healthily and well. Time allows people to grow in their love and commitment; it also allows people to drift apart without major trauma if God is not joining them together. A careful initiatory period can allow two foundations to be laid in the prospective member's life: foundational teaching about how to live as part of a Kingdom community and the cultivation of loving relationships within the Body.

2) Tying membership into becoming an integral part of one of the church's small groups. The small group can even be responsible for commending a person to the larger church for membership. This builds community and discipleship into the membership process.

3) Making the act of membering a real celebration, possibly during a weekend retreat. The celebration could include such things as baptisms, testimonies of

commitment on the part of the incoming members, testimonies of God's character revealed in that person by those who know him or her well, the laying on of hands by one or more church leaders with special prayers asking God to empower this person for a special role in the Body, and even the washing of the feet of the new members! Not all of this may fit your situation. Yet if your church community is to be the new believers' most important corporate reality, how might you make their initiation into the Body truly memorable?

4) Developing a membership covenant. While this can be legalistic, it need not be. The covenant might be at a house church or cell group level and could include simple commitments to unconditional love, availability, sharing, responsibility and accountability.

5) Some churches have found it helpful to have a two-tiered membership: *general* church membership and *community* or *covenant* membership. This allows for present members to continue as before while some people move ahead into a fuller expression of discipleship. For new people, general church membership may be a step toward community membership. Wherever the two levels are used, it is important to make the difference not so much one of privileges as of responsibilities.

f. *Expressing unity with Christians beyond our local church.* To avoid ingrownness, and to fully enter into Christ's vision for unity, we need to pursue and participate in opportunities for expressing unity with other churches in our city, state, country, and the world. As regards the latter, the Lausanne Committee for World Evangelization and the World Evangelical Fellowship are two principal evangelical expressions of unity among evangelicals.

Other means of expressing such unity can include such things as: occasional joint worship services with another church, interchurch prayer vigils, joint sponsorship of special events, shared youth group activities, standing together on clearly biblical social or political issues, and, of course, mutually supporting city-wide evangelistic crusades.

Perhaps one of the most valuable means for building inter-church community is when pastors meet together regularly for in-depth fellowship. The following model has proven helpful in some places. A group of four to twelve pastors might meet the first Monday of each month. The morning could be spent in worship, personal sharing, sharing advice with each other and praying for each other. The afternoon could be spent in deepening the group's vision in one area of church life. Everyone would have at least a month to be thinking about the topic and gathering together key points. One or two people could have an assignment of actually writing up a paper. A useful study question as background for this work could be the following: 'If we were starting a 'perfect church' from scratch, what would we want our [theme of the day] to look like?'

NOW IT IS TIME TO DEVELOP YOUR *ACTION PLAN*. TURN BACK TO PAGE 9 FOR INSTRUCTIONS ON HOW TO DO SO. YOU WILL ALSO FIND OUT HOW TO USE THE RESOURCE MATERIAL IN SECTION 3.

8

RENEWING OUR MINISTRY (SPIRITUAL GIFTS)

'What a beautiful package. Look, each side of the box is different.

'This side is white, pure white. I've never seen a lovelier young woman than the one sketched on the white paper. So innocent, so fragile, yet strong — with a trace of sadness about her face. Her features are Jewish I think.

'Turn the box around. There, that side is deep blue, midnight blue. Shepherds and their sheep. What a peaceful scene.

'I wonder why this side is so dark. Nothing but darkness. Put it on the bottom so it doesn't show. Rest the package on that side.

'That's better. Isn't this side striking? I don't think I've ever seen a more gorgeous shade of purple. It's — well — regal, especially with those man on camels in the design. I wonder where they came from, where they're going.

'This gets more interesting all the time.

'Look at this pure gold side. Those are angels, aren't they? This is by far the richest side of the whole package.

'But what a contrast, this red. You know, I never did like red, especially that shade. I wonder why whoever wrapped this package, whoever designed it, made one side that awful colour. Turn it away, turn the box so that the terrible red is on the bottom and the dark side is at the back. There, that's much better; now the red doesn't show and the black side's turned away from view.

'White, blue, gold, purple. I just enjoy sitting here looking at the beautiful package.'

'AREN'T YOU GOING TO OPEN IT?'

'Why — is there something inside?'

(Joe Bayly, 'The Present,' *I Saw Gooley Fly and Other Stories*, Fleming H. Revell Co., Old Tappan, N.J., 1968:94,95. Published in Britain by Scripture Union.)

Has anyone opened up the gift hidden inside you? Is your church evoking community? Why do so many believers settle for not opening the 'box'? Why do so many churches hesitate to stimulate, provoke and support such unwrapping of gifts?

> The identifying of gifts brings to the fore . . . the issues of commitment. Somehow if I name my gift and it is confirmed, I cannot 'hang loose' in the same way. I would much rather be committed to God in the abstract than be committed to him at the point of my gifts . . . Doors will close on a million lovely possibilities. I will become a painter or a doctor only if denial becomes a part of my picture of reality. Commitment at the point of my gifts means that I must give up being a straddler. Somewhere in the deeps of me I know this. Life will not be the smorgasbord I have made it, sampling and tasting here and there. My commitment will give me an identity.
> (Elizabeth O'Connor, *Eighth Day of Creation*, Word, Waco, TX, USA, 1971:42,43).

That kind of commitment transforms the individual — and transforms the church. For the church too must enter into being a committed community if her people are to discover the ministries God has planted in them. These seeds cannot grow apart from the watering and warmth and cultivation of a supportive community.

Are the members of your church fulfilled in ministry? Are a faithful few doing almost everything? Or is your church more like a bustling beehive? And if it is a bustling beehive, is honey being produced? Are people expending their energy in simply maintaining programmes? Or are they also bearing spiritual fruit through personal ministry in committed relationships? These kinds of questions are addressed in this chapter.

The subject of spiritual gifts intersects several areas that are dealt with in depth in other chapters. Chapter Seven on Christian community focuses on reciprocal relationships (the 'one-anothers' of the New Testament) and authentic meaningful membership. Some specific types of ministries are the focus of other chapters: intercessory prayer, giving, teaching, discipling, evangelism, social responsibility (service), missions and spiritual warfare (which includes healing and deliverance).

This chapter attempts to unleash the power that will make those ministries fruitful.

What lies ahead in this chapter? The chapter has four sections, designed for church leaders to work through together in ten to twelve hours. A retreat setting would be ideal. If this seems too large a time commitment, take into account that in this time you are: a) opening your lives to a life-changing understanding and commitment to the development of spiritual gifts; b) deepening team relationships among yourselves as leaders; c) laying foundations for the church's future; and, d) outlining the church's specific course for the next four to twelve months.

Spiritual gifts have, unfortunately, been one of the most divisive issues in recent evangelical church history. As you reflect, study and plan, may the Lord grant you real wisdom, sensitivity and grace to rise above such issues, especially if they have been a problem in your own context. Please make use of whatever is helpful in this chapter and feel free to leave behind whatever you think will cause problems.

The four sections, with the approximate time each might require, follow below.

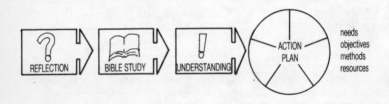

1. Reflecting on **your church's use of its people's gifts** (*1 hour*).
2. Looking at God's vision regarding spiritual gifts through an **inductive Bible study** (*3 hours*).
3. Clarifying in summary fashion your understanding of spiritual gifts (the **what, why and how** of spiritual gifts) (*1½ hours*).
4. Developing your **action plan** for renewing the church's vision and practice of spiritual gifts.

> A. Identifying **your church's needs** in this area (*1 hour*).
> B. Identifying **desired objectives** for the coming months (*1 hour*).
> C. Identifying **methods** for reaching those objectives (*2 hours*).
> D. Identifying **resources** for helping accomplish those objectives (*1 hour*).

Throughout the above process you will need to enter regularly into the Lord's presence in prayer and worship so that his Spirit can freely teach you. No structure, no human teacher, no manual will adequately communicate the truths of God apart from the Spirit's work! In fact before going any further, please stop and spend some time in prayer lifting all of this to the Lord. Appropriate prayers follow overleaf.

> *NOTE*. There is no subject which has aroused more difference of opinion in the last few years than the subject of this chapter! Some Christians believe that all the gifts of the New Testament days are intended to be used in the modern church; others argue that they are not; others feel that there are many more gifts than are listed in the New Testament. Some believe that the church should be structured according to the spiritual gifts of its members, and others feel that they have a less important place in Christian ministry. We hope that this chapter will be helpful *whatever* your church's theological position. If you need to reflect more on this subject before embarking on the rest of the chapter, the following books are representative of differing positions:
>
> Peter Wagner, *Your Spiritual Gifts Can Help Your Church Grow* (Gospel Light)
> Gene Getz, *Sharpening the Focus of the Church* (Zondervan)
> John Stott, *Baptism and Fulness* (IVCF)

* confession of your need for him to teach you in this area as only he can do.
* praise for all he is going to do in and through you in the coming weeks and months.
* intercession for the church members, that the Lord will be preparing their hearts for where he wants to lead them in the coming months.
* prayer for his wisdom to modify all that follows in this chapter to suit your context well.

---

1. REFLECTION ON YOUR CHURCH'S
USE OF SPIRITUAL GIFTS

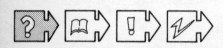

Reflect on your church's use of spiritual gifts as you answer the questions below. Do this individually first, writing your responses in a notebook. Later you will discuss some responses as a group. Continue to use your notebook to keep track of all you are learning about spiritual gifts.

A. Reflecting on your church's use of spiritual gifts.

■ How many ministry teams are there in your church? (A ministry team is a group of people planning, praying, and working *together* to serve others in a specialized way.)

■ How many people in your church have a sense of calling that they are fulfilling through ministry in or through the church?

■ What ministries do you feel are weakest or most needed in your church?

■ What is your vision for the church's using people's gifts and mobilizing people in ministry? Summarize it in one or two paragraphs.

■ What is your church's present experience of using people's gifts and mobilizing people in ministry? Summarize it in one or two paragraphs.

■ How similar or different are your answers to the above

two questions? What insights come to you in comparing them?

B. *What* do you understand a spiritual gift to be? Some people seem only to see the more manifestational or supernatural gifts of 1 Corinthians 12:7–10. Others can see no place for these gifts. Some people think the pastor should be doing all the ministry (after all, that's what he's paid for, isn't it?!). Others think the pastor should do as little ministry as possible, devoting himself to training and equipping others to use their gifts. Some people think spiritual gifts are basically sanctified talents; others think they are supernatural abilities bestowed by the Spirit at salvation or later. What do you think? Try defining the concept 'spiritual gift' in twenty-five words or less.

C. *Why* are spiritual gifts important? List at least three reasons why spiritual gifts are key for your growth in the Lord.

D. *How* can we best release people into the ministry in the church? List three 'releasing' activities which are (or could be) a regular source of strength for your life and the life of the church.

E. As a group discuss your answers to the questions in Section A above before going on together to the inductive study below.

---

2. INDUCTIVE BIBLE STUDY ON MINISTRY AND SPIRITUAL GIFTS

The group leader should now guide the group in the inductive Bible study which you will find in the Resource section (turn to page 244). Rather than talking a lot, he will seek to help others in expressing their insights. His main task is repeatedly to ask the following question: *'What does this passage tell us about ministry and gifts?'* The leader's task is simple (though it may not be easy!). Advance study will help him in asking the group pertinent questions to draw out the essence of the Bible passages. Everyone should take notes in his workbook on anything he may want to remember or review later. This kind of inductive study works well in groups ranging from four to twenty or even twenty five. The Bible study outline will require two sessions of approximately one and a half hours apiece. The leader may want to choose certain passages in advance that he might skip if there is insufficient time. Similarly, he may choose to substitute other passages.

While everyone will be responding to the same general question underlined above, each person will also have a secondary question to keep in mind. Each person should be assigned to take notes on one of these three questions to contribute to a discussion later on:

1. *What* is a spiritual gift?
2. *Why* has God given us spiritual gifts?
3. *How* can we best release and support people in developing their gifts and ministries? (If you have a large group, most of the people might focus on this area.)

 NOW TURN TO THE BIBLE STUDY ON PAGE 244.

3. DESCRIPTION OF WHAT SPIRITUAL GIFTS LOOK LIKE

A. Clarifying your perspective on spiritual gifts

Divide into your three sub-groups regarding the what, why and how of spiritual gifts. Take about fifteen minutes to develop a short presentation for the larger group. The presentation should both stimulate the larger group to consider your question further and present the sub-group's thinking. The following group process guidelines may be helpful.

1. **What** is a spiritual gift? (Group one)
   a. Share your definitions or thoughts and come to an agreement on a single definition.
   b. Write your definition where everyone can see it. In presenting this, you might ask the larger group to go back to their individual definitions written at the beginning of the study. They could compare and contrast them with your work. Encourage the larger group to note whether anything critical has been left out of your definition.
   c. As a large group reach consensus on a working definition. This is not set in concrete. We are all constantly learning. It is simply the group's working definition to use until the Spirit shows you something further.
2. **Why** has God given us spiritual gifts? (Group two)
   a. Seek to come up with a few truly compelling reasons. Real conviction is more important than a long list of reasons!
   b. In presenting this, you might ask the large group for its ideas and list them on a flip chart or blackboard. Affirm each idea before adding any of your own that the larger group overlooked.
3. **How** can we best release and support people in developing their gifts and ministries? (Group three).

NOTES FOR THE GROUP LEADER: While everyone should be taking his own notes, you might assign one person to take formal notes of the three groups' presentations. These can later be typed up and distributed to all the participants. This will be a working theology of spiritual gifts. It forms the biblical base for the action plan that will be developed by the end of this chapter. Read the comments below regarding the what, why and how of spiritual gifts ahead of time. Insert them at appropriate moments in the group's discussion, but not until the group has first done some significant thinking on each question for itself.

   a. As a group develop two lists: 1) the church's strengths in helping people develop ministries; and, 2) the church's weaknesses in helping people develop ministries.

   b. In presenting this to the group, you might ask for their ideas as you present each list. Using a separate flip chart sheet for each list, once you have a number of ideas from the group, add from the list your sub-group developed.

B. Some further thoughts on the what, why and how of spiritual gifts

1. **What** is a spiritual gift? A possible working definition might include the following elements: 'A spiritual gift is a Spirit-giving power (or grace) to build up the very spirit of others, resulting in the growth of the Body.' Two Greek words are commonly translated 'spiritual gifts': *charismaton*, from *charis* which means grace; and *pneumata* which means breath, wind or Spirit, indicating invisible power. God often uses natural abilities, surrendered to him, to effect spiritual ministry. (*If your definition is short and catchy, people will remember it more easily. You may want to have the group recall it every so often in the ongoing discussion until they have it down well.*)

2. **Why** has God given us spiritual gifts?

   a. *The gifts reveal Christ.*

     1) The gifts reveal Christ's character. Each gift reveals something about the nature of God (I Pet. 4:10,11).

     2) The gifts reveal Christ's power (John 14:2; Acts 1:8; I Cor. 4:20).

     3) The gifts reveal Christ's grace. God's gifts are a way not only of giving himself *to* us, but also a way of giving himself *through* us (Eph. 4:7–13; Rom. 12:6–8).

   b. *The gifts mobilize the Body.*

     1) Edifying or building up the Body to maturity (I Cor. 12:7; 14:12,26; Eph. 4:11–13).

     2) Equipping or training the Body for ministry (Eph. 4:11,12; Heb. 13:21).

     3) Energizing, motivating or empowering the Body (I Cor. 12:6,11; Phil. 2:13).

c. *The gifts allow us to continue God's creative work in this world.*

God works for six days, rested on the seventh, and then, as O'Connor puts it, turned the world over to us for *The Eighth Day of Creation*, the title of Elizabeth O'Connor's book (1971). Not only does God meet the Body's needs through his gifts, but he also meets our needs: the need to create, the need to be needed, the need to discover and risk. As we use his gifts, we are filled with the creator's joy. Using our gifts gives us the joy of seeing God continue to work out his purposes, his creative designs for his world — *through us!* Dormant gifts depress. Churches who fail to use the creativity and gifts of their people, in most cases eventually lose their people. The people either leave or else emotionally and mentally remove themselves even while physically staying on.

In short, throughout spiritual gifts we more fully know Christ, we edify, equip and energize the Body, and we continue God's creative work in the world!

3. **How** can we best release and support people in developing their gifts and ministries? The following elements are helpful, if not imperative.

a. *Providing a loving and supportive environment.* Love is essential for gifts to function rightly. It is also essential for people to be able and willing to risk uncovering their hidden hopes, desires and ambitions for ministering. It can be quite a revelation to study I Cor. 13:4–7 and note how each quality of love is essential to releasing people in their gifts and ministries.

b. *Teaching people how to discover/discern spiritual gifts.* Scripture encourages us to understand our gifts so we can build others up (I Cor. 12:1; 14:1,12; Rom. 14:19). Several methods can help in discerning spiritual gifts.

1) DEFINE THE GIFTS. The starting point is for the church leaders to help people have a simple (preferably written) definition of each of the gifts found in Scripture. Some pastors have found the Romans 12 gifts to be underlying motivations, while seeing the

Ephesians 4:11 gifts as ministries and the ones in I Corinthians 12:8–10 as manifestational gifts. This can then lead to more careful teaching on the seven motivational gifts of Romans 12 as a means of mobilizing the Body. Tight adherence to this model has its problems, but following it loosely has often been helpful. Whether you use this framework or not, defining the specific gifts will help people recognize the gifts in themselves and in one another.

2) DO A SIMPLE ASSESSMENT. This can take many forms. One would be to use a chart where the gifts are listed down the left hand side of the page and three columns are at the top titled:

A) I definitely feel I have this gift.
B) I might possibly have this gift.
C) I would really like to develop this gift more this year.

Doing this in a spirit of prayer will help people avoid either under-estimating or over-estimating what God has given them. Other questions that can help with self-assessment include:

— What do you do that gives you the most satisfaction and self-worth?
— What angers you? (Very possibly it may be: seeing your gift abused or used poorly.)
— How would you describe the path down which God has led you to this point? What experiences has he given you that would indicate his training you in a specific gifting or calling?
— If you knew you had the support of a Christian community who would back you completely, what would you like to give yourself to? (Assume you have no limitations financially, educationally or in any other way!)
— How would you list the church's ten greatest weaknesses? Then list your ten greatest strengths (most people have some difficulty with this!). Very possibly some of your key strengths are exactly what the church is lacking and needing.

3) SHARE WITH A SMALL GROUP. Building on some form

CHARACTERISTIC

TYPE OF GROUP

	Task-Oriented	Neighbourhood Evangelism	Fellowship	Pastoral Care	Leadership Training
Leader's Gifts and Maturity	Moderate	Moderate	Moderate	High	Very high
Training Needed by Leader	Low	Moderate	Moderate	High	Very high
Quality of Relationships Among Members	Functional	Friendly	Friendly	Strong, personal, supportive	Highly committed, especially to leader
Schedule Priority	Moderate	Moderate	Moderate	High	High
Frequency	Varies	Usually weekly	Varies from weekly to monthly	Weekly or biweekly	Weekly
Longevity	Ends when task is completed	Can be short-term or open-ended	Usually ongoing	Ongoing	Until training is completed
Composition	Based on skills needed to do the job	Mixed, changeable	Mixed, changeable	Homogeneous, stable	Homogeneous, stable

of self-assessment, a small group that knows each other well could use a similar chart or assessment tool and note what they feel might be the gifts of others in their small group (ideally four to six people). Each person can share his view of a given individual's gifting before having that individual than share his own self-assessment. When done in the Spirit, this can be a deeply affirming and exciting discovery time. Husbands and wives would also profit from discussing this together.

4) SERVE! Nothing tests and clarifies our gifts so much as trying to use them. If you do not know what your gifts are, then 'whatever your hand finds to do, verily, do it with all your might' (Eccl. 9:10; Eph. 6:7). As you get involved in the lives of others, your gifts will emerge. If you know what one or more of your gifts are, use them! Practice makes perfect (I Tim. 4:14–16; II Tim. 1:6). And you will become sure of what your gifts are as you encourage joy and fulfillment in using them, as well as finding the community's recognition.

c. *Encouraging the formation of ministry/ groups*. If pastoral care, discipling or fellowship groups already exist, they may need to be restructured to facilitate ministry. Other people may reform their present commitments to work closely with those who sense a similar calling. The formation of such groups should not be according to gifts, but according to callings or function. Thus each grouping will include many different complementary gifts. Some possible mission/ministry groups could include the following:

* evangelical ministries
* foreign missions support
* marriage enrichment
* hospitality
* worship and music
* intercession
* social responsibility/action
* healing prayer teams
* children's ministries
* political involvement
* service in the church
* service to the poor and needy
* discipling new Christians (possibly as they become members of the church and find their mission/ministry).

Gordon Cosby and Elizabeth O'Connor, both listed in the
resource section, give extensive guidelines for forming ministry
groups drawn from their experience at Church of the Savior in
Washington, D.C. Ideally these groups should be made up of
people who are called to a specific form of ministry. A key
person around whom a group is built is a prior or moderator
— a person whose chief call is to be an enabler or evoker of
gifts. Other special roles include the intercessor, the spiritual
director, the pastor-prophet and the patron. A patron is
defined as 'one chosen, named, or honoured as a special
guardian, protector, supporter, or the like.' He is gifted in
providing people an environment for risk-taking and creativity.

  d. *Seeking the anointing of the Spirit.* The Spirit is the one
     who breathes life into our efforts, empowers our
     ministry, and causes it to bear lasting fruit. The impact
     of all the above will be greatly multiplied if the Spirit is
     poured out on the congregation. This may come in the
     commissioning of mission groups through the laying on
     of hands. Or then again, as we are ardently seeking the
     Lord it may come almost unexpectedly. Scripture
     teaching regarding this could include Lk. 11:9–13; John
     7:37–39; 14:12–18; Acts 1:7; 2:1–4,17,18; 4:29–33;
     6:3,5,8,10; 8:14–19; 9:17,18; 10:44–48; 19:1–7; Eph.
     5:18–20; and II Tim. 1:6,7.

  e. *Tying people's gifts into the church leadership.* Two
     opposite and equally tragic abuses can easily arise.
     Church leaders can squash gifted people instead of
     affirming them. The authority of a leader is demon-
     strated in how high he can raise others. His calling is to
     detect and confirm gifts, facilitating them and providing
     avenues for their use. The inverse abuse of gifts is when
     gifted people begin doing their own thing, ignoring or
     overriding the appointed church leadership. This can be
     compounded when people mistake giftedness for matur-
     ity. It becomes even worse when gifted people begin
     claiming a type of 'divine authority' in and through their
     gifting that supposedly raises them up above the church
     leadership.

     A pastor and an especially gifted person need to
  balance their commitment to unity with their commit-

ment to diversity. As regards unity, they need a close personal relationship, free and regular communication, and trust. As regards diversity, they need to honour and respect one another and give each other room in which to express what God has put in each of them. A particularly gifted person does well to recognize that his greatest weaknesses are inherent in his strengths. The pastor can serve as a spiritual director to protect and guide the gifted person in his ministry.

NOW IT IS TIME TO DEVELOP YOUR *ACTION PLAN*. TURN BACK TO PAGE 9 FOR INSTRUCTIONS ON HOW TO DO SO. YOU WILL ALSO FIND OUT HOW TO USE THE RESOURCE MATERIAL IN SECTION 3.

9

RENEWING OUR FAMILY LIFE

How is the family doing? Reports over the last several decades continuously raise warning flags. The following items from census data and recent surveys in the United States indicate that:

* the overall divorce rate is now forty per cent.
* one of every three children no longer lives in an intact nuclear family (with their original mother and father).
* by 1990, more than half the United States families will be single-parent or stepfamilies.
* suicide is now the highest cause of death of young people.
* eight million children need immediate help for psychiatric disorders according to the Presidential Commission on Mental Health.
* there are one million runaway children each year.
* child pornography is growing; some thirty thousand boys and girls are being exploited in Los Angeles alone.
* in the 1970's *reported* cases of child abuse averaged 500,000 a year. Abuses included physical attack, sexual and emotional harm, and neglect. One expert believes more children die from abuse injuries than from all the common childhood diseases. In the 1980's reported cases of child abuse appear to be double that of the 1970's.
* an estimated 1.6 million women are beaten by their husbands every year — one out of six wives, and generally in a pattern of repeated abuse.
* an estimated twenty-five million homosexuals live in America. (Sources: *The Chicago Tribune*, October 16, 1983, Section 3, page 12; and *Fathergram*, March, 1984, #54, P.O. Box Z,

Mobile AL 36616 and *Christianity Today*, September 19, 1980, pp. 40,41.)

In Britain, the situation is as follows:

* on average, each year in Britain there are now 145,000 divorces. Roughly speaking, one marriage in three will end in divorce.
* one quarter of all couples who marry have been living together first.
* in 1971 33% of illegitimate pregnancies led to a marriage. In 1981 it was only 19%. In other words, the number of single parent families has almost doubled.
* in 1982 over 158,000 children under the age of sixteen went through the trauma of their parents' divorce.
* research suggests that 140,000 marriages in the United Kingdom involve violence and battering.
* there were 6388 reported instances of child abuse in Britain in 1982.
* one in eight families in Britain is a single-parent family.

(Source of these figures: HMSO.)

The condition of the family is different in some respects in every country. The above exemplifies Western civilization which is impacting almost every country in a greater or lesser degree. Some countries do not have all the above problems, but have other family problems which are just as serious.

Like the boy who cried 'Wolf! Wolf!' too often, we easily become jaded by the sheer frequency of the reports on family problems. According to a report by the National Association of Evangelicals Task Force on the Family, at its March 1985 convention, 58 per cent of evangelical pastors were aware of an increase in family breakdown in the churches. However, they seemed satisfied with their ability to handle their families' problems without outside assistance. In fact. many pastors did not respond to the task force survey, causing the task force to ask, 'Do these pastors really want help?'

How are the families of your church doing? Are they filled with peace and joy and order? Is their beauty one of the church's chief means of attracting people to Christ. Are the fathers spiritual leaders of their homes? What is the mother's role in the home? Do the children readily obey and respect adults? Do the families regularly do things together as a family? Questions such as these are addressed in this chapter.

Family life intersects several areas that are dealt with in depth in other chapters. Chapter Seven on Christian community on reciprocal relationships (the 'one-anothers' of the New Testament) which make a very revealing study when considered in light of marriage or the family. Most if not all of the functions of the church emphasized in other chapters should be reflected in miniature in a Christian family. Worship, intercessory prayer, giving, teaching, discipling, evangelism, social responsibility (service), and missions all have a place in the family! If the emphasis is healthy, every facet of church renewal will strengthen the family. Yet the family is too important to strengthen it only indirectly through good church life. Thus this chapter focuses on *intentionally renewing* family life.

What lies ahead in this chapter? The chapter has four sections, designed for church leaders to work through together in ten to twelve hours. A retreat setting would be ideal. If this seems too large a time commitment, take into account that in this time you are: a) opening your lives to a life-changing understanding and commitment to family life; b) deepening team relationships among yourselves as leaders; c) laying foundations for the church's future; and, d) outlining the church's specific course for the next four to twelve months. The four sections, with the approximate time each might require, follow overleaf.

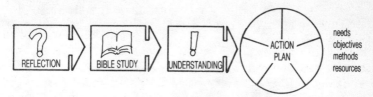

Throughout the above process you will need to enter regularly into the Lord's presence in prayer and worship so that his Spirit can freely teach you. No structure, no human teacher, no manual will adequately communicate the truths of God apart from the Spirit's work! In fact before going any further,

1. Reflecting on **your church's family life** (*1 hour*).
2. Looking at God's vision regarding family life through an **inductive Bible study** (*3 hours*).
3. Clarifying in summary fashion your understanding of family life (the **what, why and how** of family life) (*1½ hours*).
4. *Developing your* **action plan** for renewing the church's vision and practice of family life.
   A. Identifying your church's **needs** in this area (*1 hour*).
   B. Identifying **desired objectives** for the coming months (*1 hour*).
   C. Identifying **methods** for reaching those objectives (*2 hours*).
   D. Identifying **resources** for helping accomplish those objectives (*1 hour*).

please stop and spend some time in prayer lifting all of this to the Lord. Appropriate prayers could include:

* confession of your need for him to teach you in this area as only he can do.
* praise for all he is going to do in and through you in the coming weeks and months.
* intercession for the church members, that the Lord will be preparing their hearts for where he wants to lead them in the coming months.
* prayer for his wisdom to modify all that follows in this chapter to suit your context well.

1. REFLECTION ON YOUR CHURCH'S FAMILY LIFE

Reflect on the condition of your church's families as you answer the questions below. Do this individually first, writing your responses in a notebook. Later you will discuss some responses as a group. Continue to use your notebook to keep track of all you are learning about family life.

A. Reflecting on your church's family life.
- How many whole families are there in your church? (A whole family is a father, mother and — usually — at least one child.) How many partial or broken families? (Children without parents or with just one parent; couples who are separated or divorced.)
- How many singles are there in your church? How many of them live in some kind of household, share their lives together, and have a sense of belonging to a family? (A household might be defined as two or more people intentionally living together for the Lord.)
- How many fathers in your church would you say are doing a good job of leading their families and fathering their children?
- What is your vision for healthy family life? Summarize it in one or two paragraphs.
- How similar or different are your answers to the above two questions? What insights come to you in comparing them?

B. *What* do you understand distinctively Christian family life to be? Try defining the concept 'Christian family' in twenty-five words or less.

C. *Why* is healthy family life important? List at least three reasons why healthy family life is key for your growth in the Lord.

D. *How* can families function healthily? List three activities which make (or could make) family life a regular source of strength for you and the rest of the church.

E. As a group discuss your answers to the questions in Section A above before going on together to the inductive study below.

---

2. INDUCTIVE BIBLE STUDY ON FAMILY LIFE

The group leader should guide the group in the inductive Bible study which you will find in the Resource section (turn to page 247). Rather than talking a lot, he will seek to help others in expressing their insights, His main task is repeatedly to ask the following question:

'*What does this passage tell us about family life?*' The leader's task is simple (though it may not be easy!). Advance study will help him in asking the group pertinent questions to draw out the essence of the Bible passages. Everyone should take notes in his workbook on anything he may want to remember or review later. This kind of inductive study works well in groups ranging from four to twenty or even twenty-five. The Bible study outline will require two sessions of approximately one and a half hours apiece. The leader may want to choose certain passages in advance that he might skip if there is insufficient time. Similarly, he may choose to substitute other passages.

While everyone will be responding to the same general question underlined above, each person will also have a secondary question to keep in mind. Each person should be assigned to take notes on one of these three questions to contribute to a discussion later on:

1. *What* is a Christian family? To be more specific, how is a Christian family distinctive from a non-christian family?
2. *Why* has God ordained family life?
3. *How* can families function healthily? (If you have a large group, most of the people might focus on this area.)

NOW TURN TO THE BIBLE STUDY ON PAGE 247.

3. DESCRIPTION OF WHAT GODLY FAMILY LIFE LOOKS LIKE

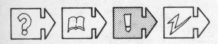

A. Clarifying your perspective on family life

Divide into your three sub-groups regarding the what, why and how of family life. Take about fifteen minutes to develop a

short presentation for the larger group. The presentation
should both stimulate the larger group to consider your
question further and present the sub-group's thinking. The
following group process guidelines may be helpful:

1. **What** is a *Christian family*? (Group one)
   a. Share your definitions or thoughts and come to agreement on a single definition.
   b. Write your definition where everyone can see it. In
   presenting this, you might ask the larger group to go
   back to their individual definitions written at the
   beginning of the study. They could compare and
   contrast them with your work. Encourage the larger
   group to note whether anything critical has been left out
   of your definition.
   c. As a large group reach consensus on a working
   definition. This is not set in concrete. We all are
   constantly learning. It is simply the group's working
   definition to use until the Spirit shows you something
   further.
2. **Why** has God ordained family life? (Group two)
   a. Seek to come up with a few truly compelling reasons.
   Real conviction is more important than a long list of
   reasons!
   b. In presenting this, you might ask the large group for its
   ideas and list them on a flip chart sheet or blackboard.

NOTES FOR THE GROUP LEADER: While everyone
should be taking his own notes, you might assign one
person to take formal notes of the three groups'
presentations. These can later be typed up and distributed
to all the participants. This will be a working theology of
family life. It forms the biblical base for the action plan
that will be developed by the end of this chapter. Read
the comments below regarding the what, why and how of
family life ahead of time. Insert them at appropriate
moments in the group's discussion, but not until the
group has first done some significant thinking on each
question for itself.

Affirm each idea before adding any of your own that the
larger group overlooked.
3. **How** can families function healthily? (Group three)
   a. As a group develop two lists: 1) common strengths of
   families in your church; and, 2) common weaknesses of
   families in your church.
   b. In presenting this to the group, you might ask for their
   ideas as you present each list. Using a separate flip chart
   sheet for each list, once you have a number of ideas from
   the large group, add from the list your sub-group
   developed.

B. Some further thoughts on the what, why and how of family life

1. **What** is a Christian family? Larry Christenson offers the
following simple definition: 'A Christian family is a family
that lives together with Jesus Christ.' He goes on to say,
'The secret of good family life is disarmingly simple:
cultivate the family's relationship with Jesus Christ. There
is no phase of family life left outside this relationship'
(1970:14). (*If your definition is short and catchy, people will
remember it more easily. You may want to have the group recall
it every so often in the ongoing discussion until they have it
down well.*)
2. **Why** has God ordained family life?
   a. *Family life tangibly communicates the mystery of God*
   (Eph. 5:22–27,32).
      1) Husband and wife enter into the mystery of being
      one, yet more than one; the mystery of more fully
      understanding the masculinity and feminity that are
      encompassed in being jointly created to be the image
      of God; and the mystery that submission brings
      freedom while leadership means servanthood.
      2) Children develop a tangible image of God through
      their parents — not so much by what their parents
      say as by what they do and who they are. The
      Fatherhood and love of God becomes incarnate, for
      better or for worse. On a small scale, the family
      should demonstrate the wisdom and gentleness of
      command, the willingness of obedience, the unity

and firmness of mutual confidence which will characterize the perfect kingdom of God.

b. *Family life is one of God's primary tools for maturing us.* Basic character traits are formed very early in children and are reinforced throughout their growing up years. At the same time, children may teach their parents more about love, patience, endurance, mercy and many other godly qualities than perhaps anyone else at this stage in the parents' lives. Together we practice and test all the principles of God in a 'safe' setting where it is okay to make mistakes, to fail, to struggle, to doubt, to laugh and cry, to slowly but surely grow up!

c. *The normal Christian needs a strong Christian environment* if he is going to live Christ's life in a vital way. This is also one of the reasons God has established the church to be a Christian community as discussed in Chapter Seven. (In fact, all the reasons for why God has called us into Christian community also apply to the family.) The family is our base for being a 'peculiar people' walking differently from the world. It is a shelter, a place of healing, of restoration, of being renewed for the challenges that face us 'outside.'

In short, **through godly families we tangibly experience more of God, we have a supportive setting in which to grow, and we are renewed to face the daily challenges that come our way!**

3. **How** can families function healthily? The following elements are helpful, if not imperative.

a. *Commitment to marriage as a covenant relationship.* Marriage needs to be built on commitment and serve rather than romance or emotional intimacy. That is to say, it is primarily a matter of the will and the mind rather than of feelings. If our wills and minds are set right, our feelings will fall into line. Commitment to our spouse should be second only to our relationship with Jesus Christ. It should come before our children, our business, our church and our friends. It has been said that familiarity breeds contempt. We need to be careful that our spouse does not fall into last place as we stretch ourselves thin in ministry, business and other pursuits.

Our schedules need to include regular quality time with each other. We need to make time together for thinking, dreaming, sharing, planning, going out together and loving. It has been said that the three most common problems in marriage are communication, communication and communication! If we invest little time in knowing and nurturing our spouse, we cannot expect a rich and life-giving relationship.

b. *Commitment to healthy parenting*. One outline of what this includes can be drawn from Lk. 2:52 regarding Christ's growth 'in stature and wisdom and favour with God and man.'

1) GROWING IN STATURE. Godly parents teach their children to eat well, exercise well, sleep well and maintain good hygiene.

2) GROWING IN WISDOM. Rather than simply relegating the job to schools, godly parents take an active part in their children's education. They guide and interact with their children regarding the input they receive from television, literature, music, movies and friends.

3) GROWING IN FAVOUR WITH GOD. This includes:

A) Bringing the children to Christ. Nothing will so draw our children to Christ as our own pursuit of him and our love. As regards the latter, physical and verbal affection should be abundant. They need to know they are loved unconditionally. As regards the former, daily family devotions are difficult to establish, but very worthwhile once the habit is in place. Responsibility for them can be rotated so each takes a turn being in charge. Even when children are four or five years old, parents can help them plan and lead a devotional time. As they get older, they will do it themselves.

B) Teaching children to obey. Many proverbs speak to the necessity of corporal punishment (Prov. 13:24; 23:13,14; 29:15). Good spankings are administered in private, and can be followed up by the child asking God's forgiveness, and the parent granting forgiveness with a big hug of affirmation. One hard spanking administered like this will eliminate hours of nagging, shouting, arguing and threatening.

C) Modelling the church in microcosm. Worship, prayer, priesthood, obedience, witness, faith, and so on, should be learned firstly and most deeply in the home.

D) Developing a positive heart attitude toward the church. This is far more valuable than developing external conformity to church attendance.

4) GROWING IN FAVOUR WITH MAN. This social realm includes:

A) Teaching responsibility through work around the house.

B) Teaching courtesy and social norms through family life.

C) Building a sense of identity, belongingness and self worth in a world marked by uncertainty and alienation. One major way of doing this is to build good memories through developing family traditions and special events like vacations. Children need time devoted to them individually as well as together as a family. Establishing a certain night or nights for special events each week is one way of doing this. Some such nights could be game nights, chef nights, heritage nights (telling stories of past events, pulling out old pictures) and scrapbook nights (pasting in pictures and highlights of recent family life).

D) Providing sex role modelling for our children. Fathers should be the spiritual heads of their families and teach their sons godly rather than cultural masculinity; mothers should be homemakers and teach their daughters godly rather than cultural femininity. For either to be taught well requires the complementary role provided by one's spouse.

What *is* 'godly masculinity' and 'godly feminity'? In every culture, it is important to remember, it will look a little different, as it is expressed in varying ways. We need to work out for ourselves what it should look like in our own culture — although obviously there will be some generic similarities, and the books in the Resources section (page 277) should help you in analysing it for yourself.

c. *Commitment to incorporating adult singles.* Interestingly enough, in both Old Testament times and New Testament times, singles found a place living in someone's household. In fact, the term most commonly translated family from the Hebrew (*bayit*) and the Greek (*oikos*) would more appropriately be translated house or household. A household commonly included some portion of extended family as well as incorporating servants, employees and others such as close friends who became attached to the family. Today more and more singles live alone. In fact, one out of five households in the United States consists of one person living alone; five per cent of British women between 18 and 49 are divorced. People are marrying later in life. More single women are striking out on their own. Many more elderly people are living alone (*Newsweek*, January 17, 1983). The church must develop an intentional strategy for incorporating adult singles. While the most common approach in America is to have one or more 'singles programmes,' some churches are beginning to work with the biblical concept of 'households' to provide meaningful community for adult singles. Such households sometimes consist of all singles (of the same sex) or may have married couples who oversee the household.

NOW IT IS TIME TO DEVELOP YOUR *ACTION PLAN.* TURN BACK TO PAGE 9 FOR INSTRUCTIONS ON HOW TO DO SO. YOU WILL ALSO FIND OUT HOW TO USE THE RESOURCE MATERIAL IN SECTION 3.

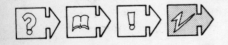

10

RENEWING OUR LOCAL EVANGELISM

'I've observed,' said the Latin American leader, 'that churches are either strong on evangelism or strong on renewal. One of the problems I have with the current emphasis on church renewal is that it invariably seems to undermine the outreach of the church. I would much rather see a church continue to reach the world for Christ than focus on how to 'renew' itself.'

What do you think of this perspective? Only too often churches that are strong on being the family of God are weak on seeing new people come to Christ. Many pastors carry a deep burden for outreach, yet cannot seem to mobilize the Body effectively.

Consider another scenario perhaps more common to some Third World countries. People are coming to the Lord faster than they can be absorbed into the Body. In some churches not ten, or twenty or thirty people a month, but hundreds of people make professions of faith each month! But maybe only a tenth of those who make a profession take the step of baptism. And maybe only a tenth of those who are baptized are still with the church a year later . . .

How is your church doing in witnessing? Do your people know how to share the Gospel simply and naturally with their friends? Do they even have nonchristian friends? Is the beauty of their lives one of the church's chief means of attracting people ot Christ? Are people coming to the Lord regularly? And are they becoming a meaningful part of your church? Questions such as these and situations such as those described above are addressed in this chapter.

Witness to the world intersects several areas that are dealt with in depth in other chapters. Chapter Eleven focuses on foreign mission strategy which is evangelism extended to areas beyond the church's local sphere. Chapter Twelve addresses our social responsibility, becoming involved in the problems and difficulties of our community, city or nation. Such involvement is an integral part of our witness. So, while witnessing through our works and through our words cannot be separated, more will be said about our works in Chapter Twelve. Almost every dimension of church life underlies, reflects and adds power to our witness. And little wonder, for a good relationship with God and a good relationship with his people are foundational to healthy witness.

What lies ahead in this chapter? The chapter has four sections, designed for church leaders to work through together in ten to twelve hours. A retreat setting would be ideal. If this seems too large a time commitment, take into account that in this time you are: a) opening your lives to a life-changing understanding and commitment to witness to the world; b) deepening team relationships among yourselves as leaders; c) laying foundations for the church's future; and, d) outlining the church's specific course for the next four to twelve months. The four sections, with the approximate time each might require, are shown opposite.

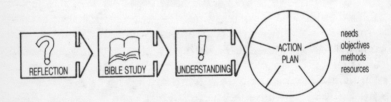

Throughout the process you will need to enter regularly into the Lord's presence in prayer and worship so that his Spirit can freely teach you. No structure, no human teacher, no manual will adequately communicate the truths of God apart from the Spirit's work! In fact, before going any further please stop and spend some time in prayer lifting all of this to the Lord. Appropriate prayers could include:

* confession of your need for him to teach you in this area as only he can do.

1. Reflecting on **your church's witness to the world** (*1 hour*).
2. Reflecting on God's vision regarding witness to the world through an **inductive Bible study** (*3 hours*).
3. Clarifying in summary fashion your theology of witnessing to the world (the **what, why and how** of witness to the world) (*1½ hours*).
4. Developing your **action plan** for renewing the church's vision and practice of witnessing to the world.
   A. Identifying **your church's needs in this area** (*1 hour*).
   B. Identifying **desired objectives** for the coming months (*1 hour*).
   C. Identifying **methods** for reaching those objectives (*2 hours*).
   D. Identifying **resources** for helping accomplish those objectives (*1 hour*).

* praise for all he is going to do in and through you in the coming weeks and months.
* intercession for the church members, that the Lord will be preparing their hearts for where he wants to lead them in the coming months.
* prayer for his wisdom to modify all that follows in this chapter to suit your context well.

1. REFLECTION ON YOUR CHURCH'S WITNESS TO THE WORLD

Reflect on your church's witness to the world as you answer the questions below. Do this individually at first, writing your responses in a notebook. Later you will discuss some responses as a group. Continue to use your notebook to keep track of all you are learning about witness to the world.

A. Reflecting on your church's witness.
    ■ How many people in your church have won someone to the Lord in the last year? How many do you think have verbally shared the Gospel in the last six months?
    ■ What kinds of structures or programmes does your church have that are specifically geared to outreach?
    ■ Of the people who have come to the Lord in or through your church in the last year, what proportion have been baptized?
    ■ What is your vision for your church's witness to the world? Summarize it in one or two paragraphs.
    ■ What is your church's present witness to the world like? Summarize it in one or two paragraphs.
    ■ How similar or different are your answers to the above two questions? What insights come to you in comparing them?
B. *What* do you understand a Christian witness to be? Try defining the concept 'Christian witness' in twenty-five words or less.
C. *Why* is our witnessing to the world important? List at least three reasons why witnessing is key for your growth in the Lord.
D. *How* can we witness effectively? List three witnessing activities which are (or could be) a regular source of strength for you and the rest of the church.
E. As a group discuss your answers to the questions in Section A above before going on together to the inductive study below.

| 2. INDUCTIVE BIBLE STUDY ON WITNESS TO THE WORLD |

The group leader should now guide the group in the inductive Bible study which you will find in the Resource section (turn to page 250). Rather than talking a lot, he will seek to help others in expressing their insights. His main task is to repeatedly ask the following question: '*What does this passage tell us about our witness to the world*?' The leader's task is simple (though it may not be easy!). Advance study will help him in asking the group pertinent questions to draw out the essence of the Bible passages. Everyone should take notes in his workbook on anything he may want to remember or review later. This kind of inductive study works well in groups ranging from four to twenty or even twenty-five. The Bible study outline will require two sessions of approximately one and a half hours apiece. The leader may want to choose certain passages in advance that he might skip if there is insufficient time. Similarly, he may choose to substitute other passages.

While everyone will be responding to the same general question underlined above, each person will also have a secondary question to keep in mind. Each person should be assigned to take notes on one of these three questions to contribute to a discussion later on:

1. *What* is a Christian witness?
2. *Why* has God commanded us to witness?
3. *How* can we witness effectively? (*If you have a large group, most of the people might focus on this area.*)

NOW TURN TO THE BIBLE STUDY ON PAGE 250.

---

3. DESCRIPTION OF WHAT GODLY
WITNESS TO THE WORLD LOOKS LIKE

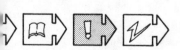

A. Clarifying your perspective on witness to the world

Divide into your three sub-groups regarding the what, why

and how of witness to the world. Take about fifteen minutes to
develop a short presentation for the larger group. The
presentation should both stimulate the larger group to
consider your question further and present the sub-group's
thinking. The following group process guidelines may be
helpful.

1. **What** is a Christian witness? (Group one)
   a. Share your definitions or thoughts and come to agree-
      ment on a single definition.
   b. Write your definition where everyone can see it. In
      presenting this, you might ask the larger group to go
      back to their individual definitions written at the
      beginning of the study. They could compare and
      contrast them with your work. Encourage the larger
      group to note whether anything critical has been left out
      of your definition.
   c. As a large group reach consensus on a working
      definition. This is not set in concrete. We are all
      constantly learning. It is simply the group's working
      definition to use until the Spirit shows you something
      further.
2. **Why** has God commanded us to witness? (Group two)
   a. Seek to come up with a few truly compelling reasons.
      Real conviction is more important than a long list of
      reasons!
   b. In presenting this, you might ask the large group for its
      ideas and list them on a flip chart sheet or blackboard.
      Affirm each idea before adding any of your own that the
      larger group overlooked.
3. **How** can we witness effectively? (Group three)
   a. As a group develop two lists: 1) strengths of your
      church's witness; and, 2) weaknesses of your church's
      witness.
   b. In presenting this to the group, you might ask for their
      ideas as you present each list. Using a separate flip chart
      sheet for each list, once you have a number of ideas from
      the large group, add from the list your sub-group
      developed.

NOTES FOR THE GROUP LEADER: While everyone should be taking his own notes, you might assign one person to take formal notes of the three groups' presentations. These can later be typed up and distributed to all the participants. This will be a working theology of witness to the world. It forms the biblical base for the action plan that will be developed by the end of this chapter. Read the comments below regarding the what, why and how of witnessing ahead of time. Insert them at appropriate moments in the group's discussion, but not until the group has first done some significant thinking on each question for itself.

B. Some further thoughts on the what, why and how of witness to the world

1. **What** is a Christian witness? A possible working definition might include the following elements: 'A Christian witness is a person who accurately and attractively communicates the Good News of the Kingdom by God by his life and by his words.' (*If your definition is short and catchy, people will remember it more easily. You may want to have the group recall it every so often in the ongoing discussion until they have it down well.*)
2. **Why** has God commanded us to witness?
   a. *For God's sake.*
   1) Only through our witness will his mission be accomplished. He came to seek and to save those who are lost (Mt. 18:11–14). He came to destroy the works of the devil (I John 3:8), deliver people from the domain of darkness and transfer them to the Kingdom of his beloved Son (Col. 1:13). But how will people hear the Good News if we do not share it (Rom. 10:13–15)?
   2) Through our witness we bring him great joy. Every one who comes to him brings Him great joy (Lk. 15:7,10,32). What greater blessing can we give him

who has given us everything, than to be part of bringing him such joy?

b. *For the sake of those who are lost without him.* God is greatly concerned for both 1) their eternal salvation (John 3:18; Mt. 10:15) *and* 2) for bringing them into the goodness of his Kingdom here and now (Mt. 9:36–10:1). For many of us the former is undermined by head knowledge that is not accompanied by heart conviction, while the latter is undermined by not seeing that our lives differ significantly from those of our nonchristian neighbours. How can we overcome these two problems? You may want to discuss this further since having a vibrant witness requires overcoming both problems.

c. *For our sake as his people.* Without effective witness, a church falls into the problems:

1) We become ingrown and stagnant, suffering from 'koinonitis.' The energy that should be going to win the world gets turned in on ourselves. We become real candidates for in-fighting, politicking and even division.

2) Our worship becomes dull. Worship is based on the great works and character of God. If we do not see him at work in changing nonchristians' lives, we begin to wonder whether our Christianity is simply another cultural expression or whether we do indeed have hold of '*the* way, *the* truth and *the* life'. Even when we do not consciously begin to doubt, unconsciously we increasingly begin to live the life of a sceptic.

In short, **through our witness we bless God, we offer others God's abundant life in the 'here and now' as well as for eternity, and we see God do mighty works!**

3. **How** can we witness effectively? The following elements are helpful, if not imperative.

a. *An effective on-the-job training programme to mobilize the congregation.* All the messages in the world, all the small group Bible studies imaginable, will not equal the impact of someone who is skilled in seeing people come to Christ intentionally training others in a reproductive way (II Tim. 2:2). The Kennedy Evangelism Explosion program is one of the best along these lines. It teaches people key memory verses, questions for stimulating conversation about the Lord, an outline of the Gospel and how to give their testimony. This is done in the context of regularly accompanying someone as they witness to others. Over the course of sixteen weeks the novice grows to the point of communicating the Gospel effectively — not in theory, but in practice!

b. *Presenting the Gospel of the Kingdom.* What Jesus preached was 'the Gospel of the Kingdom' (Mt. 4:23; 9:35). (Christ's vision for the Kingdom of God is discussed more fully in Chapter One of this section, p. 000. Too often we present a different Gospel! (See Gal. 1:6–12.) Many people have contrasted two different approaches to the Gospel. Key words identifying this contrast include:

* Becoming a Christian (*this expression occurs 3 times in the New Testament*)
* Becoming a disciple (*this word occurs 270 times in the New Testament*)
* Man-centred, emphasizing the benefits of salvation
* God-centred, emphasizing man's need to be reconciled to God
* Subjective (*feeling oriented*)
* Objective (*truth oriented*)
* Synthetic (*enriching our present lifestyle*)
* Authentic (*like the challenge given to the rich young ruler: laying down everything*)
* Saviour (*24 times in the New Testament*)
* Lord (*700 times in the New Testament*)
* Believe
* Repent and obey
* Cheap grace
* Costly grace
* Being fulfilled
* Laying down one's life

The first column describes an incomplete gospel while the second column describes the Gospel of the Kingdom. Some elements of the first column complement the Gospel of the Kingdom. Some elements of the first column complement the Gospel of the Kingdom; but whenever the first column is made primary, we have departed from the Good News of Jesus Christ. Jim Wallis comments aptly on this:

> The great tragedy of modern evangelism is in calling many to belief but few to obedience. The failure has come in separating belief from obedience, which renders the gospel message confusing and strips the evangelistic proclamation of its power and authority. The evangelistic question has become what do we believe *about* Christ rather than are we willing to forsake all and follow him. When the theology of faith is torn apart from the life of faith, what results is an evangelism that has more to do with doctrine than with transformation.
> (*Agenda for Biblical People*, Harper & Row Publ. Inc., 10 East 53rd Street, New York, N.Y. 10022, 1976).

c. *Relationally-based evangelism.* Evangelism based on friendship focuses on seeing a person's life change. This has been compared with content-oriented evangelism (focusing on how many people heard the message) and manipulative evangelism (focusing on how many people said yes). Win Arn, executive director of the Institute for Church Growth, reports on a number of studies indicating that church drop-outs commonly have been evangelized through one of the last two approaches, while those who become active church members have commonly been evangelized through friendship. He points out that effective evangelism involves the following elements:

1) MANY AND VARIED PRESENTATIONS OF THE GOSPEL (such as through music, friends' lives, Bible study, literature, a testimony, radio and so on). After many exposures, there comes a season of receptivity in his life — a time of need — when the seed that has been sown breaks into new life, sprouts, takes root, and grows.

2) DRAWING PEOPLE INTO FRIENDSHIPS IN THE CHURCH. Friendships appear to be the strongest bond cementing new members to their congregation. If new members do not immediately develop meaningful friendships in their church, many of them return to their old

friendships — and ways — outside the church. Research indicates that a visitor — whether a new Christian or a transferring older Christian — will likely become inactive unless he acquires at least four friends in the first three to six months of visiting a church.

3) DRAWING PEOPLE INTO MINISTRY. Arn says that a church should have at least 60 ministry roles available for every 100 members. A 'role' refers to a position, function, or responsibility in the church — choir member, committee member, teacher, officer and so on. However, in typical Protestant churches, for every 100 members there are approximately 25–30 roles available. Of those 30 roles, 20 are filled by 10 people — the willing workers who have more than one job. The remaining 10 are filled by an additional 8 people, thus involving 18 of the 100 members. A new member in this situation will have difficulty finding a meaningful opportunity for ministry and service.

4) DRAWING PEOPLE INTO SMALL GROUPS AND STARTING NEW GROUPS. Arn says there should be at least seven small groups for every 100 members who are 14 years or older. The consequence of having too few groups where people can build meaningful relationships is a high rate of inactive members leaving the church. Furthermore, Arn says that of the fellowship groups that exist in a church, one of every five should have been started in the last five years. Otherwise people get into a rut and stop growing. Making new groups, whether by changing the membership of the groups or starting groups that have a new purpose, provides continued freshness in the church and a place for newcomers to find a home (Win Arn, 'Can We Close the Back Door?', *Pastoral Renewal*, Vol. 10, No. 7 [February 1986], pp. 101, 117–120. Available from PO Box 8617, 840 Airport Blvd, Ann Arbor, MI 48107.

d. *Understanding the factors which can hinder or advance our witness*. Why are some kinds of people responsive, and others not? Why do some churches grow steadily, while others reach a certain level of membership and then stick there? Why are some methods effective in some areas and less than useless in others? The answers to all of these questions have been studied for over thirty years by researchers in the field of Church Growth. A mass of useful and helpful material is available (see Resources section, page 280). Unless we know the facts of the situation in which we are working, and understand the different forces at work within it, we may be much less effective than we could be. And unless we are able to appraise our own strengths and weaknesses accurately, we may invest a lot of time, money and energy for very little reward.

e. *Having a clear idea of where we want to go.* 'Aim at nothing,' goes the old saying, 'and that's what you'll hit.' In many situations around the world where Christian witness has been remarkably effective, it has been because God's people have put some thought and prayer into setting specific goals for their work. When everyone has the same vision, and is working towards the same end, the energies of the church are harnessed properly and God is able to respond to their faith with blessing. When the aim of witness is unclear, and the end result we want to see is only vaguely defined, there is a much greater chance that nothing will result. Many books on Church Growth give helpful ideas about setting goals in faith; see the Resources section (page 280).

NOW IT IS TIME TO DEVELOP YOUR *ACTION PLAN*. TURN BACK TO PAGE 9 FOR INSTRUCTIONS ON HOW TO DO SO. YOU WILL ALSO FIND OUT HOW TO USE THE RESOURCE MATERIAL IN SECTION 3.

11

RENEWING OUR MISSION STRATEGY

The young missionary closed his message: 'We all know that everyone is a missionary and that the mission field is everywhere. As we go tonight from the church, let us go out as missionaries called by God to bring the Good News to everyone we meet!' The missionary conference closed with a rousing hymn. The people energetically shook the missionary's hand at the door, thanking him for the challenging message.

This popular perspective on missions raises a question: Is the call to missions any different from the call to witness? Missionary work encompasses the call to witness, but goes beyond it. It is no more accurate to say we are all missionaries than to say 'every Christian is a pastor' or to say the whole body is an eye (I Cor. 12:17). Many churches have only a vague notion of what a missionary is. And many know even less about how to plan strategically for missions. After all, is that not the work of the mission agencies?

Many readers of this book will be citizens of countries which have traditionally been 'receiving' rather than 'sending' nations — countries to which foreign missionaries have come, rather than countries which have sent their own missionaries elsewhere. In such places, churches often find it hard to believe that they too can — and must! — be involved in the task of worldwide mission. If you are a small church, in an emergent nation, isn't it a criminal waste of your resources to send some of your best people abroad? Thus runs the thinking in many places.

What about your church? What do you think missionaries are? Do you have a missionary strategy? Do your people know how they fit into that strategy? Is missions more than a budget item and an annual conference to raise mission pledge money? Are missionaries a vital part of the life of the church or just visiting dignitaries? Are church members with a missionary calling being *recognized* in your church? *Prepared* by the church? *Tested* and *proven* before being sent? Questions such as these are addressed in this chapter.

Developing a mission strategy intersects several areas that are dealt with in depth in other chapters. Chapter Ten on witnessing lays the groundwork for sharing the Gospel. The Scripture study and perspective developed in that chapter underlie this chapter. Chapter Twelve on social responsibility treats the subject of community development and service ministries. Such involvement is an integral part of our missions strategy. Indeed, given the strategy of fielding missionary teams that will model the church in miniature, every chapter of this manual becomes an essential backdrop to missionary work.

What lies ahead in this chapter? The chapter has four sections, designed for church leaders to work through together in ten to twelve hours. A retreat setting would be ideal. If this seems too large a time commitment, take into account that in this time you are: a) opening your lives to a life-changing understanding and commitment to missionary work; b) deepening team relationships among yourselves as leaders; c) laying foundations for the church's future; and, d) outlining the church's specific course for the next four to twelve months. The four sections, with the approximate time each might require, follow below.

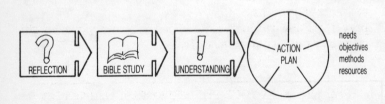

1. Reflecting on **your church's mission strategy** (*1 hour*).
2. Looking at God's vision regarding missions through an **inductive Bible study** (*3 hours*).

3. Clarifying in summary fashion your understanding of missions (the **what, why and how** of missions) (*1½ hours*).

4. Developing your **action plan** for renewing the church's vision and practice of missions.
   A. Identifying **your church's needs** in this area (*1 hour*).
   B. Identifying **desired objectives** for the coming months (*1 hour*).
   C. Identifying **methods** for reaching those objectives (*2 hours*).
   D. Identifying **resources** for helping accomplish those objectives (*1 hour*).

Throughout the above process you will need to enter regularly into the Lord's presence in prayer and worship so that his Spirit can freely teach you. No structure, no human teacher, no manual will adequately communicate the truths of God apart from the Spirit's work! In fact before going any further, please stop and spend some time in prayer lifting all of this to the Lord. Approximate prayers could include:

* confession of your need for him to teach you in this area as only he can do.
* praise for all he is going to do in and through you in the coming weeks and months.
* intercession for the church members, that the Lord will be preparing their hearts for where he wants to lead them in the coming months.
* prayer for his wisdom to modify all that follows in this chapter to suit your context well.

1. REFLECTION ON YOUR CHURCH'S MISSION STRATEGY

Reflect on your church's missions thrust as you answer the questions below. Do this individually first, writing you responses in a notebook. Later you will discuss some responses as a group. Continue to use your note book to keep track of all you are learning about missions.

A. Reflecting on your church's missions strategy.
- What is your vision for your church's involvement in missions? Summarize it in one or two paragraphs.
- What is your church's present involvement in missions? Summarize it in one or two paragraphs.
- How similar or different are your answers to the above two questions? What insights come to you in comparing them?
- How many church members has your church sent out as missionaries?
- How many missionaries does your church support so substantially that they would consider your church their 'home church', and settle down there when they are on furlough?
- What proportion of your budget is set aside for home missions? For foreign missions?

B. *What* do you understand a missionary to be? Some people feel that anyone in their congregation who wanted to go to another country in the Lord's service could be a missionary. Others feel it is such a special calling — like the apostolic calling mentioned in Eph. 4:11 and I Cor. 12:28 — that they doubt missionaries would arise from their congregation. What do you think? Try defining the concept 'missionary' in twenty-five words or less.

C. *Why* is a mission strategy important? List at least three reasons why a mission strategy is key for your church's growth in the Lord.

D. *How* can we best encourage missions (and missionaries) in our church? List three missions activities that are (or could be) a regular source of strength for you and the rest of the church.

E. As a group discuss your answers to the questions in Section A above before going on together to the inductive study below.

2. INDUCTIVE BIBLE STUDY ON MISSIONS

The group leader should now guide the group in the inductive Bible study which you will find in the Resource section (turn to page 254). Rather than talking a lot, he will seek to help others in expressing their insights. His main task is to repeatedly ask the following question: '*What does this passage tell us about missions?*' The leader's task is simple (though it may not be easy!). Advance study will help him in asking the group pertinent questions to draw out the essence of the Bible passages. Everyone should take notes in his workbook on anything he may want to remember or review later. This kind of inductive study works well in groups ranging from four to twenty or even twenty-five. The Bible study outline will require two sessions of approximately one and a half hours apiece. The leader may want to choose certain passages in advance that he might skip if there is insufficient time. Similarly, he may choose to substitute other passages.

While everyone will be responding to the same general question underlined above, each person will also have a secondary question to keep in mind. Each person should be assigned to take notes on one of these three questions to contribute to a discussion later on:

1. *What* is a missionary?
2. *Why* has God called some people to be missionaries?
3. *How* can we best encourage missions (and missionaries) in our church? (If you have a large group, most of the people might focus on this area.)

NOW TURN TO THE BIBLE STUDY ON PAGE 254.

3. DESCRIPTION OF WHAT A BIBLICAL MISSIONS STRATEGY LOOKS LIKE

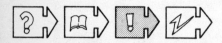

A. Clarifying your perspective on missions

Divide into your three sub-groups regarding the what, why and how of missions. Take about fifteen minutes to develop a short presentation for the larger group. The presentation should both stimulate the larger group to consider your question further and present the sub-group's thinking. The following group process guidelines may be helpful.

1. **What** is a missionary? (Group one)
   a. Share your definitions or thoughts and come to agreement on a single definition. Make a point of developing a biblical definition and not simply a cultural definition.
   b. Write your definition where everyone can see it. In presenting this, you might ask the larger group to go back to their individual definitions written at the beginning of the study. They could compare and contrast them with your work. Encourage the larger group to note whether anything critical has been left out of your definition.
   c. As a large group reach concensus on a working definition. This is not set in concrete. We are all constantly learning. It is simply the group's working definition to use until the Spirit shows you something further.
2. **Why** has God called some people to be missionaries? (Group two)
   a. Seek to come up with a few truly compelling reasons. Real conviction is more important than a long list of reasons!
   b. In presenting this, you might ask the large group for its ideas and list them on a flip chart sheet or blackboard. Affirm each idea before adding any of your own that the larger group overlooked.

3. **How** can we best encourage missions (and missionaries) in our church? (Group three)
   a. As a group develop two lists: 1) strengths of your church's missions strategy; and, 2) weaknesses of your church's missions strategy.
   b. In presenting this to the group, you might ask for their ideas as you present each list. Using a separate flip chart sheet for each list, once you have a number of ideas from the large group, add from the list your sub-group developed.

NOTES FOR THE GROUP LEADER: While everyone should be taking his own notes, you might assign one person to take formal notes of the three groups' presentations. These can later be typed up and distributed to all the participants. This will be a working theology of missions. It forms the biblical base for the action plan that will be developed by the end of this chapter. Read the comments below regarding the what, why and how of missions ahead of time. Insert them at appropriate moments in the group's discussion, but not until the group has first done some significant thinking on each question for itself.

B. Some further thoughts on the what, why and how of missions

1. **What** is a missionary? A possible working definition might include the following elements: 'A missionary is a member of a team set apart, sent and empowered for the formation of healthy churches.' This definition focuses on a missionary's gift, calling and function rather than on his nationality, cultural setting or skin colour. The definition draws from the Greek word *apostolos* translated 'missionary.' For a further study of the gift of apostleship (with a small 'a'), see my article listed in the resources section. (*If your definition is short and catchy, people will remember it more easily. You*

may want to have the group recall it every so often in the ongoing discussion until they have it down well.)

2. **Why** has God called some people to be missionaries?

   a. *A missionary is to extend the Kingdom of God beyond the local church sphere.* Our witness and service extends the Kingdom of God in the area where we live. Further discussion as to why this is important can be found in the section of chapter twelve on why God has called us to be his witnesses. Beyond this, God intends for the Gospel of his Kingdom to be preached throughout the world before he returns (Mt. 24:14). Indeed, as noted above, the Greek word 'apostle' can be and sometimes is translated 'messenger.' A fuller definition of a missionary or apostolic worker would incorporate this central function of being a messenger of the Kingdom of God. Such a definition might read like this. 'A missionary is one set apart, sent and empowered to communicate the Good News of the Kingdom of God, resulting in the formation of churches with sound doctrinal and governmental [leadership] foundations.'

   b. *A missionary is to equip local church leaders to lead their churches in healthy Kingdom living.* Paul appointed Titus to 'set in order the things that are wanting, and ordain elders in every city' (Titus 1:5). This work could involve discipling or pastoring the key leader(s) of a local church. It could also involve giving them formational teaching to use in leading their people to live rightly (righteously). A missionary team lays foundations (note I Cor. 3:10; Rom. 15:20; Heb. 6:1,2) and then moves on to let local leaders continue the work. However, the Pauline model suggests that the missionary team leader or someone he designates will continue to oversee that work in some way.

   c. *A missionary is to bring unity to the church.* One of the functions of the Ephesians 4:11 callings is to help us 'attain to the unity of the faith.' Some of these callings function in a local church, while others, like the apostolic calling, function extralocally. The neglect of this gift may be reflected in the division which has so characterized evangelicals. Missionaries, properly understood, may be used by God as 'joints' (Eph. 4:16; Col. 2:19) to help tie together the Body of Christ. This unifying work may be seen more in terms of committed relationships than in terms of organization.

In short, **missionaries are appointed by God to extend his Kingdom beyond the local church, to strengthen local church leaders in deepening Kingdom community life, and to bring unity to his church.**

3. **How** can we best encourage missions (and missionaries) in our church? Note the Association of Church Missions Committees (ACMC) in the resources section. They have superb tools for involving a congregation in all aspects of missions. Four key ways of encouraging missions in your church include: a) thinking strategically about missions, b) preparing church members to be missionaries, c) supporting a few missionaries strongly, and, d) strengthening the congregation's awareness of missions and prayer involvement. Key elements for each of these four thrusts follow below:

a. *Thinking strategically about missions.* Strategic thinking could incorporate the following elements:

   1) FOCUS ON UNREACHED PEOPLES. The largest groups of unreached peoples are in those countries that are primarily Muslim, Hindu, Buddhist or Communist. At the same time pockets of unreached peoples exist in every country and (probably) in every major city of the world. Examples include high-rise apartment dwellers in urban centres and ethnic groups within cities.

   2) THE NUMBER OF MISSIONARIES SUPPORTED. What are the advantages of supporting a few missionaries in depth? The disadvantages? For the church? For the missionaries?

   3) THE KIND OF MISSIONARIES SUPPORTED. Does church planting and evangelism have a special priority? What is the possibility of supporting national missionaries and evangelists (at one-fifth of the cost-or less-of putting a foreign missionary on the field)?
   (For further information on this you could write to Partners International [formerly CNEC], P.O. Box

15025, San Jose, CA 95112, USA
(Phone: 408/298–0965).

4) TEAMS THAT MODEL HEALTHY CHURCH LIFE. Since
church life is inherently corporate, formational work
with churches and church leaders will be more
effective as a team effort than alone. Regardless of
what we teach, what we reproduce will be our
practice. The team can both model and experience the
many benefits of corporate life (Eccl. 4:9–12). Such
benefits include corporate prayer, corporate worship,
community life, spiritual gifts, protection in warfare
and the witness to nonchristians of love and unity.
Paul's missionary work was always done in teams —
rarely fewer than three people; sometimes as many as
ten or more (Acts 20: 4,5). In fact, there were times
when he delayed or turned away from ministry until
the team was in place (Acts 18:1–5; II Cor. 2:12,13).

5) CHURCH MEMBERS' CALLINGS. What are our members'
gifts and callings? How can we affirm gifts and help
people in fulfilling their callings?

6) BUDGET. How much is given annually to missions?
What proportion of the church's budget is that? How
much would we like to be giving? (*Some churches have
found it helpful to use as a starting point a tithe of church
income.*)

b. *Preparing church members to be missionaries.* As a rough
approximation, for every one hundred church members,
the Spirit may touch at least one person for missionary
service. The church leaders need to be looking for such
people and to oversee their preparation in the following
ways:

1) DISCIPLE THEM. Since missionaries are involved in
the reproductive work of discipleship (II Tim. 2:2),
they need to experience this care in their own lives.
Many missionaries' problems can be traced to a lack
of discipleship or pastoral care — past or present.

2) INVOLVE THEM WITH MISSIONARIES' LIVES, like
Timothy with Paul. Prospective missionaries should
be encouraged to have missionaries in their homes,
travel with missionaries if they can, and enter into

short-term apprenticeship-like experiences where possible.

3) GIVE THEM MINISTRY OPPORTUNITIES TO TEST THEIR CALLING. A calling is a deeply-sensed conviction that God is setting a person aside for a special ministry. For missionaries as they are defined above, such a 'set-apartness' is proven by:
A) A growing vision for extralocal ministry
B) A testing of character, vision and ministry
C) Affirmation by the local church, church leaders, and other missionaries (see Acts 13:1,2; 16:1–5)
D) Commissioning or ordination (Acts 13:2; Titus 1:5)
E) The empowering of the Holy Spirit for putting the calling into effect (I Tim. 4:15; Eph. 3:7; Col. 1:28–29)

A good pattern to follow is for the missionary candidate to go through the progressive steps of becoming a local elder/deacon/council member; becoming a staff member of the church with a focus on outreach; developing a missionary team identity; and then being commissioned. This is roughly the model we see in Paul's life. An argument behind this kind of rigorous training is that he who is faithful in little can be given more responsibility. It is unfair to the missionary (*and* to the new converts) to put him in a responsibility in another culture that he has not yet fulfilled successfully in his own culture. The New Testament generally indicates that the missionaries were the most mature and experienced people the local church had to offer. An exception to this is the Timothy 'on-the-job' apprenticeship model of working in a discipleship relationship under a mature church planter. Certainly we need to find ways to cultivate and use the energy and vision of our young people without giving them responsibility that will be beyond their maturity and experience. Two organizations specializing in this are Operation Mobilization (headed by George Verwer, PO Box 148, Midland Park, NJ 07432, USA) and Youth With a Mission

(PO Box YWAM, Tyler, TX 75710 (Phone: 214/597–1171). British addresses are Operation Mobilization, The Quinta, Weston Rhyn, Oswestry, Shropshire SU10 7LT; Youth With A Mission, 13 Highfield Oval, Ambrose Lane, Harpenden, Herts AL5 4BX.

4) GUIDE THEM IN GETTING THE NECESSARY TRAINING. In addition to local church ministry, training for missionary work may include some form of Bible school or seminary, cross-cultural training and language learning (though the latter may wait until arriving on the mission field). The training will be effective in proportion to how much it is based in real life experience rather than simply classroom learning. Ideally the preparation period will include in-depth involvement in healthy church life. Experiential learning of the key steps involved in establishing healthy churches is invaluable. Finally, developing a 'tent-making' skill or profession as Paul did would be wise It will give the missionary candidate flexibility throughout his life, particularly if the Lord leads him or her out of active missionary work for a short of long period of time.

c. *Supporting a few missionaries comprehensively.* Ideally missionaries would be members of the church, an integral part of the life of the Body — both when they are away and when they come back on furlough (if they do). During furloughs they would have a church home in which to serve and be served rather than having to travel around the country to raise support. If they are in need of rest and restoration, the church can be a place of healing and renewal. If they are strong in the Lord, they could join the staff of the church to strengthen the outreach and foundational teachings of the church.

d. *Strengthening the congregation's awareness of missions and prayer involvement.* Materials for mobilizing a local church in missions can be ordered from the Association of Church Missions Committees listed in the Resources section for this chapter (page 281).

1) DEPTH. Little will catalyze prayer so much as personal involvement in the life of a person who

needs prayer. You will be able to pray more effectively for a few missionaries whom you know well than for a list of relative strangers. Small groups can commit themselves to a specific missionary or missionary family as 'their' missionary people, keeping in close contact with them. Church leaders (especially the pastor) can deepen this body life by periodically visiting the missionary, ministering to him and bringing back a report to the church to further encourage prayer and support of the missionary. In some cases a church may even be led to form a partnership with a Third World church.

2) BREADTH. The church should have a broad picture of what God is doing in the world and what specific part the church itself can play. This is an important context for strategic missions thinking. The resources section lists some prayer tools that can inform and encourage prayer for the Lord's work worldwide.

NOW IT IS TIME TO DEVELOP YOUR *ACTION PLAN*. TURN BACK TO PAGE 9 FOR INSTRUCTIONS ON HOW TO DO SO. YOU WILL ALSO FIND OUT HOW TO USE THE RESOURCE MATERIAL IN SECTION 3.

12

RENEWING OUR SOCIAL ACTION

A Tale of Two Boys

Stomachs protruding, bulging, sore. Two reasons.
'Mom, can I have more turkey?' 'Help yourself, there's plenty more.'
'Mom, isn't there anything to eat? My stomach's sore.' 'Maybe tomorrow.'
One mom laughs. The other mom cries.
Inflation's cutting the paycheck, we'll have to economize!
Drought-ravaged land: no game, no grain.
One dad trying to keep his standard of living alive.
The other struggling just to survive.
'I don't like sweet potatoes!' 'Well, there's plenty of mashed.'
Dad, couldn't you find anything to eat?' 'Nothing!'
'Now thank we all our God . . . 'You know I don't like pumpkin pie!' 'Then eat the mince.' 'I don't like that either!' 'Surprise, I baked a cherry just for you.'
'Nothing?' 'Nothing!' 'It's been three days!' 'Maybe tomorrow.'
'Mom, my stomach hurts!' 'That's what you get for eating like a pig. Quiet down. You won't die. Dad's getting you some Alka Seltzer.'
'Mom, my stomach hurts!' 'I know, son. Maybe tomorrow there'll be something. Dad's out looking.'

Stomachs protruding, bulging, sore. Two boys. Two reasons.
One is stuffed. The other is starved.
One mom laughs. The other mom cries.
One boy lives. The other boy dies.

(Roger G. Timmerman, in *The Banner*, Christian Reformed Church in North America, Board of Publications, November 21, 1975)

'I was hungry and you formed a humanities club and discussed
my hunger. Thank you. I was in prison and you crept off
quietly to your chapel and prayed for my release. I was naked
and you debated the morality of my appearance. I was sick and
you knelt and thanked God for your health. I was homeless and
you preached to me the shelter of the love of God. I was lonely
and you left me alone to go home and pray for me. You are so
holy and close to God. I am hungry and cold. You prayed, but
your prayers were unanswered. Where did your prayers go?
What have your prayers done? What profit a man if he page the
prayer book when the rest of the world is crying for help?'
(Old Town Window)

Liberal church leaders have been characterized as urging
Christians 'to empower minority people, end the war and
racism', and conservatives have been characterized as 'urging
Christians to seek inward peace and renewal'. This stereotype
is changing, but we evangelicals still have a long way to go in
understanding — and acting on — our social responsibility.

What about *your* church? What social involvement do you
have? Do you have a strategy (other than evangelistic) for
making an impact upon the community? Is 'helping the poor'
more than a nominal 'deacon's fund', or a request for a second
offering on occasional Sunday mornings? Could or should
your church be a visible sign of solidarity with the poor? Is
your church doing anything to respond to world hunger?
Anything to try to get at some of the root causes of world
hunger? Are church members with a calling for social ministry
being recognized in your church? Equipped by the church?
Backed by the church? Hard questions such as these are
addressed in this chapter.

The church's social responsibility intersects a number of
areas dealt with in depth in other chapters. Extending the
Kingdom of God (Chapter 1 of this section) is the framework
for all our involvement in the world. Our social involvement in
many ways is an extension of the Kingdom community we
experience together (Chapter 7) and our calling as stewards
(Chapter 4). Of course, the Gospel and our verbal witness
(Chapter 10) must be inseparably woven together with our
works. And finally, the burden and challenge for partnering in
some fashion with the Lord in his worldwide missions work

(Chapter 11) ties together with extending our social involvement beyond our local sphere.

What lies ahead in this chapter? The chapter has four sections, designed for church leaders to work through together in ten to twelve hours. A retreat setting would be ideal. If this seems too large a time commitment, take into account that in this time you are: a) opening your lives to a life-changing understanding and commitment to social responsibility; b) deepening team relationships among yourselves as leaders; c) laying foundations for the church's future; and, d) outlining the church's specific course for the next four to twelve months. The four sections, with the approximate time each might require, follow below.

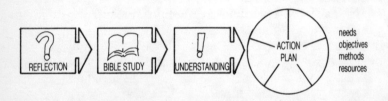

1. Reflecting on **your church's social involvement** (*1 hour*).
2. Looking at God's vision regarding social responsibility through an **inductive Bible study** (*3 hours*).
3. Clarifying in summary fashion your understanding of social responsibility (the **what, why and how** of social responsibility) (*1½ hours*).
4. Developing an **action plan** for renewing your church's vision and practice of social responsibility.
    A. Identifying **your church's needs** in this area (*1 hour*).
    B. Identifying **desired objectives** for the coming months (*1 hour*).
    C. Identifying **methods** for reaching those objectives (*2 hours*).
    D. Identifying **resources** for helping accomplish those objectives (*1 hour*).

Throughout the above process you will need to enter regularly into the Lord's presence in prayer and worship so that his Spirit can freely teach you. No structure, no human teacher, no manual will adequately communicate the truths of God apart from the Spirit's work! In fact before going any further, please stop and spend some time in prayer lifting all of this to the Lord. Appropriate prayers could include:

* confession of your need for him to teach you in this area as only he can do.
* praise for all he is going to do in and through you in the coming weeks and months.
* intercession for the church members, that the Lord will be preparing their hearts for where he wants to lead them in the coming months.
* prayer for his wisdom to modify all that follows in this chapter to suit your context well.

---

1. REFLECTION ON YOUR CHURCH'S SOCIAL RESPONSIBILITY

Reflect your church's social involvement as you answer the questions below. Do this individually first, writing your responses in a notebook. Later you will discuss some responses as a group. Continue to use your notebook to keep track of all you are learning about social responsibility.

A. Reflecting on your church's social involvement.
  ■ How many people in your church are directly involved in helping the poor and needy in an ongoing way? How many are seriously involved in political or other means to see greater justice and more godly values prevail?
  ■ What programmes does this church have for serving and transforming the community or society? Does the

church's budget reflect the priority the church gives to social responsibility?

■ Who in the church might be key people for catalyzing the church in social responsibility? Are they, or could they be, present for the study and reflection and planning that follows?

■ What is your vision for your church's social involvement? Summarize it in one or two paragraphs.

■ What is your church's present social involvement? Summarize it in one or two paragraphs.

■ How similar or different are your answers to the above two questions? What insights come to you in comparing them?

B. *What* do you understand the church's social responsibility to be? Some people consider that the church has no such responsibility, that such work is neither spiritual nor eternal. Others think it is central to being God's people. Among these people would be those who would consider the church's responsibility to be largely acts of mercy. Yet others would feel that the church must challenge and help change structural or systemic (social and political) injustices. What do you think? Try defining the concept of Christian social responsibility in twenty-five words or less.

C. *Why* is the church's social involvement important? List at least three reasons why such involvement is key for your church's growth in the Lord.

D. *How* can the church's social responsibility be expressed? List three social responsibility activities that are (or could be) a regular source of strength for you and the rest of the church.

E. As a group discuss your answers to the questions in Section A above before going on together to the inductive study below.

---

2. INDUCTIVE BIBLE STUDY ON SOCIAL RESPONSIBILITY

The group leader should now guide the group in the inductive Bible study which you will find in the Resource section (turn to page 283). Rather than talking a lot, he will seek to help others in expressing their insights. His main task is repeatedly to ask the following question '*What does this passage tell us about social responsibility?*' The leader's task is simple (though it may not be easy!). Advance study will help him in asking the group pertinent questions to draw out the essence of the Bible passages. Everyone should take notes in his workbook on anything he may want to remember or review later. This kind of inductive study works well in groups ranging from four to twenty or even twenty-five. The Bible study outline will require two sessions of approximately one and a half hours apiece. The leader may want to choose certain passages in advance that he might skip if there is insufficient time. Similarly, he may choose to substitute other passages.

While everyone will be responding to the same general question underlined above, each person will also have a secondary question to keep in mind. Each person should be assigned to take notes on one or these three questions to contribute to a discussion later on:

1. *What* is biblical social responsibility?
2. *Why* has God called us to social responsibility? (Why can we not simply focus on verbal proclamation of the Gospel to the world?)
3. *How* can we work out our social responsibility to the world? In addition to winning people to the Lord, how can we be extending the Kingdom of God into the world? (If you have a large group, most of the people might focus on this area.)

As you reflect on these passages, try to put yourself in the shoes of the earth's disinherited, oppressed, weak and destitute. If you are white, try imagining yourself as non-white.

NOW TURN TO THE BIBLE STUDY ON PAGE 283.

3. DESCRIPTION OF WHAT SOCIAL
RESPONSIBILITY LOOKS LIKE

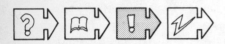

A. Clarifying your perspective on social responsibility

Divide into your three sub-groups regarding the what, why and how of social responsibility. Take about fifteen minutes to develop a short presentation for the larger group. The presentation should both stimulate the larger group to consider your question further and present the sub-group's thinking. The following group process guidelines may be helpful.

1. **What** is (the church's) social responsibility) (Group one)
   a. Share your definitions or thoughts and come to agreement on a single biblical definition.
   b. Write your definition where everyone can see it. In presenting this, you might ask the larger group to go back to their individual definitions written at the beginning of the study. They could compare and contrast them with your work. Encourage the larger group to note whether anything critical has been left out of your definition.
   c. As a large group reach consensus on a working definition. This is not set in concrete. We are all constantly learning. It is simply the group's working definition to use until the Spirit shows you something further.
2. **Why** has God called us to social responsibility? (Group two)
   a. Seek to come up with a few truly compelling reasons. Real conviction is more important than a long list of reasons!

b. In presenting this, you might ask the large group for its ideas and list them on a flip chart sheet or blackboard. Affirm each idea before adding any of your own that the larger group overlooked.
3. **How** can we work out our social responsibility to the world? (Group three)
   a. As a group develop two lists: 1) strengths of your church's social involvement; and, 2) weaknesses of your church's social involvement.
   b. In presenting this to the group, you might ask for their ideas as you present each list. Using a separate flip chart sheet for each list, once you have a number of ideas from the large group, add from the list your sub-group developed.

NOTES FOR THE GROUP LEADER: While everyone should be taking his own notes, you might assign one person to take formal notes of the three groups' presentations. These can later be typed up and distributed to all the participants. This will be a working theology of social responsibility. It forms the biblical base for the action plan that will be developed by the end of this chapter. Read the comments below regarding the what, why and how of social responsibility ahead of time. Insert them at appropriate moments in the group's discussion, but not until the group has first done some significant thinking on each question for itself.

B. Some further thoughts on the what, why and how of social responsibility

1. **What** is social responsibility? A possible working definition might include the following elements: 'Social responsibility means extending the mercy, justice and healing power of Christ's Kingdom into the world, particularly to the poor and need.' This definition highlights the place of the poor, but indicates that our mandate should touch every sphere of life — our work, our recreation, our neighborhood and

so forth. Healing is further discussed in chapter fifteen under spiritual warfare. Often mercy and justice are interwoven (Ps. 85:10,11; Micah 6:8. In mercy we respond to immediate needs, while in justice we seek to remedy the underlying causes of those needs. (*If your definition is short and catchy, people will remember it more easily. You may want to have the group recall it every so often in the ongoing discussion until they have it down well.*)

2. **Why** has God called us to social responsibility? Since our social responsibility is an expression of Kingdom life, the reasons given in Chapter One of this section, for why the Kingdom is important, would be worth repeating here. Similarly the reasons for witness (Chapter 10) and mission (Chapter 11) underlie our mandate for social responsibility as well. In addition to all this, our social mandate is extremely important because:

   a. *Our words without our works are hollow* (James 2:14–20). The Kingdom of God does not consist in words, but in power (II Cor. 4:20). Our works authenticate the Gospel (Mt. 11:2–5). Furthermore, he who knows how to do good and does it not, to him it is sin (James 4:17). God's righteous wrath will be poured out on us if we do not extend his justice and mercy to the poor and needy. Why will he be angry? Because we have betrayed him and the Kingdom he has entrusted to us (Ezek. 22:29–31; Mt. 25:34–46).

   b. *Our works, done in love, have a power in and of themselves.* We share Christ's compassion for the physical, social and emotional needs of the multitudes (Mt. 9:36; 14:14–21; 15:32). True, our present bodies will not enter eternity (I Cor. 15:50), nor will emotional wounds (Rev. 21:4,5?, nor yet structural injustice and the wrongs of the nations (Rev. 21:24–22:3). Yet man in his entirety — body, soul and spirit — is confronted by the Kingdom of God in the here and now. The health, wholeness and holiness of the Kingdom reaches every aspect of our lives to reveal a foretaste of the new order (II Cor. 5:17–19). Extending God's healing power, justice and mercy beyond the church through our good works will lead nonchristians to glorify God (Mt. 5:13–16; I Pet. 2:12).

c. *We have been redeemed to do good works* (Eph. 2:10; Titus 2:14). Such works are as natural to our new nature as swimming is to a fish or flying is to a bird. In leaving behind the old way of life, we become 'useful to the Master, prepared for every good work' (II Tim. 2:21). Our attitude toward those in authority is not to be contentious but rather 'to be ready for every good deed' (Titus, 3:1,2). We are to be careful to devote ourselves to doing what is good (Titus 3:8). By engaging in good works to meet pressing needs, we will be fruitful rather than barren (Titus 3:14).

In short, **in his compassion for all people, God calls us to social responsibility in order to authenticate the Gospel, extend the Kingdom of God beyond the local church, and work out the salvation that God has worked into us**!

3. **How** can we work out our social responsibility to the world? Some churches may feel they are so poor they are exempt from this responsibility. However, hardly any church is so poor that there is not a poorer church or poorer people somewhere else — be it nearby or in another country. In fact, the poor a church and the people around it, the more important this whole are of social responsibility becomes. God does not want us to be impoverished. If we are, we have a responsibility to help ourselves and those around us achieve a higher quality of life.

Four key ways of encouraging missions in your church are discussed in Chapter 11. The ideas may be worth reviewing since they have application here as well. Without repeating the discussion in Chapter 11, the same four ways of encouraging missions are applied to the area of social responsibility below:

---

a. thinking strategically about social responsibility:
b. preparing church members for effective social impact;
c. supporting a few causes strongly, and,
d. strengthening the congregation's awareness of social responsibility and the impact of corporate prayer (discussed in Chapter 2).

---

a. *Thinking strategically about social responsibility.*

   1) TARGETING A SPECIFIC GROUP OF POOR OR NEEDY PEOPLE. Where are the needy people? What are their principal needs? (According to *them*?) What are they doing about those needs? Who is already involved in helping them? What are God's intentions for how these people should live? Socially? Physically? Spiritually? If they are not meeting their own needs and/or are not organized, how could they be encouraged to take responsibility for their situation? How can they be encouraged in self-help development rather than ongoing dependency? How can you avoid their becoming dependent on you even while you enable them to overcome their problems? What agencies could be tapped as resources? Christian development agencies such as those listed in the resource section (page 283) can be of great help in working through these kinds of questions.

   2) PARTNERING WITH A CHURCH IN A NEEDY AREA. Christ has shown us that ministry begins with service (Mt. 20:25–28). And service begins with identifying with those whom we would serve, just as he did. Though he was rich, for our sake he became poor — so that he might raise us out of our poverty (II Cor. 8:9)! He emptied himself and became one of us (Phil. 2:5–8). Identification in its truest sense requires this. Their struggles must become our struggles. Our involvement becomes our credibility. How can we identify with the poor and come alongside them? Simplifying our lifestyle is a starting point. Reorienting our ministry to the poor is another step. Relocation may be an option or even a calling that needs prayerful consideration. Another excellent step would be to partner with a church already identified with the poor because her members *are* the poor! Harvest (further described in the resources section, page 283) has developed excellent guidelines for churches partnering together in circumstances like this. Harvest's focus on North American churches partnering with

Third World churches can be adapted to churches partnering in the same country of city.

Some readers may be tempted to skip over this suggestion because they come from a country in which there are tremendous internal needs. Why should a church in an already needy area concern itself about need in other parts of the world, when there is a massive job to do right on the doorstep, and barely enough resources in the church to supply the needs of its own members?

The answer is that giving help to others is an expression of fellowship, without which our Christian experience is stunted and poor. Giving even out or our scarcity can be a joyful experience, as the early Christians in Macedonia discovered (II Cor. 8). The privilege of generosity need not be restricted to the wealthy countries alone.

This is not to deny that the wealthy Christians of the world have a far greater responsibility to share! In telling the story of the Macedonians, Paul made it clear that God's will was *equality* — 'not that others might be relieved while you are hard pressed' (v. 13). But the history of missions teaches us that when one group of Christians becomes dependent on another richer group for handouts, their independence and self-respect is sapped, and they become pale, inadequate 'rice-Christians' with little spiritual power or joy. What we have to share with others may be extremely meagre. But then so was five loaves and two fishes, as a lunch for five thousand people!

3) FOCUSING ON KINGDOM ISSUES IN THE PUBLIC DOMAIN. What are the most pressing social, political and economic matters that are (or could become) contrary to the Kingdom of God? What can you do about them? If there is a clearly unbiblical situation (such as abortion, homosexuality, pornography, abuse of human rights, poverty, or clear injustice) can churches be encouraged to act together in some meaningful way? Other issues may be less black and

white, but still be very important (such as issues related to the family, education, religious freedom, war, and peace, agrarian reform, nuclear arms, media bias, crime and prison reform, or world hunger). Where possible, courses of action may include legislative pressure (voting, writing to politicians, lobbying, even running for office!), protesting (petitions, picketing, peaceful resistance) and public unified boycotting (such as boycotting stores that sell pornography, or not buying products from a clearly unjust corporation).

This will not be possible for some readers of this book, who live under authoritarian regimes where there is no opportunity for Christians to be involved in the political process. This was the case in New Testament days, too, and rather than fighting a lonely, hopeless battle against the authorities, the early Church found it more strategic to concentrate on spreading their revolutionary message which would one day challenge the structures of power that oppressed and imprisoned people. The exact way in which Christians can engage in action in the public domain will vary from society to society, but there are some overriding principles which can be studied in some of the books in the Resources section (page 000).

We need also to be careful about the way in which we protest about the problems of other countries. While it is right for Christians to stand against unrighteousness and inequality wherever it occurs, we need to be careful that we have understood the issues properly and listened to all sides of the argument; and we need to ensure that we do not create difficulties for people whom we are trying to help. For example, it is possible for Christians living under a dictatorship to suffer because Christians in other parts of the world are protesting and causing problems for the oppressive government. It is possible for Christian initiatives to bring about trade embargoes and sanctions as a protest against a corrupt regime — only to produce chaos and anarchy in the country these Christians are trying to help.

b. *Preparing church members for effective social impact.* The church leaders need to be looking for people burdened to extend Christ's mercy, justice and healing power to the world. They need to encourage such people both individually and corporately to find avenues for ministry. At the individual level, a sense of calling may be sufficient to warrant certain vocational choices. At the corporate level, people may be drawn together around a common ministry to form a mission/ministry group (discussed further in Chapter 8 regarding spiritual gifts). This group can raise the congregation's awareness of certain issues and be a catalyst for activities such as those mentioned above. The group's work can also include research, writing, networking, strategizing, coordinating activities (within the church and with other churches), speaking, praying, and involvement with like-minded civic groups. In some cases they may even become leaders in such civic groups.

c. *Supporting a few causes strongly.* This is in keeping with developing mission/ministry groups. As a church you do not want to be spread so thinly that you touch only the surface of people's lives, or have only token involvement with a broad range of issues. You may want to seek the Lord together for where he would have you make a significant impact.

d. *Strengthening the congregation's awareness of social responsibility and prayer involvement.* Little motivates us to pray so much as personal involvement in the life of someone needing help. Being deeply involved in a few areas of social responsibility will strengthen prayer. Special occasions can combine prayer with raising the congregation's awareness of our call to extend justice, mercy and God's healing power to the world.

e. *Guidelines for political involvement.* Mark Amstutz in the April 1983 issues of *InForm* (the Bulletin of Wheaton College, Wheaton, IL 60187) gives the five following guidelines:

   1) Become informed biblically and politically. To speak in the name of the Lord and of the relevant political issue. It is one thing to advocate a general moral

principle such as peace, justice, the sacredness of life.; it is quite another to apply such principles to specific situations.

2) Remember that all political choices ultimately bear the consequences of human fallenness. Because of the radical nature of sin, our understanding of issues and policies will always bear the results of human sin and finiteness. There can therefore rarely be a single Christian policy on the dominant issues of societies. Realizing this should not lead us to inaction but towards humble political activity.

3) Use the utmost care in applying specific moral and biblical principles to public policy issues. Since moral authority tends to decline with the increasing specificity of the policies advocated by groups, it would seem generally unwise for any church body or significant part of its membership to advocate a specific political course of action. The specific issues need to be addressed and advocated, but it should be undertaken through individual and small informal associations. The moral authority of the church ought not to be compromised as a result of its advocacy of particular issues *unless* the Bible speaks clearly to a certain issue.

4) Avoid the fallacy of dichotomous thinking — that is, viewing political alternatives in mutually exclusive categories (*either/or*). We need to remember that most political debates are not between saints and sinners but *among* sinners. Moral criteria and Biblical principles are of course relevant, but no group has a monopoly on Christian ethics.

5) Relate Christian political action to the non-political aspects of evangelism. If, for instance, the state comprises one-ninth of our society, no more than one-ninth of our incarnational witness should be addressed to the political sphere. (For instance, a constitutional amendment permitting prayer in the schools has been hotly debated in the U.S. But many Christian parents do not pray regularly with their children. The implication is clear: if a Christian

worldview is to be infused in our society, it will be up to the church and its members to do so. We ought not to overload the state with moral responsibilities.)

NOW IT IS TIME TO DEVELOP YOUR *ACTION PLAN*. TURN BACK TO PAGE 9 FOR INSTRUCTIONS ON HOW TO DO SO. YOU WILL ALSO FIND OUT HOW TO USE THE RESOURCE MATERIAL IN SECTION 3.

13

RENEWING OUR SPIRITUAL WARFARE

Recently a story was told of a Christian who was flying to a conference and noticed that the young man next to him was not eating the meal which had just been served. Inquiring, he discovered that the man was fasting. For some religious purpose? Yes, indeed! He was a devoted member of a church of Satan, and had banded with other members of his church to seek the destruction of the marriages of selected Christian leaders. So far, the young man reported, more than a dozen of the marriages had ended in divorce. Yet, not willing to be content with their success to date, here he was continuing his fasting and prayer to undermine other Christian leaders.

Is this simply a strange isolated event? In her book *Today's Witches*, Suzy Smith says: 'The truth is that witchcraft is having its greatest resurgence since the Middle Ages.' Is such a resurgence basically a jungle phenomena among 'uncivilized' peoples? The *San Francisco Chronicle* estimates that six million Americans are devoted followers of the occult. It reports 30,000 witches in England and 60,000 sorcerers in France, countries where Christianity is making very little headway. Alex Sanders, self-styled King of the Witches in Britain, estimates that there are 120,000 British witches. And the occult is not confined to hidden groups operating largely in secret. In January of 1986 for ten days the headlines of the Brazilian newspapers focused on a supernatural healing. The Brazilian president used Air Force planes to fly herbs, a jungle chief and a shaman to heal a naturalist dying of toad poisoning. With the help of hallucinogenic herbal 'cigars,' chants and massage, the Indian chief appeared to extract a green strong-smelling paste identified as the poison. The naturalist is reported healed.

For a number of years movies on the occult and exorcism have consistently drawn crowds. In bookstores it is not uncommon to find a section devoted to paperback novels on the occult. In a country like Brazil voodoo and the occult play a prominent role in the television soap operas. Astrology, of course, features in a regular column in most major newspapers. Little wonder that a book entitled *Satan is Alive and Well on Planet Earth* (Hal Lindsey, Zondervan, 1972) could sell a million copies!

What about your church? Is there a spiritual warfare around your church or are you somehow being 'overlooked' by Satan? Are you aware of spiritual attack? Do your people know how to recognize Satan's attacks? Do they know how to defend themselves from those attacks? Do they know how to take the offensive and claim territory from Satan? When was the last time your church or church leaders corporately battled with the Enemy and defeated him? Do you have church members gifted in deliverance or healing? Are they recognized in your church? Equipped by the church? Backed by the church? Questions such as these are addressed in this chapter.

The church's spiritual warfare intersects a number of areas dealt with in depth in other chapters. Extending the Kingdom of God (Chapter 1 of this section) is the framework for all of our involvement in the world. Our weapons include intercessory prayer (Chapter 2), worship and praise (Chapter 3) and the Word (Chapter 5). Other areas that deeply affect the effectiveness of our warfare include walking in the unity of Christian community (Chapter 7), using our spiritual gifts (Chapter 8) and effectively penetrating the world (Chapters 10, 11 and 12). That is to say, warfare has an impact upon, and draws from, practically every area of church life.

What lies ahead in this chapter? The chapter has four sections, designed for church leaders to work through together in ten to twelve hours. A retreat setting would be ideal. If this seems too large a time commitment, take into account that in this time you are: a) opening your lives to a life-changing understanding and commitment to spiritual warfare; b) deepening team relationships among yourselves as leaders; c) laying foundations for the church's future; and, d) outlining the church's specific course for the next four to twelve months. The four sections, with the approximate time each might require, follow below.

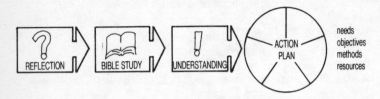

---

1. Reflecting on **your church's experience** of spiritual warfare (*1 hour*).
2. Looking at God's perspective regarding spiritual warfare through an **inductive Bible study** (*3 hours*).
3. Clarifying in summary fashion your understanding of spiritual warfare (the **what, why and how** or spiritual warfare) (*1½ hours*).
4. Developing an **action plan** for renewing your church's vision and practice of spiritual warfare.
   A. identifying **your church's needs** in this area (*1 hour*).
   B. Identifying **desired objectives** for the coming months (*1 hour*).
   C. Identifying **methods** for reaching those objectives (*2 hours*).
   D. Identifying **resources** for helping accomplish those objectives (*1 hour*).

Throughout the above process you will need to enter regularly into the Lord's presence in prayer and worship so that his Spirit can freely teach you. No structure, no human teacher, no manual will adequately communicate the truths of God apart from the Spirit's work! In fact before going any further, please stop and spend some time in prayer lifting all of this to the Lord. Appropriate prayers could include:

* confession or your need for him to teach you in this area as only he can do.

* praise for all he is going to do in and through you in the coming weeks and months.
* intercession for the church members, that the Lord will be preparing their hearts for where he wants to lead them in the coming months.
* prayer for his wisdom to modify all that follows in this chapter to suit your context well.

---

1. REFLECTION ON YOUR CHURCH'S SPIRITUAL WARFARE

Reflect on your church's understanding and experience of spiritual warfare as you answer the questions below. Do this individually first, writing your responses in a notebook. Later you will discuss some responses as a group. Continue to use your notebook to keep track of all you are learning about spiritual warfare.

A. Reflecting on your church's spiritual warfare.
- In the last three months how many people in your church do you think have been intentionally and consciously involved in spiritual warfare? (Among other things, this could include power encounters with Satan's forces, emotional and physical healing, deliverance, reconciliation and invoking God's presence to dispel demonic power or presence.)
- What indicators of victory in spiritual warfare have been evident in your church over these last three months?
- What are some of the principal fronts on which Satan needs to be overcome in your culture or context? How well is your church doing in these areas?
- What is your vision for how your church should engage in spiritual warfare? Summarize it in one or two paragraphs.
- What is your church's present approach to spiritual warfare? Summarize it in one or two paragraphs.

■ How similar or different are your answers to the above two questions? What insights come to you in comparing them?

B. *What* do you understand (the church's) spiritual warfare to be? Some people feel it is rare and unusual, confined to the occult. Others feel that Satan is actively at work in daily ways ot undermine and destroy our lives. Some limit it to demonic activity; others see it as the Christian's fight against the flesh and the world as well as Satan. What do you think? Try defining the concept 'spiritual warfare' in twenty-five words or less.

C. *Why* is the church's involvement in spiritual warfare important? List at least three reasons why such involvement is key for your church's growth in the Lord.

D. *How* can the church enter into spiritual warfare? List three warfare activities that are (or could be) a regular source of strength for you and the rest of the church.

E. As a group discuss your answers to question number four above before going on together to the inductive study below.

┌───┐
│ 2. INDUCTIVE BIBLE STUDY ON SPIRITUAL WARFARE │
└───┘

The group leader should now guide the group in the inductive Bible study which you will find in the Resource section (turn to page 261. Rather than talking a lot, he will seek to help others in expressing their insights. His main task is repeatedly to ask the following question: '*What does this passage tell us about spiritual warfare?*' The leader's task is simple (though it may not be easy!). Advance study will help him in asking the group pertinent questions to draw out the essence of the Bible passages. Everyone should take notes in his workbook on anything he may want to remember or review later. This kind of inductive study works well in groups ranging from four to twenty or even twenty-five. The passages below require two sessions of approximately one and a half hours apiece. The leader may want to choose certain passages in advance that he might skip if there is insufficient time. Similarly, he may choose to substitute other passages.

While everyone will be responding to the same general question underlined above, each person will also have a secondary question to keep in mind. Each person should be assigned to take notes on one of these three questions to contribute to a discussion later on:

1. *What* is spiritual warfare?
2. *Why* has God called us to spiritual warfare? (What difference does it make if we ignore spiritual warfare?)
3. *How* can we walk victoriously in spiritual warfare? What are our tactics and weapons? And what are Satan's tactics and weapons which we must thwart in order to defeat him? (If you have a large group, most of the people might focus on this area.)

NOW TURN TO THE BIBLE STUDY ON PAGE 261.

---

3. DESCRIPTION OF SPIRITUAL WARFARE

A. Clarifying your perspective on spiritual warfare

Divide into your three sub-groups regarding the what, why and how of spiritual warfare. Take about fifteen minutes to develop a short presentation for the larger group. The presentation should both stimulate the larger group to consider your question further and present the sub-group's thinking. The following group process guidelines may be helpful.

1. **What** is spiritual warfare? (Group one)
   a. Share your definitions or thoughts and come to agreement on a single biblical definition.
   b. Write your definition where everyone can see it. In presenting this, you might ask the larger group to go back to their individual definitions written at the beginning of the study. They could compare and contrast them with your work. Encourage the larger group to note whether anything critical has been left out or your definition.
   c. As a large group reach consensus on a working definition. This is not set in concrete. We are all constantly learning. It is simply the group's working definition to use until the Spirit shows you something further.
2. **Why** has God called us to spiritual warfare? (Group two)
   a. Seek to come up with a few truly compelling reasons. Real conviction is more important than a long list of reasons!
   b. In presenting this, you might ask the large group for its ideas and list them on a flip chart sheet or blackboard. Affirm each idea before adding any of your own that the larger group overlooked.
3. **How** can we walk victoriously in spiritual warfare? What are our tactics and weapons? (Group three)
   a. As a group develop two lists: 1) strengths of your

NOTES FOR THE GROUP LEADER: While everyone should be taking his own notes, you might assign one person to take formal notes of the three groups' presentations. These can later be typed up and distributed to all the participants. This will be a working theology of spiritual warfare. It forms the biblical base for the action plan that will be developed by the end of this chapter. Read the comments below regarding the what, why and how of spiritual warfare ahead of time. Insert them at appropriate moments in the group's discussion, but not until the group has first done some significant thinking on each question for itself.

church's spiritual warfare; and, 2) weaknesses of your
church's spiritual warfare.

b. In presenting this to the group, you might ask for their
ideas as you present each list. Using a separate flip chart
sheet for each list, once you have a number of ideas from
the large group, add from the list your sub-group
developed.

B. Some further thoughts on the what, why and how of spiritual warfare

1. **What** is spiritual warfare? A possible working definition
might include the following elements: 'Spiritual warfare is

Claiming territory

What do we mean by 'claiming territory from Satan'? Basically, this describes the activity of wrestling in prayer to
loosen the grip, and counteract the designs, of the powers of
evil on various areas of life. Michael Green once wrote that
he used to be puzzled by the prayer of the apostles in Acts 4
('They took no social or political action . . . even in that
prayer meeting they scarcely made a request of any kind').
It seemed to be an irrelevant response to their situation:

> But now I see that they were doing the most effective thing
> open to them. They were ascribing glory to Almighty God in
> the face of all pretended claims from other sources to exercise
> power over them. No wonder the place was shaken where they
> were assembled, and they were filled anew with the Holy
> Spirit. They had taken on the principalities and powers in
> prayer, and had prevailed.
>
> (*I Believe in Satan's Downfall*, Hodder/Eerdmans.)

'Claiming territory' is a progressive thing. It needs to begin
in our individual life. Until Satan's strongholds within
ourselves are destroyed, we can hardly pray with effect in
any other area. The next sphere to be prayed about is our
family life, and then the church fellowship with which we
are involved. But then the concerns spill over into society at
large: the world of our work, the impact of the forces of evil
upon world politics and the government of society, the
spiritual struggle of the church worldwide as God brings
about his Kingdom in human lives.

---

the cosmic conflict between Satan and God, especially focused on overcoming and destroying the other's power and work in the human race. The Fall was Satan's greatest work; redemption is Christ's greatest work. Satan and Christ both claim the same territory, of human lives. As Christians we fight to stand firm on the territory Christ has won and expand his Kingdom day by day. (*If your definition is short and catchy, people will remember it more easily. You may want to have the group recall it every so often in the ongoing discussion until they have it down well.*)

2. **Why** has God called us to spiritual warfare? Through our warfare:
   a. *God overcomes Satan*, destroying his works (I John 3:8) and freeing those in bondage to him — be it physical, emotional, social or spiritual bondage. God not only destroys Satan's work, but replaces it with his redeeming, liberating, healing work (Acts 26:18; Col. 1:13,14). Victory in warfare further extends the Kingdom of God into our lives, our families, our church and our society.
   b. *God matures us.* We grow from spiritual infancy to mature manhood through the testing we experience as we learn to be overcomers (I John 2:12–14). Testing procedures endurance, proven character, hope, maturity and growth in wisdom (Rom. 5:3–5; James 1:2–5). A wise person perceives the root cause of a problem and understands how to deal with that rather than just with symptoms (Eph. 6:12). Even when God gives Satan permission to hurt us, God uses this for his glory and for our perfection (II Cor. 12:7–10).
   c. *God effects his purposes in history.* Satan is the ruler of this world (John 12:31,32; 16:8–11). He has mighty principalities and powers over the nations of the world (Dan. 10:13,20,21) and possibly over certain cities as well. He works in and through those who are not Christians (Eph. 2:2). The havoc and destruction of the end times will come as Satan realizes that his other more subtle means of destruction are not adequate to ruin God's purposes (see Mt. 24:3–24; Rev. 11:7–12). Many countries today face political chaos, a shattered economy, guerilla wars and rumours of wars, unparalleled physical

calamities and increased lawlessness. Satan is very present, whether we recognize his hand or not.

Where is the Church? God is looking for her to stand in the gap to thwart Satan's destructive work and extend God's righteous healing (Ezek. 22:29–31). In fact Paul Billheimer boldly contends, 'It is clear that . . . God intends the true church, not Satan, to be the controlling factor in human affairs . . . She, not Satan, holds the balance of power in human affairs' (*Destined for the Throne*, Christian Literature Crusade, Fort Washington, PA 19034, USA, 1975:57,62). Can this be? Probably not, if we continue in our present divided state. Probably not, if we neglect spiritual warfare. And probably not, if we do not exercise the power of intercession. Moses' intercession and faith brought an end to the pride of Egypt's army (Ex. 14:10–31), saved the whole nation of Israel from the Amalekites (Ex. 17:8–13), and later saved the nation from God's wrath (Ex. 32:9–14). If one man's intercession can change the course of such nations, what might the unified intercession of the church of Jesus Christ accomplish? In short, **God calls us to spiritual warfare in order to overcome Satan and his work, develop strength and maturity in us, and effect his purposes in history!**

3. **How** can we walk victorious in spiritual warfare? Victorious Christian warfare rests on the premise that the battle is not ours, but the Lord's (Ex. 14:13,14; Ii Chron. 20:15–29; Eph. 6:12). Furthermore, the critical battle has already been won by Christ at Calvary (Eph. 3:18–23; Col. 2:13–15). Our job is to stand firm in that victory and see the salvation of our God. How then can we banish Satan from territory that rightly belongs to Christ? What are our tactics and weapons? How do we render Satan's tactics and weapons ineffective? While the focus below is on Satan, the discussion is intended to encompass his allies as well. His allies include the world's system of thinking (I John 2:15–17; John 16:33) and the flesh (Gal. 5:16,17; Rom. 7:23–25; James 4:1–4).

a. *Our weapons*

    1) PRAISE AND WORSHIP. Our praise silences the Enemy

(compare Ps. 8:2 with Jesus' interpretation in Mt. 21:16). When he is silenced, most of his weapons (tempting, deceiving, lying, accusing) are stilled. Satan has a hard time harrassing someone who is filled with gratefulness and praise. When the battle is clearly the Lord's, the choirs can lead the way with their worship (II Chron. 20:20–23).

2) THE NAME OF THE LORD. What we ask in Christ's name, he will do (John 14:14; 16:23,24; Mk. 16:17,18). His name is above every other name; all others must submit to him (Phil. 2:9–11). David defeated Goliath 'in the name of the Lord of hosts' (I Sam. 17:45).

3) THE WORD OF OUR TESTIMONY (Rev. 12:10,11). Confessing Christ, his power, his goodness, his victory at the cross, causes Satan great distress. Words have meaning. Words have power. Even as Satan can hurt and destroy through words, we can extend strength and power through speaking truth about God.

4) THE BLOOD OF THE LAMB (Rev. 12:11). The blood cleanses us, removing sins that Satan could use to undermine us. The blood brings us into Christ's presence, the holy of holies, and Satan must flee.

5) THE WORD OF GOD (Eph. 6:16; Heb. 4:12). We can move forward into victory by responding in faith to the promises God has made us in his Word. Our obedience to the Word of God is one of the most strategic components of victory in spiritual warfare. One of the reasons that the Bible's power is not fully released in our lives can be that we are hearing *but not obeying*. And ingesting Biblical information without living it out in reality is a harmful, dangerous practice, a recipe for disaster. C.S. Lewis once wrote, 'We have a tendency to think without acting. The more we do this, the less becomes our capacity to act.' James 1:21–25 speaks pointedly about this principle.

6) THE ARMOUR OF GOD (Eph. 6:10–18). We should individually and corporately put on the armour of

God, especially in times of stress or difficulty. Excellent insights into Satan's tactics can be gained by considering what each piece of armour is intended to withstand.

b. *Our tactics.*

1) INTERCESSORY PRAYING. Intercession moves the hands of God Some battles are won only through prayer and fasting (Mk. 9:29; Mt. 17:21), sometimes prolonged prayer (Dan. 9). Guidelines for effective intercessory prayer are given in Chapter 2 of this section (p. 48).

2) SUPPORTING OUR LEADERS. Without Aaron and Hur's support of his arms, Moses would have failed in his prayers and Israel would have been defeated by the Amalekites (Ex. 17:8–13). When King David sinned, the whole nation suffered (I Chron. 21:1ff). If Satan can undermine or destroy a leader, the people will be scattered (Mt. 26:31). One of Satan's most devastating tactics is to do whatever he can to destroy godly leaders (Zech. 3:1–5; Lk. 22:31–34; I Tim. 3:6,7).

3) WALKING IN FORGIVENESS.

A) *Strongholds.* When we walk in Christ's forgiveness toward us, we can readily forgive those who hurt or wrong us. To harbour no wrong or hurt or sin takes away Satan's most effective way of neutralizing and eventually destroying us. Satan looks for our vulnerable points (I Tim. 3:7). A hurt or sin undealt with becomes a foothold for Satan (Eph. 4:26,27). A foothold is an area in which Satan can gain leverage in our lives. A foothold undealt with becomes a stronghold (II Cor. 10:3–5). A stronghold is an ungodly pattern of system of thinking leading to sinful attitudes and actions. Some common strongholds are a spirit of rejection (negative thinking), a bitter unforgiving spirit, dabbling in the occult, addictions, and worry. Finally, strongholds undealt with become areas of enemy control. Such control, if not dealt with, enables Satan to undermine all the rest of a person's life and the lives of others around him (Heb. 12:15; Joshua

7). If a person is unrepentant, church discipline
may be necessary (Mt. 18:15–18; I Tim. 1:19,20;
Titus 3:10,11).

B) *Deliverance and emotional healing*. Many adults,
perhaps most adults, carry with them wounds
and unresolved hurts with accompanying anger,
and sometimes unforgiveness. In the early centuries of the church's history it became standard
practice for new members to receive a deliverance
ministry. Such ministry can involve identifying
problem areas, confessing sin, forgiving others,
renouncing (which means 'withdrawing permission from') Satan, prayers of deliverance
(rebuking, binding and sending away any spirits
that may have been afflicting the person), and
healing. The healing of emotions comes through
forgiving and through receiving Christ's love and
forgiveness. 'To forgive is to set a prisoner free
and discover that the prisoner was you. To
forgive is to reach back into your hurting past
and recreate it in your memory so that you can
begin again . . . Our only escape from history's
cruel unfairness, our only passage to the future's
creative possibilities, is the miracle of forgiving'
(Lewis B. Smedes, 'Forgiveness: The Power to
Change the Past', *Christianity Today*, January 7,
1983).

4) PHYSICAL HEALING. Much (though by no means all!)
physical illness is caused by sin and the devil. Satan
can even take life (Job 1,2; Acts 10:38; II Cor. 12:7).
Christ has taken on himself our infirmities and
diseases (Is. 53:3–6; Mt. 8:16,17). Some hold that
God never heals today, others hold that he always
heals in response to a prayer of faith. Neither is true.
In praying for physical healing therefore we seek to
understand what the Father is doing and join into
that work (John 5:19). John Wimber describes this as
visualizing what God is doing so we can pray toward
that end. The Spirit puts inklings or pictures in our
minds of what he is doing, and we seek to pray these
into reality. Sometimes we hear or see nothing; at

other times we do not understand what we hear or see in our spirit, but we try to express it anyway. People who pray in this way, humbly and in dependence on God, make mistakes and stumble as they learn. At the same time, many are testifying to seeing God work in supernatural ways through such prayers of faith. (Further guidelines for hearing from God are discussed in Chapter 2 of this section.)

5) WALKING IN UNITY.

a) *Repenting of our division.* God never intends Christians to walk alone, independent of other Christians. Similarly, God never intends a local church to walk alone, independent of other churches. United we stand, divided we fall (Eccl. 4:9–12). The Reformation had its blessings, but it also had its failings: the Church has been afflicted by division and a spirit of independence ever since. Satan has used this as a doorway to wreak havoc in the Church. It has been said that those who spend their lives in pastoral ministry will experience an average of three major church divisions. Many leave the ministry, devastated by such internal warfare. Like Nehemiah (ch. 1) we need to identify with the Church's sin in this regard and cry out in repentance (II Chron. 7:14). As we do so, God may be gracious and deliver us from the division and independence that is so deep-rooted in us.

b) *Protecting one another.* The spiritual armour Paul prescribes for us to wear has no protection for a person's back. Roman soldiers fought side by side, linking their shields together into a solid wall if necessary. If surrounded, they would move into a back-to-back position. Hence, in spiritual terms, the seriousness of 'back-biting' (Ps. 15:1–3;. Prov. 25:23; Rom. 1:28,30; II Cor. 12:20). Little will so quickly destroy a person or a church as not being faithful to the Mt. 18:15–17 injunction to talk *directly* with a brother if we have a problem with him. We are to protect and cover for one another, not expose each other's weaknesses (see Gen. 9:18–27). Satan is the Accuser (Job 1,2; Zech. 2:1–5; I Tim. 5:14). When we refuse to listen to accusations against another person, and redirect people to talk directly with the person they are accusing, we take away one of Satan's major weapons.

c) *Taking the corporate offensive*. Both Ephesians 6 (on spiritual warfare) and I Pet. 5:8 (warning that the devil seeks to devour us) are written in the context of church life. Spiritual warfare is to be a corporate reality, not just an individual struggle. Several ways of taking the offensive include:

* Concerts of prayer, praying in unity with other churches for a city or nation. According to Korean leaders, one of the reasons the Gospel has spread so far in Korea is that the principalities and powers over that country have been broken. In areas of strong resistance to the Gospel, breakthroughs await the binding of evil powers. These powers are so great, in many places, that they will not be bound apart from a united offensive on our part.

* Rising up against major forces that are destroying people — such as the chaos and corruption that cause hyper-inflation in many third world countries, or abortion in the United States; or persecution and abuse of human rights in some places.

* A way of quickly mobilizing the Body to pray. For instance, a prayer chain can be activated by the pastor or a church leader when someone needs corporate prayer.

* 'Spiritual house cleaning.' When someone moves into a previously occupied house, it can be helpful to ask God to cleanse the house of any spirits that may have had influence there previously. This can be especially important if lingering illness, death, addiction or other signs of destructive forces accompanied the previous residents.

6) ENDURING PERSECUTION. For some readers of this

book the Devil's attacks will be immediate, personal and unavoidable — because they live in countries where Christians suffer persecution. Enduring under persecution is not just a lamentable necessity, a harsh fact of life; it can also be an effective means of spiritual warfare. Tertullian, one of the early Christian leaders, wrote, 'The blood of martyrs is the seed of the church'; and history shows that wherever Christians have resisted Satan by remaining faithful when persecuted, the church has grown tremendously. Revelation 12 specifically links the overthrow of Satan with the endurance of persecuted Christians:

> Now have come the salvation and the power and the kingdom of our God, and the authority of his Christ. For the accuser of our brothers, who accuses them before our God day and night, has been hurled down. They overcame him by the blood of the Lamb and by the word of their testimony; they did not love their lives so much as to shrink from death.

Jonathan Chao tells the story of an American youth who came to Hong Kong to study the church in China, asking, 'If God loves the Chinese church so much, why did he let so much persecution come upon it?' After seeing the reality of Chinese church life, he went away asking a different question: 'If God loves the American church so much, why does he not allow persecution to come upon it?' Suffering can be a source of spiritual dynamism.

NOW IT IS TIME TO DEVELOP YOUR *ACTION PLAN*. TURN BACK TO PAGE 9 FOR INSTRUCTIONS ON HOW TO DO SO. YOU WILL ALSO FIND OUT HOW TO USE THE RESOURCE MATERIAL IN SECTION 3.

SECTION 3

RESOURCES

This section is to be used as back-up material for the other sections. To understand how to use it, first read SECTION 1 (pp. 1–25).

HOW TO EXPRESS YOUR GENERAL NEED

> THIS WILL HELP YOU WITH *STEP B* OF
> THE PLANNING PROCESS (SEE P. 12)

Here are some ideas for ways in which the *general need* you
want to address might be expressed. (See page 14).

Chapter One: 'Our Church needs Christ's vision of — and
commitment to — the Kingdom of God.'

Chapter Two: 'Our church needs to be mobilized to incorporate prayer so that our lives and the lives of others around us
will be effectively transformed.'

Chapter Three: 'Our church needs to experience corporate
worship in such a way that we regularly encounter the living
God and are changed by these encounters.'

Chapter Four: 'Our church members need to become the kind
of stewards that make the most resources possible available for
the growth of God's Kingdom.'

Chapter Five: 'Our church needs the Spirit to be central in
teaching God's Word so that lives will be effectively transformed.'

Chapter Six: 'Our church needs pastoral care leaders who will
personally guide others into individual and corporate ministry
and maturity.'

Chapter Seven: 'Our church members need to enter into the

kind of community life that will make the church the central corporate reality of their lives.'

Chapter Eight: 'Our church members need to discover and use their gifts to carry out the ministries God wants our church to have.'

Chapter Nine: 'Our church members need to strengthen their families to reflect the Kingdom of God in the midst of a world whose families are falling apart.'

Chapter Ten: 'Our church members need to become confident and effective witnesses, regularly leading people to enter the Kingdom of God.'

Chapter Eleven: 'Our church needs to develop a missions strategy that effectively sends and supports people called to extend the Kingdom of God to new areas.'

Chapter Twelve: 'Our church needs to become socially

TURNING NEEDS INTO OBJECTIVES

To turn your *general need* into an *objective* (which is the next stage of the planning process — see page 15), simply express it as a goal. For instance:

Chapter Five: 'Our church needs the Spirit to be central in teaching God's Word so that lives will be effectively transformed' becomes 'Our church *will* make the Spirit central . . .'

Chapter Ten: 'Our church members need to become confident and effective witnesses, regularly leading people to enter the Kingdom of God' becomes 'Our church members *will* become confident and effective witnesses . . .'

And so on.

responsible in extending Christ's mercy, justice and healing power into the world.'

Chapter Thirteen: 'Our church needs to become victorious in spiritual warfare to free people from Satan's many-faceted bondage.'

HOW TO SELECT ACTION STEPS

> THIS WILL HELP YOU WITH *STEP D*
> OF THE PLANNING PROCESS (SEE P. 17)

POSSIBLE ACTION STEPS FOR CHAPTER ONE
(THE KINGDOM OF GOD)
(*See page 29*)

As a stimulus to developing your action plan, consider the following possible six-month *teaching and training outline* on the subject of the Kingdom of God. Its aim is to mobilize the entire church to a vision of the kingdom, and commitment to it. The most effective way to use it is to combine Sunday sermons with linked small group discussion (in adult Sunday School, or some similar setting).

a. The eternal purposes of God (6 weeks).
   1) Expressed in creation (1 week)
   2) Ruined by the Fall (1 week)
   3) Restored by Jesus Christ
      — a study of the Kingdom in Matthew (2 weeks)
      — a study of the Kingdom in Acts (1 week)
      — a study of the Kingdom in the Epistles (1 week).
b. The expression of the Kingdom of God in the here and now (7 weeks). (This could introduce the major areas to be covered after this series on the Kingdom.)
   1) The Kingdom expressed through personal pastoral care (discipling)

2) The Kingdom expressed in spiritual disciplines (devotional life)
3) The Kingdom of God expressed in the family
4) The Kingdom of God expressed in Christian community
5) The Kingdom of God expressed in ministry (spiritual gifts)
6) The mission of the Kingdom of God — impacting society
7) The Kingdom of God and church unity (catholicity)

c. Understanding and following the will (the government) of God expressed in three ways, in order of their importance (7 weeks).
1) The Holy Scriptures
   a) How to study the Bible (inductive Bible study steps of observation, interpretation, application: one week explanation, one week demonstration, then ongoing practice).
   b) Interpreting the Scriptures (hermeneutics: one week explanation and one week demonstration; then ongoing practice).
2) Our conscience: being sensitive to the Spirit (one week).
3) Delegated authority (delegated by God) (two weeks).
   a) People: government, family, church leaders and employers.
   b) Gifts: authority expressed in and through spiritual gifts.

d. Commitment to obeying the will (the government) of God (4 weeks)
1) Challenge to obedience (outlining consequences of obedience and disobedience).
2) Challenge for each person to commit himself to the Kingdom of God and to grow in the seven areas of point B above.
3) Defining a covenant — for individuals to covenant themselves to pursue the Kingdom of God above all else.
4) Celebration of the covenant, preferably in a one-day or weekend retreat. If the Spirit so leads, the church leaders will now have a group of people committed to being formed in the ways of the Kingdom. Once people

have made the mental and spiritual transition from informational teaching to formational teaching, the foundation is laid for the ongoing process of re-formation!

POSSIBLE ACTION STEPS FOR CHAPTER TWO (PRAYER)
(*See page 40*)

Here are **three** possible action steps you could consider in putting together your plan.

a. *Set up a prayer pyramid* for mobilizing the whole church quickly to pray about any issue. The way it works is as follows. The pastor passes the word to his main leaders, who in turn pass it on to three or four designated people; they continue to repeat the process until everyone has been reached. (You can use the system to pass along information, as well as prayer requests and answers.)

b. *Sunday teaching topics* could include one or more teaching sessions on the 'what', 'why' and 'how' of prayer. You might consider a one– or two–month concentration on 'hearing from God', and another on 'intercession'. Studying the Lord's prayer in depth supplies an excellent structure for a series on how to pray. If the sermons can be backed up by small group discussion *and practice*, their effectiveness will be multiplied!

c. *Structuring the church for prayer*. Consider how to revitalize present prayer meetings, if necessary. Consider how to make prayer a major part of meetings and structures that already exist — especially elders' meetings and business meetings. Be sensitive to the Spirit's leading in starting new prayer structures: early morning prayer, lunch time prayer meetings, special prayer places, prayer partnerships, small group prayer, intercessory ministry teams, prayer vigils, prayer teams after the Sunday church services — many things are possible. (The last of these suggestions is especially effective in reinforcing the sermon through immediate action for those who need empowering, healing, release or intercession for whatever reason.) But do not start too many new enterprises at once. Indeed, you will probably want to restrict yourselves to one — the one where you as leaders will deeply invest yourselves. If the Spirit moves others in the congregation to start other prayer activities — great!

POSSIBLE ACTION STEPS FOR CHAPTER THREE (WORSHIP)
(*See page 52*)

Here are **four** possible action steps you could consider in putting together your plan.

a. *Teach*. Sunday teaching topics could include one or more teaching sessions on the 'what', 'why' and 'how' of worship. You might consider a one– or two–month concentration on 'preparing for worship', 'participating in worship', and 'the Lord's Supper'. If the sermons can be backed up by small group discussion *and practice*, their effectiveness will be multiplied!
b. *Structure church services for better worship*. Consider how to revitalize present worship meetings if necessary. Consider how to celebrate high points of the church year in a big way!
c. *Celebrate the Lord's Supper* as a central part of church life. The early church shared the Lord's Supper at least once a week. If you do so less frequently, you might consider the early church pattern. Some study of church history or discussion with leaders of churches with a liturgical tradition (e.g. Anglican) could be helpful in this.
d. *Make worship central to any important decision-making*. This could tie together with hearing from God as discussed in Chapter Two.

POSSIBLE ACTION STEPS FOR CHAPTER FOUR
(STEWARDSHIP)
(*See page 65*)

Here are **four** possible action steps you could consider in putting together your plan.
a. *Teach*. Sunday teaching topics could include one or more teachings on the what, why and how of stewardship.

You might consider a one– or two–month concentration on celebrating the first day of the week, on celebrating the first hour of the day, and on celebrating our first fruits (tithes and offerings). If the sermons can be backed up by small group discussion and practice, their effectiveness will be multiplied! Aim at seeing one focus lived out before going on to another.

b. *Structure church services for more celebrative giving.* For instance, some churches have everyone sing songs of praise as they bring their offerings to the front.

c. *Provide financial management guidelines for the people.* Since finances are a part of the Kingdom, people should be free to bring their financial problems to whomever is pastoring/ discipling them. The pastoral leader/discipler needs to be equipped to give basic counsel and know where to turn if the issues are unusual or very complex. Having our finances in order is a part of bringing all parts of our lives under the Lordship of Christ. Aim not only at teaching this, but also at equipping people to live it.

d. *Provide time management guidelines for the people.* Our time is our most valuable resource. Most of us need help in periodically thinking through our priorities and scheduling our time to reflect our priorities. We need to move from the 'tyranny of the urgent' to living by Kingdom priorities. Jesus clearly had priorities and did not allow others to dictate how he would use his time or what he would do (see Mt. 12:46–50; 16:21–23; 26:51–53; Lk. 2:48,49; 4:42–44; 9:51; John 7:3–9). Once again a discipler/pastoral leader can be invaluable in helping us with our priorities and schedule. He can help people in thinking through management issues, and in the more difficult task of encouraging and holding them accountable to change old habits that have been destructive.

POSSIBLE ACTION STEPS FOR CHAPTER FIVE
(TEACHING AND STUDY OF THE WORD)
(*See page 78*)

Here are **four** possible action steps you could consider in putting together your plan.

a. *Deepen Sunday sermons through small group Bible studies.*
Such studies could come *before* the sermon, in preparation
for it, or *afterwards*, in deepening and applying the lessons.
It is important for Christians to concentrate on an area until
they are living it victoriously, rather than jumping from
one topic to another every week or dealing with several
topics at once every week.

b. *Train small group Bible study leaders.* Without training,
church leaders may simply turn a small group Bible study
into a small church service. Training is indispensable.
(Some training resources are listed on page 000.) The best
resource is to have a skilled small group Bible study leader
train others. If every qualified Bible study leader will train
others at the same time as actually leading Bible studies,
the Bible study approach can become a movement. A good
training process often has three steps:

1) The trainer does the task while the learner observes.
2) The trainer and a learner do the task together, while
   both observe.
3) The learner does the task while the trainer observes.

c. *Concentrate on inductive Bible study.* If the Spirit is leading
you to make this a major focus of concentration, both the
content of the Sunday sermons and the way they are taught
can illustrate and instruct in this regard. An overhead
projector, blackboard and/or handouts may help. Another
way of concentrating would be to focus also on teaching
people more about personal devotional Bible study methods
during these months. The goal, of course, would not be to
teach about Bible study, but to see people doing Bible
study that changes their lives. Sunday teaching topics could
include one or more teachings on:

1) What spiritual teaching is (instruction that reaches our
   spirits, changing our lives).
2) Why spiritual teaching is essential.
3) How spiritual teaching/learning is done. It would help if
   this teaching on 'how-to's is slow enough to master a
   given approach or method before giving much more.

d. *Continue on one topic until it is being practised well.* For
instance the following discussion questions might easily be
asked in one discussion session. On the other hand if the

group does not move on to the next question until it is
practising the first one relatively well, lives will be changed.
1) What helps me to prepare my heart to hear from God?
2) What helps me to hear from God in a Sunday teaching?
3) What helps me to hear from God in small group Bible
study?
4) What helps me to respond to God, by obeying what I
heard him saying?

POSSIBLE ACTION STEPS FOR CHAPTER SIX
(DISCIPLING AND PASTORAL CARE)
(*See page 89*)

Here are **three** possible action steps you could consider in
putting together your plan.
a. The pastor might look for someone wiser and more mature,
who can extend pastoral care to him — that is, if he does
not have such a person already. He probably should not
commit himself to such a relationship until the church
leaders are in agreement with his doing so. This may be a
process of months or years. In some ways, it is similar to a
courtship!
b. The pastor might invite between four and six church
leaders to be part of the first pastoral care group, under his
leadership. As they consider this invitation, it would be
good for them to understand fully the responsibilities and
privileges involved. For instance, they might be invited to
commit themselves to this 'pilgrimage' for a year, with the
understanding that it would take about four hours a week.
For the first three months or so, they would be largely on
the receiving end.
   At the same time they would be giving the pastor
feedback which would help him to refine his approach to
pastoral care and the meetings involved. When they are
ready to begin their own caring groups, they might devote
about an hour a week to preparation, an hour a week to
individual one-to-one meetings and two hours a week to
meeting with the whole caring group. Once they have their
own caring groups, they might meet only once a month

with the pastor's caring group and possibly once a month alone with the pastor for pastoral care and for further refining of the pastoral care model. (If necessary, you may decide to pursue this in a less time-consuming way. The reasons for allocating this much time to the system is that it can thus be the primary means of discipling everyone in the Body. Whatever amount of time is given to pastoral care, it would be wise consciously to cut back on about the same amount of time given to other activities.)

c. When some or all of the first pastoral care group are ready to begin their own caring groups, a training or orientation day could be held for those who might want to come into the caring groups. There could be an open invitation, or specific invitations could be given by caring group leaders to those whom they feel God might want to be in their group. The day could be used to orient those present to the biblical vision of discipling and pastoral care (possibly using the inductive study from earlier in this chapter). The leaders could share some of their personal experience of the benefits and responsibilities of coming into such a group. If the day were to be viewed as a 'training course,' the same course could be repeated in the future when more leaders were ready to begin caring groups. If group members are carefully chosen, they will be among those most ready to lead their own groups in the future. However, it may take most of this second group of people longer than three months before they are ready to begin their own caring groups, since presumably they are not quite so mature and skilled as the group first chosen by the pastor.

POSSIBLE ACTION STEPS FOR CHAPTER SEVEN
(CHRISTIAN COMMUNITY LIFE)
(*See page 100*)

Here are **three** possible action steps you could consider in putting together your plan.

a. *Strategize how to develop stronger community among the leaders.* You might focus on this for several months before raising this area to the congregation's attention.

b. *Teach*. Sunday teaching topics could include one or more teachings on the what, why and how of Christian community. You might consider a one– or two–month concentration on a Christian environment or culture, or a series focusing on the 'one another' commandments. You might take the whole church through a series of foundational teachings for membership. If they have already been through this when they become members, this can help them review the basics again. If the teachings are new, the series could be climaxed by a re-commitment retreat. Backing the sermons up by small group discussion and practice, will multiply their effectiveness! Remember to aim at seeing one focus lived out before going on to another.

c. *Re-structure the church life for cell groups*. If you do not already have a small group structure in place, you might consider changing or adapting the mid-week church meeting to make a transition toward it being a night for cell groups. This needs to grow organically, not be imposed organizationally. Further guidelines for starting small groups, selecting small group members and so forth are discussed in the chapter on discipling/pastoral care (pages 96–99). A good way to pace small group growth is not to start new groups until leaders are trained. Every leader, once trained, should begin training one or two of the most promising people in his group so that his group can multiply into two groups in the future. The more you try to put people who live close to one another into the same cell group, the easier it will be for them to practise community life between meetings.

POSSIBLE ACTION STEPS FOR CHAPTER EIGHT
(MINISTRY, SPIRITUAL GIFTS)
(*See page 114*)

Here are **two** possible action steps you could consider in putting together your plan.

a. *Assess and affirm your spiritual gifts as leaders*. As leaders, you might 'pre-test' the discovery process into which you want to lead the congregation.

b. *Teach*. A possible teaching outline follows below. Such a

series may change the very structure of your church. May
Isaiah 43:18,19 be very real to you! Some topics below
might require more than one week. The over-all purpose is
to lay a foundation that will mobilize the whole church in
ministry. Remember that backing your teaching up by
small group discussion and practice will multiply its
effectiveness! Aim at seeing your teaching not only
understood but also put into practice in people's lives.

Following is a possible teaching outline based on the
'motivations, ministries, manifestations' framework:

1) What are spiritual gifts?
2) Why has God given us our spiritual gifts? What are
their purposes?
3) How do we discover our spiritual gifts?
4) Love — the environment we need for developing gifts
(I Cor. 13)
5) Prophecy
6) Serving
7) Teaching
8) Exhortation
9) Giving
10) Leading
11) Mercy

Romans 12:6–8:
* What this gift is
* Why God has given the Body
this gift
* Possible characteristics of one
with this gift
* Dangers of this gift when walking
in the flesh
* Guidelines and resources for
further developing this gift

12) Manifestational (or sign) gifts: what and why (I Cor.
12:7–10)
13) Manifestational gifts: how they should and should not
be used (I Cor. 14)
14) Ministerial gifts: their special role (Eph. 4:11–13;
I Cor. 12:28–31)
15) Ministry groups and calling: what and why
16) Ministry groups and calling: how they might function
17) The anointing/outpouring of the Holy Spirit
RETREAT: focusing on affirming gifts and launching (or
re-affirming) some initial ministry groups. Not all ministry
groups will be ready to launch at this point; most of them

will emerge in the coming months and years if the basic
supportive environment and structure is in place.

POSSIBLE ACTION STEPS FOR CHAPTER NINE
(FAMILY LIFE)
(*See page 129*)

Here are **six** possible action steps you could consider in
putting together your plan.

a. *Assess and affirm your family life as leaders*. If you want to
lead the congregation into new ideas and norms for family
life, it could be good to 'pre-test' them in your own
families.

b. *Teach*. Below is the outline of Larry Christenson's excellent
book *The Christian Family* (1970); it could form the outline
for a teaching series to clarify God's divine order for the
family. Erroneous teaching about the family is common
today, even in Christian circles; influences from egalitarian-
ism, individualism and some forms of feminism can create
wrong ideas. Remember that backing up your teaching by
small group discussion and practice, will multiply its
effectiveness! Aim at seeing your teaching not only
understood, but also put into practice in people's lives.

  1) Understanding and following God's order for the
    family.
    A) God's order for marriage partners
    B) God's order for husbands
    C) God's order for wives
    D) God's order for parents
    E) God's order for children.
  2) Practicing the presence of Jesus in the family
    A) Jesus, the family's Saviour and Lord
    B) The Priesthood of parents
    C) Our family, a witness for Jesus

c. *Make sure church activities reinforce family life*. Are church
activities consuming all of a family's time? Are they
scattering the family in different directions rather than
reinforcing family solidarity? Does the church protect and
affirm the pastor's time with his own family? The family

and the church are God's two unique social creations. The church is to be a family of families. In a sense, a family is to be a church in miniature. Healthy families and a healthy church should reinforce and strengthen each other.

d. *Provide support, guidance and counsel for hurting family members.* Many adults, perhaps most, have some significant areas in which they need healing. Many parents had *inadequate parental models* while they were growing up. *Child abuse* is much more rampant in the church than we realize. *Teen rebellion*, of course, is only too common. Good counselling and instruction combined with healing and/or deliverance ministries and good modelling can release people to be the kind of parents they want to be.

e. *Intentionally teach men how to lead their families.* The head of the family is the husband. Western culture is increasingly undermining this, both philosophically and practically. Many, if not most, family problems have their root in the head of the family. Men commonly do not know how to husband and father well. They need to see good models and be taught God's vision for the family and for their role in particular. This kind of teaching works particularly well in the context of discipling or pastoral care relationships. As men are pastored well, they can in turn pastor their families well.

f. *Develop some family-oriented ministry teams.*

   1) **Marriage enrichment team.** These seminars or retreats can both strengthen church families and be a key tool for serving nonchristians in a way that will draw them to Christ.

   2) **Family ministry team.** This team could help the church in giving special emphasis to family activities and education. Possible activities include stimulating and/or coordinating:
      — adult Sunday School electives for parents who have children of different ages
      — Father's Day, Mother's Day and possibly a 'Children's Day'
      — A Christian home week-long emphasis once a year
      — Encouraging everyone in the church to set aside one night a week as 'family night'. In some cases it may

work well for everyone to aim at the same night and thus reinforce and protect one another by not scheduling anything else on that night.

3) **Fatherless families ministry team**. There are a high number of single parent families (nine out of ten of which are headed by women), in addition to outright orphans. The Scripture repeatedly calls us to a special care for the fatherless. (The Hebrew *yathowm* and Greek *orphanos* often translated 'orphans' could equally be translated 'fatherless'; they come from a root word meaning 'to be lonely' or 'bereaved'.) See Ex. 22:22–24; Deut. 16:14; Job 31:16–23; Ps. 68:5,6; James 1:27.)

POSSIBLE ACTION STEPS FOR CHAPTER TEN
(LOCAL EVANGELISM)
(*See page 141*)

Here are **four** possible action steps you could consider in putting together your plan.

a. *Assess your witness to the world as leaders*. If you want to train the congregation or introduce them to different methods of witnessing, it might be good to 'pre-test' the training and methods yourselves.

b. *Teach*. Sunday teaching topics could include one or more teaching sessions on the 'what', 'why' and 'how' of being a witness. You might consider a one– or two–month concentration on clarifying the Gospel of the Kingdom, and on friendship evangelism. Remember that backing up your teaching by small group discussion *and practice* will multiply its effectiveness! Your aim should be to see people not only *understanding* your teaching, but also *putting it into practice* in their lives. In achieving this goal — as we mentioned earlier — there may be nothing quite as effective as a good discipling/training programme in evangelism.

c. *Structure the church for witness*. Most churches have some structure for worship and some structure for strengthening the Body. Unless the church also has some kind of structure to encourage and channel outreach to the world, it will be difficult to develop strength in witnessing. Possible structures include the training programme mentioned earlier, and a variety of mission/ministry teams (discussed in Chapter Eight on spiritual gifts). Existing fellowship groups can be challenged to seek and then implement some kind of mission/ministry together. If the church has activities almost every night, it may need to consider cutting back in order to allow its people to develop friendships with nonchristians. People could even be encouraged to use Sunday nights to spend with nonchristian friends rather than come to the evening service . . .!

d. *Structure the church for strong follow-up discipleship.* The test of evangelism is not how many seeds get scattered, nor yet how many seeds take root, but how many seeds grow up to be fruit bearing (Mt. 13:–9,18–23). While God causes the seed to grow, we have a role in nurturing that growth (I Cor. 3:6–9). As discussed above, friendship and small groups are key to this. Equally important is intentional discipling that combines a one-on-one relationship with a small group growth process. The whole church may be structured for discipling (as discussed in Chapter Eight). If so, the discipling of the new Christian will be part of entering into an ongoing new way of life rather than a programme to get him to the baptismal waters.

POSSIBLE ACTION STEPS FOR CHAPTER ELEVEN
(MISSIONS STRATEGY)
(*See page 153*)

Here are **three** possible action steps you could consider in putting together your plan.

a. *Assess the missions potential present in the church leadership.* As God did in Acts 13:1–3, he may want some of the best leaders you have to head a missions team!

b. *Teach.* Sunday teaching topics could include one or more teachings on the what, why and how of missions. You might consider a one– or two–month concentration on the Lord's work worldwide, and a series on the church members' role in supporting missionaries (spiritually, emotionally, intellectually, socially, and physically). Remember that backing your teaching up by small group discussion and practice will multiply its effectiveness! Aim at seeing your teaching not only understood, but also put into practice in people's lives.

c. *Structure the church for missions support.* A number of ideas are listed a little earlier in the 'How' section of thinking through a missions strategy. Other structures that various churches presently use include prayer teams, reading missionary letters from the pulpit, missionary conferences, sending short-termers, and missionary pledge giving. Think of all the ways you can maintain close relationship with your missionaries on the field, so that when they come back to you they come as family, not as strangers.

POSSIBLE ACTION STEPS FOR CHAPTER TWELVE
(SOCIAL ACTION)
(*See page 166*)

Here are **three** possible action steps you could consider in putting together your plan.

a. *Assess the actual and potential leadership the church has in the area of social responsibility.* Consider how to involve these people in further exploring the ideas you have developed in your study of social responsibility.

b. *Teach.* Involvement with the poor will lead to a new reading of Scripture, being able to see in some measure from their perspective. Sunday teaching topics could include one or more teachings on the what, why and how of social responsibility. You might consider a one- or two-month concentration on mercy, justice and/or God's healing power. Nehemiah would make a good 'case study' if you are becoming involved in community development. As the Lord leads, you might consider a similar concentration on a major social issue or problem or on our responsibility for political awareness and involvement. You would want to do this only if you intend to mobilize your congregation in that area. Be careful not to jump on a bandwagon or push a certain issue simply because it is currently popular. You want to build lasting foundations for social responsibility in your church. When the Lord leads you on to a new emphasis some months from now, you want the church's social involvement to continue strong, not simply fade away as the people run after the 'new' teaching. Backing your teaching up by small group discussion and practice will multiply its effectiveness! Aim at seeing your teaching not only understood, but also put into practice in people's lives.

c. *Structure the church for social involvement.* You might review the ideas listed a little earlier in the 'How' section of thinking through the church's social responsibility. What role could the office of deacon/deaconess play in the church's social involvement?

POSSIBLE ACTION STEPS FOR CHAPTER THIRTEEN
(SPIRITUAL WARFARE)
(*See page 182*)

Here are **three** possible action steps you could consider in putting together your plan.

a. *Assess the actual and potential leadership the church has in the area of spiritual warfare.* Consider how to involve these people in further exploring the ideas you have developed in your study of spiritual warfare. Encourage and recognize those gifted in intercession, deliverance, discernment and healing. Often people gifted in areas related to spiritual warfare need added protection and care (see I Cor. 12:22–24). This may be either because Satan attacks them in a special way or because they are simply more aware of his work.

b. *Teach.* Sunday teaching topics could include one or more teachings on the what, why and how of spiritual warfare. You might consider a one– or two–month concentration on our weapons, our tactics or our armour (Eph. 6:10–18). Backing your teaching up by small group discussion and practice will multiply its effectiveness! Aim at seeing your teaching not only understood, but also put into practice in people's lives. You want to build lasting foundations for spiritual warfare in your church. When the Lord leads you to a new emphasis some months from now, you want the church's spiritual warfare to continue strong, not simply fade away as your people concentrate on the 'new' teaching.

c. *Structure the church for spiritual warfare.* You might review the ideas listed a little earlier in the 'How' section of thinking through the church's spiritual warfare. Some churches have found it helpful to have healing prayer teams regularly available for people wanting ministry, following the Sunday service and at other times during the week as they are needed.

INDUCTIVE BIBLE STUDIES

HERE ARE BIBLE STUDY OUTLINES
FOR EACH CHAPTER IN SECTION 2.

This first page of guidelines should be read before starting any of the thirteen Bible studies which follow. Then review this page again before starting any subsequent study.

The leader's work is not to explain the passage, much less preach! The leader 1) *asks questions*, and 2) *affirms the responses* of the group as much as possible. the key question to be repeated dozens of times in a study is: 'What does this passage tell us about the theme [*specify it*] on which we are focusing)?' If there is a key idea in the passage that the group has not discovered, try to help them discover it by asking 'What *else* does this passage tell us about the theme?' Once you sense the group is ready to move on to the next passage, if there's still a key idea undiscovered, feel free to share it in half a minute to a minute before continuing. A guideline you should explain to the group is that no one should talk more than about a minute at a time. You as the leader need to demonstrate this guideline so that the group can follow your example.

Remember that the questions and commentaries below are secondary to the main question above. At times the group itself will raise the points indicated below; at other times the group's discussion will be animated and well-focused so that you don't need to raise these points. The ideas below are to stimulate the discussion. You don't need to raise them if the group is doing a good job of discovering the important truths of these passages. You would do well to read over the passages, and the ideas below, ahead of time so that you are familiar with them.

When you ask the group a question regarding a certain passage, if they do not answer right away, do not be too quick to give them the answer. It will often help to ask the question *at least twice* to get them thinking seriously toward discovering the answer for themselves. Often the question is as important as the answer. Sometimes a good question is worth leaving unanswered so that people will continue thinking about it!

If several passages are grouped together in the study below, they should be read together before asking the key question of the study as noted above. Below follow the passages of the various Bible studies, with some suggestions and key questions to stimulate the discussion of each passage. (There are thirteen sections, for the thirteen themes of the handbook).

CHAPTER ONE: BIBLE STUDY OUTLINE

WHAT DO THESE PASSAGES TELL US
ABOUT THE KINGDOM OF GOD?

> *Remember to review the leader's instructions on page 219 before going ahead with the study.*

As you get started in this study, someone may ask what the

difference is between the Kingdom of Heaven and the Kingdom of God. If the question comes up, explain that Matthew primarily uses the first phrase while Luke uses the second, but that both means the same. In Matthew 19:23,24 both terms are used in an interchangeable way.

Mt. 3:1–3: What is the doorway to the Kingdom of God? (Answer: Repentance; this is a continual doorway, not just a doorway of conversion. Note that Rev. 3:19,20 is written *to the church*). Is John announcing the Kingdom as present?

Mt. 4:17–23: Were the disciples volunteers? (Answer: v. 20,22 indicate not). And as Christians today, do we see ourselves more as volunteers or as people under orders, simply obeying our Lord and King? V. 23 can be seen as a job description. Why does the announcement of the Kingdom of God come so often hand in hand with healing — as it does here? What *is* the Gospel of the Kingdom? Could it be different from the Gospel we so often hear today? (Note the frequency of these paired words in the New Testament:

1) Saviour	24 times	Lord	700 times
2) Christian	3 times	Disciple	270 times

We often hear a man-centred Gospel rather than a God-centred Gospel. The emphasis is much more commonly on *believing* than on *obeying*.

In v.17, the Kingdom of God is still 'at hand' rather than present. Why? (You do not need to get a good answer to this question; just arouse people's curiosity and let them know that the answer is important . . . and will be found as the study progresses).

Luke 4:42,43: Note the sense of urgency. What determined Christ's agenda — the people's needs or the Kingdom of God? (*Note that the two are not synonymous!*)

Mt. 6:9,10: Christ is praying 'Thy Kingdom come', even though he was present. Why? Could it be that the petition 'Thy Kingdom come' is repeated and explained in the rest of the verse? What light does this shed on the Kingdom?

Mt. 6:33,34: The heart of the Sermon on the Mount. In the context of v. 34, when Jesus calls us to seek first the Kingdom, is he calling us to look for something in the future? What does it mean to seek first the Kingdom of God? Why is righteousness (*or, as it could be* *translated, 'justice'*) included hand in hand with the Kingdom of God?

Mt. 7:21–23: A Kingdom riddle. Why are these men rejected? (*They have the right words; they have signs and wonders that surpass the efforts of most of us.*) Note the last phrase, 'you who practice lawlessness'. This means 'you who are under no law or authority' . . . workers who are not submitted. *Can* Kingdom people be unsubmitted?

Mt. 9:35–10:8,40: V. 35 repeats the job description. Why did Christ have compassion? (*Because of the eternal damnation awaiting these people? No, because of their temporary problems!*) Up to 10:1 the Kingdom of God had a name (Jesus) and had a face (that of Jesus). What happens in 10:1? (*Answer: the Kingdom explodes! Vv. 2–4 — twelve names, twelve faces [note v. 40]*). Vv. 7,8 indicate the same job description. Note that the Kingdom of God and healing appear hand in hand again. Is the Kingdom of God present? (*Answer: No, it's still only at hand [10:7]*).

Mt. 11:11,12: Two Kingdom riddles. V. 11 — How is it that the smallest in the Kingdom of God is greater than the most important prophet that ever lived? (*Answer: To be a son is far greater than being the greatest servant!*) V. 12 — What is the relationship between violence and the Kingdom of God? (*Answer: How many of the group have seen someone give birth? Is it violent? What connection might there be between this and entering the Kingdom of God?*) Perhaps some of our soft, easy 'conversions' fail in actually entering the Kingdom of God.

Mt. 12:25–29: A riddle. In Mt. 3:2; 4:17; and 10:7, the Kingdom of God was 'at hand'. Now it 'has come upon you'! What is happening here that would catapult the Kingdom of God into the present? (*Answer: Christ's government or authority is being recognized and obeyed*).

Luke 17:20,21: Is the Kingdom of God present or future? (*It is actually past, present and future, but the focus here is on the present.*) Why might we also focus on the *present* Kingdom of God? (*Answer: because we cannot do much to change either the past or the future apart from our present actions.*)

Mt. 13:10–13: A Kingdom riddle. What justice is there in v. 12? (*The key to this verse is to understand what thing or quality one needs in order to receive more and what it is that if one lacks it, even what he has* *will be taken from him. The secret is in the context of the passage and v. 10. Mt. 5:6 gives a possible clue.*)

Mt. 13:44: This whole chapter is comprised of parables of the Kingdom. Note here a complete break with the past, a selling of everything. Can we sacrifice everything for something other than the Kingdom? (*It has been said that religion is selling everything to buy the wrong field.*) What attitude accompanies such sacrifice? (*Answer: joy!*) Why?

Mt. 16:15–19: What might be the keys of the Kingdom? (*Mt. 18:15–18 indicates that these keys are given to the church and not just to Peter.*) What connection might there be between the confession of Peter and the keys of the Kingdom? What connection is there between the church and the Kingdom of God?

Mt. 20:25–28: The values of the Kingdom of God are often the opposite of the values of the world. Is Jesus explaining here an *ideal* of the Kingdom, or the *reality* of the Kingdom? (*Answer: the reality — not what ought to be, but what is!*) How does service equal authority? (*In the Kingdom of God, to rule is to raise; a person's rank is in his power to uplift.*)

Mt. 21:43: Can we possess the Kingdom of God? Can we be confident that the Kingdom of God will never be taken from us? Were the chief priests and Pharisees confident that the Kingdom would never be taken from them? (*We do not possess the Kingdom of God so much as it possesses us! We are more members of it than owners of it.*)

Mt. 28:18–20: What is the base, so often ignored, of the Great Commission (v. 18)? What is the only imperative in these verses? (*Answer: in the Greek, 'make disciples'; 'Go' is a participle in the Greek, better translated 'While going'.*) What connection is there here between making disciples and the church? (*That of baptism.*)

Acts 1:3–8: Christ's last days on earth. What was the focus of this 'graduate school' for the disciples? (*Answer: the Kingdom*). What is the connection between the Holy Spirit and the Kingdom? With all that the disciples understood, what percentage of the Kingdom would you estimate they had grasped? And us? (*The question is not how much we have grasped, but whether we are continually pressing on in the attitude of seeking more and more of his Kingdom. Thus the importance of Mt. 6:33.*)

Acts 17:6,7: Does the Kingdom of God by its very nature turn the world upside down? Does it turn *my* world upside down?

Acts 19:8–10: (*Note also Acts 20:24,25.*) Is extending the Kingdom of God exclusively God's work, or does it also include human factors and strategies? What strategy do we see here in Paul?

Acts 28: 23,30,31: What was Paul's theme? The book of Acts opens with this theme. It finishes with this theme. Christ's life opens with this theme. It breathes this theme. It finishes with this theme. And our lives?

This is a good place to finish the study with a time of prayer and worship. If you wanted to go on at some point to look further at some of what the Epistles say about the Kingdom, some key Scriptures include: Rom. 14:17; I Cor. 4:20; I Cor. 15:50; Gal. 5:19–21; and Rev. 11–15.

CHAPTER TWO: BIBLE STUDY OUTLINE

WHAT DO THESE PASSAGES TELL US ABOUT PRAYER
AND THE DEVOTIONAL LIFE?

Remember to review the leader's instructions on page 219 before going ahead with the study.

Ex. 17:8–13: Why did Moses' upraised hands bring victory to God's people? (*Answer: role of intercessor, and possibly his posture also*). Was Moses' physical posture important? Why or why not? What role did Aaron and Hur play, and how important was it? Who won the battle? (*Answer: Joshua . . . thanks to Moses . . . thanks to Aaron and Hur . . . thanks above all to the Lord! Any one person or any one role alone would have lost the battle.*)

II Chron. 7:12–14: Almost every promise has a condition. Could any of the four conditions of this promise be considered optional? Why or why not? Is this a promise to us as individuals, or is it to us corporately? Are there ways in which our land needs healing?

II Chron. 20:1–4,12–24: Being afraid, what did Jehoshaphat do? How critical was the *corporate* prayer? (*Answer: it released the Spirit and the gift of prophecy.*) How critical was the *corporate* worship of vv. 21–22? (*Answer: it demonstrated obedience and faith; it released the Lord's ambushes.*)

Eccl. 4:9–12: How might these verses apply to prayer? (*The answer might focus on prayer partners — anyone without a prayer partner is weak and vulnerable. Or also prayer teams — prayer ministry done in teams will be much more effective.*) How might 'a cord of three strands' be woven together in prayer?

Is. 59:15–18; 63:4–6; Ezek. 22:28–31: What characterizes the missing intercessor God cannot find? What is the result of God's not finding an intercessor? (*Answer: wrath, judgement and destruction.*) How might an intercessor have changed this? (*By interceding for God's mercy and patience, resulting in salvation and a renewed covenant, as illustrated by Moses (Ex. 32,33; Num. 14) and Jesus (Is. 53:12).*)

Mt. 6:9–15: What indications are there that this is a corporate prayer more than an individual prayer? (*Answer: plural use of 'Our' and 'us'*). In what ways could this prayer be used in a corporate context? Why are vv. 14 and 15 so vital to praying rightly? (This indicates a corporate dimension even when we pray alone!)

Mt. 9:36–10:1: What is Christ's response when overwhelmed with people's problems? What is the connection between the prayer of 9:39 and the commissioning of 10:1? What is involved in 'beseeching' (9:38)? How would you describe it? What is the best way of mobilizing effective workers? (*Answer: get them praying regarding the needs (9:38) and have God's anointing come on them (10:1).*)

Mt. 18:18–20: What can we bind and loose on earth that will also happen in heaven? How *do* we bind and loose such things? What does it mean to agree in prayer? (*Answer: It is much more than saying 'Hey, that sounds good!' It involves a communing in spirit, and having God's Spirit urge us or release us to pray as one.*)

Mk. 9:25–29: How can prayer increase our spiritual power and authority? How can fasting (added by many manuscripts in v. 29) increase our spiritual power and authority?

John 5:19,20 and John 14:12,13: Can we do anything 'of ourselves'? (*Answer: yes, but the result would be human, not divine.*) How important is it for us to take the role of the Son in 5:19? How do we 'see' what the Father is doing? (This question, while not easy to answer, is *critical*. The answer may involve sanctified imaginations; it may involve 'hearing from God'; it may involve spiritual gifts — thus reinforcing once again the role of *corporate* prayer).

Acts 1:14; 2:42,43; 6:1–4: The early church was devoted to prayer. Why? What would have changed if they had allowed their prayer life to become nominal? What might a church devoted to prayer look like? (Some churches have such things as a prayer centre for prayer retreats of all kinds, prayer every day at 4 to 5 a.m. at the church, all-night prayer vigils, intercessory prayer teams, healing prayer teams, and ministry prayer teams that are available after each Sunday service.)

Acts 4:18,23–33: How do we life our voices to God in one accord (v. 24)? What gave this church the confidence to pray with boldness and expect God to act? What did those early Christians have that many Christians today do not? (*Possibly: experience with Christ . . . the Holy Spirit's filling . . . confidence in the resurrected Christ . . . singlemindedness . . . unity . . . signs and wonders . . .*)

Acts 12:5,11–17: Does fervent prayer require knowing what God wants to do? (*Answer: no; the church did not know God would release Peter.*) What in this passage might lead us to think God has a sense of humour? Is there a place for hilarity and great laughter in prayer?

Eph. 6:10–13,18,19: Since the rest of Ephesians focuses on the church, what possibility is there that this is a *corporate* call? How does one become strong in the Lord and in the strength of his might? How do we 'pray in the Spirit' (v. 18)? From what are we to be on the alert (v. 18)?

I Tim. 2:1–4,8: Why do we need to pray for those in authority? (Remember, Satan seeks to undermine or destroy leaders because then the followers are much more vulnerable.) In praying for those in authority, are we simply to seek quietness and tranquility? (*Answer: according to v. 2, we are also seeking that their rule be characterized by godly qualities such as justice, mercy, and righteousness, and human dignity (freedom from oppression, meeting of basic needs, etc.).*) What does it mean to lift up holy hands?

James 5:13–18: Is it *always* God's intent to heal? If not, how can we tell when to pray for healing with confidence? What connection is there between healing and forgiveness of sins (in both vv. 15 and 16)? Why is v. 16 among the most ignored verses in the Bible? (*In part perhaps, because of an over-reaction to the Catholic and Episcopal tradition of confession.*)

CHAPTER THREE: BIBLE STUDY OUTLINE

WHAT DO THESE PASSAGES TELL US
ABOUT CORPORATE WORSHIP?

Remember to review the leader's instructions on page 219 before going ahead with the study.

II Chron. 5:11–14: How important is it to be sanctified (v. 11) before leading others in worship? How did God respond to this rehearsed and carefully planned, well executed worship performance? (*Note that our plans must allow room for the Spirit's to supersede them — v. 14!*)

Ps. 27:4,8: What is the Psalmist's basic attitude which the Lord encourages? (*Answer: seeking, hungering heart.*) How do we 'behold the beauty of the Lord'?

Ps. 51:9–19: Why is *confession* so vital to entering God's presence? What kind of spirit should we have in order to enter into worship? (*Answer: v. 10 — steadfast, v. 12 — willing, and v. 17 — broken.*) Does God delight in visible tangible sacrifices and offerings? (*Compare v. 16 with v. 19.*)

Ps. 95:1–8: How important are our feelings in worship? (*Answer: we do not fully encounter the living God in a reasoned, dispassionate way (vv. 1,2); at the same time, we worship him for who he is and what he's done (vv. 3–8), not on the basis of our fluctuating feelings!*) How would you summarize the type of worship of vv., 1–5? (*Possibly: exuberant, celebrative, joy-filled, shouting.*) How would you summarize the type of worship of vv. 6–8? (*Possibly: humble, meditative, hungering, listening.*) A good worship service will commonly have a time for each of these types of worship.

Is. 1:11–18: How many different forms of worship are expressed in vv. 11–15? Why is this worship, so abundant and rich, unacceptable to the Lord? (Cf. Hosea 6:6.) What are the two basic prerequisites to being acceptable worshippers? (*Answer: v. 16 — cleansing; v. 17 — loving action for the needy and weak.*)

Jer. 9:23,24: Is wisdom, physical strength, wealth (or, one might add, beauty) an asset in worship? (Cf. Mk. 10:23; I Cor. 1:26–31). One who truly knows and understands God would not boast of how much he has attained; what would his boasting be like? Does God take special delight in heavenly expressions of praise and extolling of his attributes? (*According to these verses, his delight is in very earthy expressions of godly relationships! Cf. Micah 6:8.*)

Jer. 17:21–27: Why was 'keeping the sabbath holy' so important to God? What blessings does God promise to those who keep his sabbath? (*Answer: strong leadership, perpetuity, the attraction of surrounding peoples, and prosperity.*) How do we know that God really meant what he said in v. 27? (Cf. II Chron. 36:17–21, especially v. 21.) How likely is it that God no longer feels that 'keeping the sabbath holy' is important?

John 4:20–24: Is there any importance in the *place* where the people of God gather? What does it mean to worship in spirit? What does it mean to worship in truth? What happens if the church ignores either one?

Acts 2:42–47: What indications of worship do we see in this picture of the early church? The 'breaking of the bread' is commonly viewed as the Lord's Supper (vv. 42,46) compare with ours? (*Note: Not until the sixteenth century did the Lord's Supper cease to be a daily, or at least weekly, highlight of church life.*) How much of the rest of the church's life described in this passage might have been diluted by taking the Lord's Supper lightly or very occasionally?

Rom. 12:1,2: Why is offering up our bodies important to God? How are our bodies tied into worship? How do we renew our minds?

I Cor. 10:1–4, 15–22: What makes food or drink spiritual? What does it mean (in vv. 15–22) to share or participate in the blood and body of Christ? The *physical* speaks of the *spiritual*. Are any of the great events of the faith purely 'spiritual'? (The Creation, Fall, Incarnation, Passion, Redemption, Resurrection, Ascension, Pentecost, the Second Coming, Baptism, the Lord's Supper . . .)

I Cor. 11:17–22: What can make our church meetings into a gathering 'not for the better but for the worse' (v. 17)? What connection is there between being a part of the Body of Christ, and taking part in the Body of Christ in the Lord's Supper?

I Cor. 11:23–26: What is Christ calling us to, when he says, 'Do this in remembrance of [participation in] me' (v. 24,25)? What is this new covenant we celebrate in the Lord's Supper? What is the significance of proclaiming the Lord's death until he comes (v. 26)?

I Cor. 11:27–34: V. 29 indicates a heavy curse or condemnation if we do not discern the Body of Christ rightly. What does it mean to 'judge' (or 'discern') the body rightly? Why is this so important to God that he would punish the lack of it so strongly?

I Cor. 14:1–6,26: How can a prophecy contribute to our worship? How can the teaching of the Word contribute to our worship? How can our worship be structured to allow every member to contribute something, as v. 26 calls for?

I Cor. 14:14–16,39,40: What does v. 15 mean, when it distinguishes between singing with the spirit and singing with the mind? What is lost when we function exclusively at either level? In vv. 39,40, which is more important: ardour or order? (*Answer: Both! They need to be kept in continual creative balance and harmony.*)

II Cor. 3:12–18: We can speak of a veil behind which we hide (as in v. 13) and a veil behind which God is hidden. How might these be related? What does it mean that the Spirit of the Lord grants liberty? How do we unveil our faces to behold the glory of the Lord?

Eph. 5:18–21: How often should we be filled with the Spirit? (The command 'be filled' is in the present continuous tense.) What is the evidence of such fullness (vv. 19–21)? At what points do vv. 19–21 begin to fall apart unless the Spirit is filling us?

Heb. 10:19–25: What allows us to come to God with confidence? What connection is there between the two commands of vv. 22, 23 and the commands of vv. 24, 25? (*Answer: the first are vertical; the second set are horizontal; neither set can be carried out successfully without the other.*) What motivation is it that 'the day [of the Lord] is drawing near' (v. 25)?

Heb. 13:15,16: A priest has two main functions: to offer up sacrifices to God and to mediate, or intercede, between God and man. What sacrifices do these verses call us to offer up? Why does God consider doing good and sharing as key expressions of sacrifice and worship? (*Once again we see that God looks for earthly expressions of our heavenly love.*)

I Pet. 2:4–10: How does this priesthood of believers express itself in our worship services? How do we express being *one* holy nation, a nation that transcends social class, cultures and nationalities? According to v. 9, what is the purpose of our having such a high calling? On the basis of these verses, what should be our attitude? (*Answer: gratitude, praise, humility.*)

I John 3:2,3: Is it possible that we are continually becoming like our image of God? (Cf. Jer. 2:5; Ps. 135:18.) What hope is v. 3 referring to? How does this hope purify us?

Rev. 5:8–14: Is falling down (vv. 8, 14) an acceptable form of worship? Is it perhaps sometimes a necessary form of worship? What do the three declarations of worship have in common?

CHAPTER FOUR: BIBLE STUDY OUTLINE

WHAT DO THESE PASSAGES TELL US ABOUT STEWARDSHIP?

> *Remember to review the leader's instructions on page 219 before going ahead with the study.*

Gen. 1:27–30: In what sense are we living in the 'eighth day of creation'? Will we be accountable for our stewardship of the earth?

Ex. 35:5,10; 36:2–7: Why the stress on having a willing heart? What may have caused the people's contributions to overflow? (*The passage does not tell us. Possibly: obedience . . . inspiration . . . love . . . abundance . . . the number of people contributing . . .*) In addition to people's contributions, what other forms of stewardship are evident here? (*Answer: time and skills*).

Lev. 25:2–6: To whom did the sabbath year belong? In what ways was this a form of stewardship? (*Answer: stewardship of both the land*

and the people . . . granting both rest.) How do we carry over these concepts into our culture today? How might this apply to the church?

Lev. 25:10–16: Was the jubilee year spiritual or economic? (*Answer: it was both, the one reflecting the other.*) In what ways do our economic policies and habits (and problems) reflect our spiritual state? In what ways was the jubilee year a foretaste of heaven? (*Note Lk. 4:18,19, where 'the acceptable year of the Lord' is commonly understood to mean the jubilee year, and the fact that the present Kingdom of God is a foretaste of heaven.*)

Lev. 25:23–28: How does it change our perspective if we view the land (or our means of livelihood) as the Lord's rather than ours? How responsible are we to be for others in the Body who have financial trouble? What did the jubilee year guarantee? (*Answers: Hope! Dignity . . . a measure of equality . . . resources for living.*) What might the church do to express a type of jubilee?

Mal. 3:7–12: The people of Israel were religious and saw themselves as devout. What was the missing proof of true devotion? Is the basic concept of stewardship different from the Old Testament to the New Testament? (*Answer: No.*) Can we today fall under the same curse of 'robbing God' as Israel did? Should we under grace respond less than, equally with, or more fully than those under the law?

Mt. 6:19–24: Why is it better to lay up treasure in heaven? (*Regardless of other reasons, the most important is in v. 21.*) What does it mean (v. 22) to have a clear eye? Do we really have to hate riches in order to love God (v. 24)? (Cf. Lk. 14:33.)

Mt. 6:25–34: What kinds of things can cause us to be anxious? (The word 'anxious' is repeated five times in this passage.) Is it really possible to be care-free? (*Answer: yes!*) If so, how do we do it? (*The secret is in v. 33.*) What does it mean to seek first his Kingdom? What does this have to do with stewardship?

Mt. 25:14–30: Is stewardship voluntary? (Cf. I Cor. 9:16–18.) Which is more important, the extent and breadth of our stewardship, or our faithfulness? What are we to be doing with all the resources put in our hands? (*Answer: investing them for Kingdom purposes, so that they might yield Kingdom fruit.*) Of what are we stewards? (*Everything that is in our hands or in our care! In addition to obvious physical possessions –*

car, house and money – there is the more crucial stewardship of our time, gifts, the Gospel and those put in our care, such as children or employees.)

Lk. 6:34–38: In what sense are we to give unthinkingly? (*Answer: in terms of expecting nothing in return, not even gratitude.*) According to these verses, in what sense are we *not* to give unthinkingly? (*We are to give, first, in love, and second, to do good. This means: not simply maintaining someone in dependence or immaturity.*) Is there anything here to support the idea of giving out of our need? (*Answer: yes, v. 38. Whatever measure we deal out to others (be it love, money, companionship, or time) we will be given back in abundance. This has been called 'seed faith'.*)

Lk. 16:10–15: How do we demonstrate faithfulness? What are some ways of being unrighteous stewards of what God has put in our hands? What are 'the true riches' to be entrusted to us (v. 11)? Do you give better care to that which is someone else's or that which is your own? In this study, do you find yourself being cautious and occasionally justifying yourself, or is your heart hungry to find ways in which to be a better steward (v. 15)?

Acts 4:32–37: Was this lifestyle idealistic naïvety? Are there any similarities between this, and God's intentions underlying the jubilee year? Any similarities between this, and how Jesus lives with his disciples? What are some of the principal things that stand between us and this kind of lifestyle?

Acts 5:1–5,11: In what ways are physical realities reflecting spiritual realities here? What was Ananias' sin? Why would God take this so seriously as to kill him? What was the effect on the church? (*Answer: fear of God; purifying motives to be singleminded.*) Has God changed so that he no longer acts in this way? (*Or might it be we who have changed so much that God can no longer deal with us on the same basis as with the early church . . .?*)

Rom. 12:1,2; I Cor. 6:19,20: Why are we to be good stewards of our bodies? How can we be good stewards of our bodies? Why are we to be good stewards of our minds (Rom. 12:2)? How can we be good stewards of our minds?

I Cor 3:21–4:2: How can all things belong to us, especially when we have clearly stated we own nothing but are only God's stewards? (*The secret is in v. 23; remember Mt. 6:33: 'and all these things shall be* *added unto you'! Cf. I Tim. 6:17b.*) How many people regard you as a servant of Christ (4:1)? What are the mysteries of God? How can we be found trustworthy (or faithful) as regards the mysteries of God?

II Cor. 8:1–5: What was the grace of God given in the churches of Macedonia (v. 1)? (*Answer: the ability to meet needs, while being poor.*) Affliction proves our character. What kind of character did the Macedonians demonstrate in the midst of financial hardship? Why did the Macedonians give so liberally? (*Vv. 4,5 — giving flows along relationship lines.*)

II Cor. 8:12–15: In what ways does this reflect God's intentions as expressed in the jubilee year? Which is a more relevant consideration according to this passage — how much we give, or how much we have left over? If the church took this passage seriously, would there still be needy people, lacking the basics of life, in the church? Worldwide? (Cf. I John 3:16–18.)

II Cor. 9:6–9: We can have a lifestyle of buying what we want . . . or of buying what we can afford . . . or of buying what we need. Which gives us the greatest freedom to sow bountifully? Which is more important, how much we give or the attitude with which we give it? (Remember I Cor. 13:3.) In v. 9, with what qualities is *unshakeable righteousness* linked?

Phil. 4:10–19: What is the secret of being content in any circumstance, be it abundance or be it suffering need? (See v. 13!) Why could Paul be so confident that the Philippians' needs would be amply met (v. 19)? (Because he knew they would reap as they had sown.) Can v. 19 be taken as a promise outside of its context?

I Tim. 6:6–11: What kinds of temptations can afflict those who want to get rich? Is money a root of all sorts of evil? (*Answer: no, the love of money is.*) From what are we to flee (v. 11)? Why? (*Answer: because we cannot pursue the rest of v. 11 if our hearts are not single.*)

I Pet. 4:8–11: How is hospitality a form of stewardship? Can we be hospitable in a way that is poor stewardship? (*Note v. 8 and the end of v. 9.*) How are spiritual gifts related to stewardship? Once again, how can we use our gifts in a way that is poor stewardship? (*Answers: lack of fervent love (v. 8), a complaining spirit (v. 9), using our gifts not for service but for our own ends (v. 10), using our gifts apart from God's enabling power (v. 11).*)

CHAPTER FIVE: BIBLE STUDY OUTLINE

WHAT DO THESE PASSAGES TELL US ABOUT TEACHING
AND STUDY OF THE WORD?

> *Remember to review the leader's instructions on page 219 before
> going ahead with the study.*

Joshua 1:7–9: What is the most important command here regarding
God's Word? (*Answer: be careful to do it! Repeated in vv. 8, 9.*) What
does it mean not to have God's Word 'depart from your mouth'
(v. 8)? What connection is there between keeping God's word, and
the promise of God's company? Does the call to be strong and
courageous apply to God's people today? Why or why not? Does
keeping God's word guarantee success? (*Answer: perhaps not directly;
cf. Heb. 11:35–40; it guarantees wisdom.*)

Ps. 19:7–11: What would be a synonym for each of the seven
adjectives describing the Word in vv. 7–9? What effect does God's
Word have (vv. 7,8,11)? Are these effects really true, or is this just
fine poetry?

Ps. 119: 25–32: According to these verses, what does God's Word do
for us? What do we have to do, to allow the Word really to take hold?
In v. 32, why does the Psalmist want or need an enlarged heart?

Ps. 119:97–104: According to these verses, what does God's Word
do for us? What do we have to do, to allow the Word really to take
hold? How might we title this passage? (*One possibility: 'God's Word
surpasses all competition'.*)

Prov. 1:1–7: Which of the benefits of God's Word listed here would
be the most helpful to you? What is the fear of the Lord (v. 7)? Why
is that the beginning of knowledge?

Is. 55:8–11: What would be some other ways of expressing how
different God's thoughts are from ours (vv. 8,9)? Given that God's
thoughts are so different, what attitude should we have? Are vv. 10
and 11 telling us that God's Word is magical, automatically changing
people? Why or why not?

Mt. 7:24–27: What is the basic difference between the wise men and the foolish man? (*Answer: obedience.*) How important are good foundations? According to this passage, what kind of foundations do we need? (*Much more than deep sermons, high ideals or grand theology, we need clear guidelines on how to live.*)

Mt. 13:10–16,36: In vv. 13–16, is Jesus abandoning some people to their damnation? What enables some eyes to see while others stay blind? What quality in v. 12 will give us yet more or, by its absence, cause us to lose even what we have? (The key is in v. 10 and v. 36 — a questing, hungering, seeking heart.)

Mt. 13:18–23: What might be 'the word *of the kingdom*' in v. 19? What can we do to make the soil of our hearts receptive to the Word? Why do Sunday morning sermons so often make no noticeable change in people's lives?

John 5:39,40: Can the Scriptures give life? (*Answer: no. They merely point us to Christ who is our source of life.*) What problems come when we fall into thinking that the Scriptures give life? If the Scriptures do not, in and of themselves, give life - how do we draw on Christ's life?

John 14:16,17,26: In what way is the Spirit a Helper? (The Greek word *parakletos* means 'one called alongside to help' or 'intercessor'.) Why is the Spirit called the 'Spirit of truth'? If the Holy Spirit is indeed the Great Teacher, how can we give him more opportunity to be active in teaching us?

John 16:12–16: How might we follow the Spirit's example of not speaking on our own initiative (v. 13)? (Cf. John 5:19,20.) How do we 'hear from God' that we might, like the Spirit, speak what we hear (v. 13)? How important is v. 12 to teachers and pastors today? (Cf. I Cor. 3:2.)

John 17:7,8,17–20: What does it mean to be sanctified in the truth? Christ sanctified himself for the Twelve (v. 19). Are we like him supposed to sanctify ourselves for a specific small group of people? (V. 18 indicates we are sent as he was sent . . .) What does this have to do with communicating God's Word? (*Answer: true communication of the Word forms lives more than it informs minds.*)

I Cor. 2:1–5: What support is there here for the KISS ('Keep it simple, stupid'!) principle? Does v. 3 indicate an unusual period of illness or discouragement, or should we consider it the norm of a teacher's spirit? How can we as teachers experience and demonstrate vv. 4 and 5?

I Cor. 2:10–3;3: What is the difference between words taught by human wisdom and words taught by the Spirit (v. 13)? How might we summarize what makes up the mind of Christ that is given to us (v. 16)? (Cf. Phil. 2:5–8; John 5:19). What distinguishes spiritual men from the men of flesh in 3:1?

Col. 3:16: This is a parallel passage to Eph. 5:18–20. In what ways is the first phrase of v. 16 parallel to Eph. 5:18's command to be filled with the Spirit? How could we make better use of psalms, hymns and spiritual songs for teaching? For admonishing?

II Tim. 2:14,15; 3:5,7: What might be the results of bypassing the presence of God, spoken of in v. 14? In light of v. 15's call to diligence, someone has said that salvation is by grace while knowledge of the Word is by works. What do you think of this statement? (*Answer: knowledge of the Word is also a profound work of grace!*) How can one be always learning and never come to the knowledge of the truth? (Cf. John 8:31,32; 17:3.)

II Tim. 3:10,11,14–17: As in v. 14, how do we teach in such a way that others become convinced of the truth rather than just taking our word? Of what importance was it for Timothy to know from whom he had learned (v. 14)? Does this suggest anything to us about our teaching methods? How do we 'train in righteousness' (v. 16)? (*Answer: by aiming at obedience–oriented results.*)

Heb. 4:2,6,12: As powerful as the Word is, what can annul its power? (*Answer: unbelief and disobedience.*) Philips' translation begins v. 12 in this way: 'The Word that God speaks is . . .' Does this way of expressing things add anything further to the verse? (*It takes us beyond thinking merely in terms of the written Scriptures, to thinking also in terms of the Spirit's voice today.*) What might it mean to pierce as deeply as the division of soul and spirit?

Heb. 5:11–14: What might cause dullness of hearing? Does v. 12 imply that all of us over time should become teachers? According to v. 14, what is the key to maturity? Is it worth teaching more, if that key is not working?

James 1:19–27: How might v. 19 be applied to the Word that God speaks? Why do we not always obey the Word? How do we look intently at the perfect law (v. 25)? (*Answer: by focusing on one thing until we are practising it reasonably well.*)

I John 2:20,21,27: How important is this anointing? Does the anointing rest on every Christian automatically all the time? If not, how do we get it? (Cf. I John 1:9.) If this anointing of the Holy Spirit is such an effective teacher, how might we better honour and release the Spirit in our students? How important is this?

CHAPTER SIX: BIBLE STUDY OUTLINE

WHAT DO THESE PASSAGE TELL US ABOUT DISCIPLING AND PASTORAL CARE?

> *Remember to review the leader's instructions on page 219 before going ahead with the study.*

Ex. 18:13–23: In what ways do vv. 13–18 characterize many pastors or church leaders? What are the benefits of a pastoral care structure? (V. 18 gives at least two benefits.) How important are the criteria in v. 21 for leaders who will be responsible for others?

Ps. 23:1–6: What are some of the key functions of a shepherd? Does good pastoral care prevent us from having difficulties and dealing with evil? (*Answer: yes and no. Yes, in terms of vv. 1–3,6, which include a good deal of preventive measures; but vv. 4 and 5 indicate that death, evil and enemies are a part of life. We do not avoid them so much as overcome them.*) How can church leaders bring people to experience Ps. 23? (*By bringing them continually to Christ, especially through regular significant times in his presence.*)

Ezek. 34:1–10: What is the heart of false shepherding? (Answer: Vv. 2,3 — selfish profiting from the sheep; shepherds become wolves!) What are the functions of a shepherd? Why does God take it so seriously when his pastors do not care well for the sheep? (*That's the whole reason they were appointed! If they are not going to do it, he'll find someone who will.*)

Ezek. 34:11–23: This passage stresses three main functions:

gathering the scattered sheep (vv. 11–13a), feeding them (vv. 13b–16) and judging them (vv. 16–22). How can we today effectively gather the scattered sheep? How can we effectively feed others? Is it a shepherd's job to judge? Why or why not?

John 10:1–5: Why is it so important to know the shepherd's voice? How important is it that a shepherd normally lead rather than push, normally go before rather than follow behind? What is involved in calling one's sheep by name? (*Answer: it suggests individualized, personal care, not just group care.*)

John 10:10–16: How can pastoral leaders give life to their followers? What are the differences between a hireling and a shepherd?

John 21:15–17: What is to be our primary motive in caring for others? (*Answer: the love of God.*) Why is that primary motive so important? Why would loving Jesus be connected with caring for his sheep?

Mt. 28:18–20: Someone has said, 'Disciples are made, not born.' Do you agree? Why is making disciples the heart of the Great Commission? Is the stress in v. 20 on teaching doctrine, or is it on teaching how to obey and how to live rightly?

Acts 20:28–31: To be alert, what should we focus upon first of all? (*Answer: ourselves — lest we fall.*) Why is this so vital? How might it help a pastor to have someone pastoring and overseeing him? (*Answers are: v. 28 — helping guard his life; v. 29 — mediating and judging when division arises in the church; and v. 31 — admonishing him with tears.*) How do we learn to admonish with tears?

Eph. 4:11–16: What is the function of the v. 11 callings? In v. 12 what added perspective do we gain from the word 'equipping' when we know that it can also be translated 'perfecting' or 'mending' (as in mending torn nets)? What insights does this passage give us as to *how* the v. 11 callings equip the saints? (Note especially vv. 15,16.)

Phil. 3:10–17: How can Paul speak in v. 12 of not being perfect, and in v. 15 of being perfect? (*The answer is that two different ideas are involved. V. 12 — being sinless, faultless, fully like Christ; v. 15 — allowing no gap to grow up between what we know we should be doing and what we actually do.*) Paul is boldly calling people to follow his example. How can he do this without being presumptuous? (*He's* *calling them to follow his pattern (v. 17) of growth (vv. 12–14), not the level or state of growth that he has reached.*) Is Paul calling them to model after his life alone? (*No . . . after Jesus, as seen in his life, and after the pattern of Christian life observable in many people — note the end of v. 17.*)

I Thess. 1:1,5–7; 2:7–12: Whose example did the Thessalonians follow? (*Note: not just Paul's, but also Silvanus' and Timothy's.*) What are the advantages of a corporate example rather than just an individual example? In what ways can a pastoral care relationship be likened to that of a loving father or mother with his or her children?

I Tim. 3:1–7: Are pastoral leaders' qualities related to their character or their gifts? (*Note: being 'able to teach' is usually considered a character quality of sharing truth well, rather than the gift of public teaching. Some elders/overseers teach publicly and some do not (I Tim. 5:17).*) Why is *character* the key, rather than *gifting*? Which classic pitfalls that can ruin a pastoral leader are warned against here? (*Answers: v. 2 — women (or the opposite sex), v. 3 — money, vv. 4–5 — putting ministry before family, and v. 6 — pride.*) What are some key lessons for caring for the church that are learned in the family?

I Tim. 4:14; II Tim. 1:6: How important might it be for a pastor to have the backing of a presbytery? of a prophetic utterance? of an overseer like Paul? How might we neglect, or conversely kindle afresh, a gift that is in us?

I Tim. 5:17–22: We know Timothy was under Paul's care. What indications do we have that Timothy in turn was to appoint and care for other overseers/elders? (*Recall 3:1–7; note Titus with a similar role in Titus 1:5ff.*) Why should a pastoral leader receive extra protection (v. 19)? Why should those who continue in sin be treated severely (v. 20)? What seems to be involved in the laying on of hands (v. 22; recall 4:14 and II Tim. 1:6)?

Heb. 13:6–8: Is there any inconsistency in calling us to rely on Christ in vv. 6 and 8, and then 'sandwiching' in between a call to follow Christian leaders? What is it about our leaders that we imitate? (*Answer: their faith.*) What do we not imitate? (*Their mannerisms, personalities, faults . . .!*)

Heb. 13:17: Why would God call us to obey our leaders and submit to them) How many people can one person 'keep watch over', and give good account for? (*Answer: in a serious committed or covenanted way, up to about six perhaps; highly gifted and mature people might manage more (Jesus had twelve). Even secular management says that managing more than about six people directly tends to be counter-productive.*) What can I do that would bring my leader(s) joy?

I Pet. 5:1–4: What three things are shepherds to avoid? Why is it so important to pastor *not* by compulsion *but* because we believe God has called us to pastor? (Remember the hireling of John 10?) How is *being an example* the opposite of lording it over others) How does Peter illustrate the way to be an example instead of lording it over others (note v. 1)?

I Pet. 5:5–8: Why is there a special exhortation to the younger men? In what ways might a humbler follower receive grace that an unsubmissive follower might not? In what ways might a humble *leader* receive grace that a proud leader might not? What added dimensions does v. 7 take on when placed in the context of humbly following and leading? What connection is there between v. 7 and v. 8? (*Answer: the anxiety of v. 7 provides a foothold for Satan to work destructively in and through our lives.*)

CHAPTER SEVEN: BIBLE STUDY OUTLINE

WHAT DO THESE PASSAGES TELL US ABOUT
CHRISTIAN COMMUNITY LIFE?

> *Remember to review the leader's instructions on page 219 before going ahead with the study.*

Eccl. 4:9–12: What are some other situations when two are better than one? According to these verses, is just being together beneficial? (*Answer: the stress here is on the benefit of doing things together, not so much on just being together.*) Speaking of community, someone has said that unless we need to be alone, we do well to take advantage of doing things with others whenever possible. What do you think? (*These verses, of course, support this perspective.*)

Mt. 18–15–20: Vv. 15–17 — why is this so important to preserve Christian community? (*Sin must be treated seriously; at the same time* *we must protect one another, being committed together in the new covenant.*) What is the relationship between vv. 15–17 and v. 18? (Note John 20:22,23.) And the relationship of these verses with vv. 19,20?

John 17:11,20–23: Why is it so important to Jesus that we be one? Was Jesus' prayer for unity more a wish or a prophecy? According to these verses, what causes unity?

Acts 2:38–47: How important are the three requirements of entering the church in v. 38? V. 42 — are any of these four activities, to which the early church devoted themselves, optional? In which of these characteristics of vv. 42–47 would you most like to see your church grow?

Acts 4:31–37: A Communist slogan says: 'To each according to their need; from each according to their ability'. In what ways do these verses reflect or surpass this slogan? What contemporary values does this passage confront? (*Possible answers: materialism, individualism* . . .) Is this mind of life an other-worldly dream, or can we take some steps in this direction?

Rom. 14:1–6: How should we handle differences in convictions? (*Answer: with honour and respect.*) What are some such convictions among Christians today? Why is Paul so strongly against judgementalism? How can we demonstrate *acceptance* (the opposite of judging)?

Rom. 14:13–21: In v. 17, what would be some synonyms for these three key characteristics of the Kingdom? (*Examples: justice or right relationships . . . harmony . . . gladness, celebration.*) What might be some things that are good in your mind, but could hurt a brother who views them differently? Picking one of these areas of difference, how could you 'make for peace and the building up of one another' (v. 19)?

Rom. 15:1–7: Do we sometimes need to bear the strengths of others as well as their weaknesses? How can we avoid becoming people who simply accept or tolerate everything? (*Answer: accepting and affirming diversity is actually the key to being alive and vibrant; when we try to be all the same or all tone down so that nothing surfaces except what we have in common, we will indeed become salt that has lost its savour.*) What insights can we gain from Christ's acceptance of us, as to how we should accept others?

Rom. 16:5,23: The church met in homes (Cf. I Cor. 16:19; Col. 4:15; Philemon 2). What advantages were there in this?

II Cor. 6:14–7:1: How important is clear separation in order to have meaningful community? What does it mean to be 'bound together' or 'yoked' with unbelievers? (*One way of defining this is in terms of being covenanted or legally obligated in a joint venture like a marrriage or, some would say, a business partnership*.) Do we have some difficulty in feeling conviction about being separate? (If we are honest, most Christians have some difficulty because our lives are not all that different from those of morally upright unbelievers.) If we have difficulty in really grasping how different we are, what might we need to remedy our dullness of self-concept? (*7:1 has several suggestions*.) What might it mean to be 'bound together' or 'yoked' with a local church?

Gal. 5:13–18: Can we love others well if we do not love ourselves well? (*Answer: no; v. 14*.) What is the difference between loving ourselves well, and fleshly selfishness? (*In the former, God is the centre of our universe and we enter into his acceptance and love of us; in the latter we are the centre of our universe and demand that everything conform itself to our desires*.) Why are the Spirit and the flesh so radically opposed)? (*Answer: because we can have only one centre, one source of life, one guide at a time*.)

Gal. 5:19–21: How many of the deeds of the flesh listed here have to do directly with how we relate to each other? (*Answer: at least eight, from enmities through to envyings*.) Why does Paul say that to hold any of these things can be done only by letting go of the Kingdom of God? Is the trade worthwhile?

Gal. 5:22–26: How many of these nine fruits are inherently relational? (*Answer: properly understood, most if not all of them*.) How does fruit grow? (*Not by its own training or work, but by drawing on the life sap of the tree or vine . . .*) If we do not live in the Spirit, is there any point in trying to walk in the Spirit? (*It will be extremely frustrating and discouraging!*) What would be the opposite of v. 26, that we should walk in?

Gal. 6:1,2: What are the consequences of not obeying v. 1? What qualities are central to restoring a person who has fallen into sin or error? What connection is there between v. 1 and v. 2?

Eph. 2:14–22: When there is division or barriers, how can they be

overcome? Thomas Merton has said, 'Our greatest spiritual director
is the person with whom we have the most friction.' How does God
bring growth through our frictions? How important is it to know
that it is *God* who is fitting us together (v. 21)?

Eph. 4:1–6: Is the 'unity of the Spirit' something we should be
seeking? Or is it something we already have which we should be
preserving? How many bonds of unity do we have according to
vv. 4–6? When the world looks at us, what does it see as regards the
unity in our church? How good are we at expressing this unity with
other churches in our city?

Eph. 4:25–32: Why is truth so essential to being members of one
another? Rubbing up against each other will almost inevitably
irritate or anger us from time to time. How can we handle this so as
not to let Satan have a foothold in our lives? In v. 29, what room is
there for saying negative things about other brothers and sisters?
How do we 'put away' bad feelings or thoughts as in v. 31? (*Much, if
not all, of the key lies in vv. 30 and 32.*)

Eph. 5–18–21: How might someone characterized by vv. 19 and 20
be confused with someone who is drunk with wine? Is Paul stating
an unrealistic ideal when he calls us *always* to give thanks in *all*
things? (*Answer: yes, if one is not filled with the Spirit!*) What
connection is there between being filled with the Spirit and v. 21?
What connection is there between being submitted to one another,
and the fear of Christ (v. 21)?

Phil. 2:1–5: Why does Paul raise these questions in v. 1? Are any of
the qualities in v.- 2 optional in expressing Christian community?
Why is the servant attitude of vv. 3–5 so necessary to Christian
community?

Heb. 10:24,25: What are some ways in which we can stimulate each
other to love? To good deeds? Why is it important to gather together
regularly? At what point might we be gathering together too much?
(*Answer: when we are straining our family life, or making it difficult for
friendships to develop with others in the Body and in the world.*)

Heb. 12:11–15: What guidelines for pursuing emotional healing
does this passage give? Comment on this sentence in light of the
passage — 'No one can stay whole or emotionally healed, apart from
a loving community.'

James 5:9,13–16: Why does James tell us to call for the elders? Why is healing associated with confession and forgiveness? Why is v. 16 so ignored — what do so many churches have little confession of faults, sins and struggles? (*Lack of pastoral models? Lack of caring with the depth of relationship to warrant such trust and to minister to the needs . . .?*)

I Pet. 5:5–8: What key roles do elders or pastors play in Christian community? What connection is there between being subject to our elders in v. 5 and v. 7? What connection is there between letting go of our anxieties and v. 8? (*Answer: Satan will consume us in our anxieties if we give him a foothold.*)

I John 1:6–9: What does it mean to walk in the light? (*Answer: to be transparent, hide nothing . . .*) Why is walking in the light vital for fellowship? What does confession and cleansing have to do with walking in the light?

I John 3:16–18: What measures of love are expressed in these verses? V. 18 calls us to love in truth. What does that mean? (*Cf. II John 1.*) How do we experience love — today?

I John 4:11–12: What connection is there between love, and the fact that no one has seen God at any time? Can we worship God well, apart from a loving community? Can we experience God well, apart from a loving community? In what ways would growing up in a weak, broken or bad family trend to affect our view of God?

CHAPTER EIGHT: BIBLE STUDY OUTLINE

WHAT DO THESE PASSAGES TELL US ABOUT
MINISTRY AND GIFTS?

Remember to review the leader's instructions on page 219 before going ahead with the study.

Ex. 35:30–35; 36:1,8: What gifts did God give Bezalel? (*Four gifts are listed in v. 31.*) Given the work he had to do (vv. 32–35), why did God give Bezalel more than just the gift of craftmanship? (*He was much more than a technician; he was an artist. He was a teacher, and*

36:1,8 suggests he had to coordinate and supervise the work of others.)
Does this passage support the saying 'Whom God calls, he equips'?

I Chron. 16:4–7,37: What gifts are indicated here? What is the
equivalent in our church?

I Chron. 16:4–7,37: Why might prophecy have been so important to
David and the army commanders? Why was prophecy linked here
with musical instruments? (*Answer: it appears to be particularly related
to stimulating praise and worship — v. 3.*) Why is it important that the
gift of prophecy be under direction or authority? (*So that it can be
judged and controlled if need be.*)

II Chron. 5:11–14: Why did the priests sanctify themselves before
entering this ministry? What indications are there here that gifted
people need many hours of practice to make their gifts really serve
well? Does God still respond today to this kind of praise by revealing
his presence?

Mt. 25:14,15,20,21,27–30: What happens to gifts we do not use?
What is it in v. 31 that if one has, one will be given more, and if one
does not have, he will lose even what he has? (*Responsibility?
Faithfulness? Initiative?*) What is the key quality the Master looks
for? (*Faithfulness, even more than success.*)

Lk. 11:9–13: How liberal is God in giving gifts? Of all the gifts for
which we might ask, what is the greatest gift the Father could give
us? (*Answer: the Holy Spirit.*) Does this passage support the
statement: 'We are as holy and Spirit-filled as we *want* to be, though
perhaps not as much as we *wish*'?

Rom. 12:3–8: Why do we need to understand v. 3 well in exploring
and using our gifts? While possibly we have a number of gifts, do
you see any indication here that we might each have one primary or
motivational gift as some scholars think? (*There seems to be an
emphasis here on concentrating on one gift or another, but it is not
definitive. Cf. I Pet. 4:10.*)

Rom. 12:9–16: It has been suggested that the seven verses starting
with v. 9 can be applied in a special way to each of the seven
respective gifts of vv. 6–8. What insights flow from considering v. 9
to be a special word for someone gifted with prophecy, v. 10 for one
gifted with service, v. 11 for one gifted with teaching and so forth
through v. 15? Why is *humility* so stressed in v. 16?

I Cor. 12:4–11: Why is it important to keep in mind how very varied the use of gifts is? What is the purpose of the gifts listed here? (*Answer: v. 7: manifestations of the Spirit for the common good, not to promote individual status.*) Might the gifts listed here be considered more *manifestational* than *motivational*? ('Manifestational' means that they appear occasionally; 'motivational' means that they are a continual underlying part of who we are and how we function.)

I Cor. 12:20–22, 25–27: What happens to a member when it does not function? What happens to a member when it sets itself up as independent of the rest of the members? What happens to the Body when a member does not function? In the Body of Christ, how is it that those members which appear the weakest are the most necessary?

I Cor. 12:28–31: Why are the apostles put first, prophets second and teachers third, each in a special role? What relationship do these three gifts (or those of Eph. 4:11) have with the rest of the gifts? (*Answer: they are the key to training and mobilizing the other gifts.*) What role do these gifts play, or could they play, in your circles?

I Cor. 13:1–10: Why does the absence of love leave the gifted servant empty? What qualities in vv. 4–7 might be especially important as an environment for someone just beginning to risk using his gifts? According to vv. 8–12 why must even the greatest gifts or the most obviously supernatural ones be exercised with great humility?

I Cor. 14:1–6: Why is prophecy so valuable and important? (*One answer: it is like the rudder to the ship of the church.*) What are the benefits of prophecy (v. 3)? What are the benefits of tongues (vv. 2 and 4)?

I Cor. 14:26–33,39,40: V. 26 indicates that *every* member is to come prepared to offer something to the Lord when the church gathers. Why is this so important? What is needed to enable this to work well in practice? Why should prophecy be judged? Why should a prophet not defend his prophecies? According to vv. 39,40, which is more important — ardour or order? (*Answer: both are necessary.*)

Eph. 4:11–16: According to vv. 11–13, what is the purpose of the gifts/callings of v. 11? According to these verses, when will these gifts cease? Who should be doing 'the work of the ministry'? In vv. 15,16, thinking of the image of the body, what is the role of a joint? Which people in your church have that role? (Not in the sense of just *programmes*, but in the sense of being involved in other's lives, tying or joining them into other parts of the body.)

I Tim. 4:14; II Tim. 1:6: How might the laying on of hands be related to receiving a spiritual gift? What difference might it make if those laying their hands on us are over us in the Lord? When we receive a new spiritual gift or ministry, how valuable might a prophecy be?

Heb. 2:3,4: Why are gifts so important in connection with extending the Gospel? Why is it critical to keep in mind that manifestations and gifts are 'according to His will' (v. 4)?

I Pet. 4:8–11: What is the most important once again? (*Hint: v. 8, 'Above all . . .'*) What guidelines are there here for using gifts? According to this passage, what is the purpose of our gifts? (*Answer: v. 11: 'so that in all things God may be glorified . . .'*)

CHAPTER NINE: BIBLE STUDY OUTLINE

WHAT DO THESE PASSAGES TELL US ABOUT FAMILY LIFE?

Remember to review the leader's instructions on page 219 before going ahead with the study.

Gen. 2:18,22–25: Why is it not good for man to be alone? How does this apply to singles? (*Generally it is not good for them to live alone.*) What three things should a man (or woman) do when getting married (v. 24)? What does it mean to cleave to one's wife? (*Answer: the meaning is something other than merely sexual because that is covered in the next phrase — 'and they shall become one flesh'.*)

Deut. 6:1,2,5–9: What is the purpose of the teaching? (*Answer: v. 1 — obedience, and v. 2 — fear of the Lord, which will lead us again to obedience.*) Does love and fear of God cause us to obey him or does obedience lead us to love and fear him? (*Answer: both. It is a growing and deepening circle.*) What title might you give to vv. 5–9? (*Example: 'Establishing a godly culture/environment'.*) What would be modern equivalents of the teaching methods in vv. 7–9?

I Sam. 1:11,21–28: Why did Hannah give Samuel to the Lord? Why might we want to dedicate our children to the Lord? What sacrifice is involved on our part in dedicating our children to the Lord? (*Answer: recognition that the children no longer belong to us, they belong to the Lord. We are the Lord's stewards, representing him to the children.*) Of what value might it be to review or rehearse the dedication with the children periodically?

I Sam. 3:11–14: Why was God angry with Eli, the high priest? Is living in sin an individual issue or a family issue? (*Answer: both.*) Why is the Lord's judgement in v. 14 apparently irrevocable, leaving no room for repentance? (*Vv. 12 and 13 indicate that Eli knew his sons were doing wrong, and he did not correct them; then God spoke to Eli about this and got no results . . . now comes the judgement. Cf. Mt. 18:15–17; I Tim. 5:20.*)

Prov. 22:6, 23:13,14; 29:17,18: Who is responsible when a teen or young adult walks in sin? (*Answer: the individual is fully responsible, yet Prov. 22:6 suggests the parents share a secondary responsibility.*) According to these verses, why is discipline so important? How does Prov. 29:18 apply to the family?

Prov. 31:10–31: Is this an impossible ideal? (*Answer: yes, if a woman tries to do it alone in her own strength.*) What does a wife need to be like this?) (*Empowering from on high . . .! A supportive, encouraging, loving husband who helps her have time to develop her potential . . . Training . . . Discipling . . .*) What should such a woman be given? (*V. 11 — her husband's heart, vv. 28–31 — blessing, praise, recognition, the fruit of her work.*)

Mt. 19:3–12: Why does God view marriage as sacred and unbreakable? Is Jesus affirming the Mosaic provision for men's hardness of heart, allowing divorce when our hearts are hardened? In vv. 10–12 is Jesus saying that singles would do well to consider staying single for the Lord and for his Kingdom?

John 19:25–27: Why did Jesus give Mary to John and John to Mary? Why did Jesus not leave Mary in the hands of her other sons? Today, is the household of faith (the church) more committed to caring for one another than most families?

Acts 11:11–15; 16:27–34; 18:8; I Cor. 1:16: Is God's promise of salvation in Acts 11 and 16 directed to an individual? (*Answer: yes and no. An individual and his household.*) Who commonly might be included in a first century household? (Cf. Acts 10:7,24,27,44.) Why would God want to save entire households? Does our present evangelism lend itself to this?

I Cor. 7:1–7: Why is sexual fulfillment in marriage important? Why might prayer be a reason for abstaining from sex in marriage? What is Paul conceding rather than commanding? (*Answer: marriage.*)

I Cor. 7:12–16,39: What does it mean that the unbelieving spouse is 'sanctified' by the believing spouse? What does it mean that a Christian parent makes the children holy? If a Christian is abandoned or divorced by his or her spouse, does this passage indicate they have the freedom to remarry? Why or why not?

I Cor. 7:32–35: If one is single, should one consider oneself single for the Lord until otherwise called? What kinds of things can someone who is single for the Lord do, that would be much harder or impossible for married people to do? (*Possibilities: itinerant or travelling ministry; having a schedule filled with ministry; a variety of ministries to singles, including freely bringing those of the same sex into his or her household . . .*) Remembering Gen. 2:18, how seriously should we consider encouraging Christian (Protestant) orders of brothers and of sisters? Alternatively, how seriously should we consider including singles in our households?

Eph. 5:18–21: Why is *being filled with the Spirit* essential to vv. 19–21? How can we stimulate vv. 19,20 in our families? How does v. 21 apply to the family?

Eph. 5:22–27: Is this kind of marriage somewhat difficult, very difficult or humanly impossible? (*Answer: humanly impossible — thus the context of v. 18!*) Is there a difference between being submitted and obeying? (*Yes, the first is always a voluntary choice.*) Is a wife's submission limited? (Cf. v. 24.) Is a husband's love limited? (Cf. v. 25). In what ways might a man sanctify and cleanse his wife?

Eph. 5:28–33: What kind of care do you give to your body? What kind of care do you give to your spouse? What difference does it make to a marriage to be an active part of a healthy church? (In the U.S. where the divorce rate is over 50%, less than one half of one per cent of couples actively involved in a church together get divorced . . .)

Eph. 6:1–4: Why is honouring our parents important? (*Answer: here* *we learn to honour everyone else, including God.*) Is there any significance in Paul's switching from parents in v. 1 to fathers in v. 4? Do fathers have a special responsibility beyond mothers? (*Yes, as the head of the home. Weak fathers result in weak families . . . which result in weak churches!*)

I Tim. 3:1,4,5,12: Why is *managing one's household well* a key criterion for church leadership? If a man is very gifted but has an unruly family, what should be do? (*Answer: devote himself to bringing peace and order to his family.*) Beyond managing one's children, what might be entailed in being a good manager of one's household?

I Pet. 3:1–6: Which is more powerful in tense family situations, the spoken Gospel or the lived Gospel? Where does our hope lie when our family situation is tense? (*Answer: in God — v. 5.*) How can we be freed from fear as in v. 6? (*By having our eyes on Christ — which is the context of the paragraph before this one.*)

I Pet. 3:7–9: How is the woman a weaker vessel? How is she *not* weaker? What is a key motivation to having a good relationship with one's spouse? (*Answer: v. 7 — to have greater freedom and power in our prayers.*) When our spouse is less than perfect, what should be our response? (Vv. 7–8.)

CHAPTER TEN: BIBLE STUDY OUTLINE

WHAT DO THESE PASSAGES TELL US ABOUT
OUR LOCAL EVANGELISM?

Remember to review the leader's instructions on page 219 before going ahead with the study.

Ps. 34:1–10: This Psalm was written when David had to pretend he was insane before King Abimelech, who then drove him away. What kind of witness is joy and praise and waiting on the Lord in the midst of adversity? How effective is our witness when we complain and get angry or depressed in the midst of adversity? If we have grumbled or become angry in adversity, what can we do to restore our witness? (*Answer: repent and ask those who were present to forgive us.*)

Ps. 103:1–5: What do we have to give witness to? If we are not aware of God's recent and present work in our life, do we have much heart for witnessing? Much reason?

Ps. 145:1–7,10–12: In how many different ways does David express that he or others will give verbal testimony to God's greatness? (*Examples: extol . . . bless . . . praise . . . declare . . . speak . . . tell . . . eagerly utter . . . shout joyfully . . . talk . . . make known . . .!*) Is verbal witness something we 'turn on' when we are with non-christians? Is verbal witness something we 'turn off'? (*It needs to be a consistent daily lifestyle, with God's greatness more real and relevant to us than who we are with.*) What are some ways in which we can make God's mighty acts known to the sons of men (v. 12)?

Mt. 5:13–16: What makes us tasty salt? Why are we called the light of the world? Do we want to put our light on a lampstand for all to see? If so, how might we better get our light up and out where it can be seen?

Mt. 9:35–10:1: What is the Gospel of the Kingdom? Could it be different from the Gospel we so often hear today? Note the frequency of these paired words in the New Testament:

1) Saviour	24 times	Lord	700 times
2) Christian	3 times	Disciple	270 times

We often hear a man-centred Gospel rather than a God-centred Gospel. Too often we are called to *believe* more than to *obey*.
Did Jesus feel compassion because of the multitude's eternal plight? (*Answer: no, because of their temporal distress.*) What is the starting point of reaching the multitudes? (*Answer: v. 36 — being aware of their crying needs; v. 37 — being aware of the great potential; v. 38 — beseeching prayer.*) How does Christ often answer such prayers? (10:1). What would have happened if the disciples had tried to minister to the multitudes without the process of prayer and anointing?

Mt. 10:32–40: In what ways can we deny Christ in front of others? What is the sword that Christ brings (v. 34)? (*Answer: a sword of cutting all loyalties that would compete with loyalty to him.*) What does it mean to take up our cross and to lose our life? What relationship is there between this and witnessing? When is it that someone who receives us also receives Christ (v. 40)? (*When we come in his Name, as his representative.*)

John 3:1–8: How valuable are signs and wonders in evangelism? (v. 2). Is natural birth fairly painless and easy, with little significant change for the baby? How about spiritual birth? In v. 8, why does Jesus liken those born of the Spirit to the blowing of the wind?

John 17:14–18: What should be the church's relationship with the world? (*Answer: v. 14 — separated from; v. 15 — in; v. 18 — sent to.*) In what ways are Christ's being sent into the world and the church's being sent into the world parallel? (Look at v. 18.)

John 17:20–23: How important is the unity of the church? What are some of the barriers we encounter in seeking unity in our context? What secrets for finding unity can we discover in these verses? What difference is there between being one *in the midst of* the world, and being one *isolated from* the world?

Mt. 28:18–20: In bringing a nonchristian to the Lord, when is our task finished? (*Answer: when he is a solid disciple and/or under someone else's care who will continue to disciple him . . .*) The call to baptism indicates that witnessing should flow from and to the church. What happens to our witness when it is divorced from the church? Did Jesus originally give this commission to great spiritual giants? (*No, to eleven total failures who knew just how weak they were . . . and how strong Jesus was!*)

Luke 24:49; Acts 1:8: What kind of witness do we have if we are not clothed with power from on high? Are we clothed now? If not, how can we get clothed? Is getting clothed with power something we just need once?

Acts 4:18–20; 29–35: What keys accompanied the power and grace of the apostles' witness? How would it have affected their witness to drop the activities of vv. 32, 34 and 35? (*Answers: lack of integrity, tangible unity, resources for ministry, being weighed down with helping needy people. . .*) How might the outpouring of the Holy Spirit (v. 31) lead naturally to actions such as those in vv. 32, 34 and 35?

Acts 20:24–27: Paul did not consider his life as of any account, nor as being dear to himself. How does this help in witnessing? Paul was an apostle and unique even among apostles. Is there any sense in which we can say with him that we have a 'ministry which I received from the Lord Jesus, to testify solemnly of the gospel of the grace of God' (v. 24)? How might we start with a clean slate so as to be able to join Paul in saying vv. 26 and 27? (*Answer: through prayers of* *confession, repentance and renewed commitment — perhaps right now or at the end of this study . . .)*

Acts 26:1,12–13: Why do we witness? (Cf. v. 18.) According to vv. 20–22, how can we tell if someone has been born again? Clearly this heavenly vision (v. 19) transformed and redirected Paul's life and was pivotal for the rest of his life. Might God still be interested in giving such visions today? If so, how might we encourage this possibility when someone comes to the Lord?

Rom. 1:14–18: Is v. 14 unique to Paul, or common to every believer? We can be heavy and weighed down by such a debt or obligation; or we can be excited and eager to know that we have an opportunity to discharge a debt. What guides our attitude? (*Answers: v. 16 — our understanding of the Gospel; v. 17 — being right with God or filled with His Spirit; v. 18 — having a vision of the consequences of sin and of God's wrath.*)

Rom. 10:9,10: Is there a difference between believing in your *heart* and believing in your *mind*? Does believing in our mind result in righteousness and salvation? Why is confessing with our mouths so important for our salvation?

Rom. 10:13–17: How many beautiful feet are there in your congregation? In your family? Is the potential unbelief of others something that should cause us to be cautious or reluctant in sharing the Good News? (*Would we be cautious or reluctant to throw a drowning person a life saver because they might not take it?*) What do we need to hear to grow in faith? (*Answer: v. 17 — Christ's voice.*)

I Cor. 9:19–23: What similarities are there between Paul's attitude here and Christ's incarnation? Why are many Christians often rigid and inflexible, finding it very hard to understand nonchristian ways or walk in the shoes of nonchristians? Is God calling you to become like a certain group of nonchristians?

I Cor. 13:1: Why is an eloquent witness, without love, like a noisy gong? Is it worth sharing the Gospel if it is not flowing from a heart of love? As God's representative, speaking for Him, are there ever tears in our voice? Should there ever be? (Cf. Lk. 13:33,34; 19:41.)

Phil. 1:12–14: Was Paul reviewing his circumstances to see if they were working out for his good? (*Answer: no, for the good of the*

Gospel!) Is there something like Paul's praetorian guard in our lives, that seems like a hindrance or limitation to the Gospel? Might it be turned to become a vehicle for the Gospel? What gives you courage to speak the word of God without fear (v. 14)?

Phil. 1:15–18: How concerned should we be with people's motives in preaching the Gospel? Paul was appointed for the defence of the Gospel. Do you know anyone in your church appointed as an evangelist? How many people do you know in your city that have been appointed as evangelists? Should such a practice be more common?

II Tim. 1:6–8,12: How can the spirit God has given us help us in witnessing? (*Power . . . love . . . sound judgement . . .!*) In v. 8, did Timothy have a third option to either being ashamed or joining in with suffering for the Gospel? What enabled Paul to suffer for the Gospel fearlessly?

Heb. 2:1–4: Scripture says that in the mouth of two or three witnesses a thing is confirmed (Deut. 19:15; Mt. 18:16). What three witnesses in verses 3 and 4 blend to make the message hard to deny? Does God still bear witness to his salvation today? What effect does it have on our evangelism if signs, wonders, miracles and super-natural gifts manifest themselves? What effect does it have on our evangelism if these manifestations are never present?

I Pet. 3:13–17: What does it mean to sanctify Christ as Lord in our hearts (v. 15)? What kind of attitude should we have when witnessing (v. 15)? Does God sometimes will that we suffer? (*Answer: yes, v. 17; cf. Heb. 5:8,9.*)

I John 1:1–4: Can we in some way have the conviction, vibrancy and authenticity of the first-person witness described here? If we do not communicate a first-person witness, how convincing are we likely to be?

Rev. 12:10,11: According to these verses, how can we overcome Satan? Is the blood of the Lamb alone sufficient to overcome Satan? What might be the 'word of our testimony' that has such power?

CHAPTER ELEVEN: BIBLE STUDY OUTLINE

WHAT DO THESE PASSAGES TELL US ABOUT MISSIONS?

> Remember to review the leader's instructions on page 219 before going ahead with the study. Most of the other chapters of this manual are vital to missions. Perhaps the most fundamental is the chapter on witness to the world. Many of the passages in the Bible study on witness are not repeated here, but would be very important to be included for anyone planning to become involved in missionary work.

Mt. 10:1–16,40: What ideas for missionary strategy do you see here? (*Possibilities include: supernatural authority . . . cultural or geographic focus . . . preach and also demonstrate . . . finances . . . entering a new place . . . not allowing cultural or personal matters (v. 40) to distort our representation of Christ.*)

Luke 10:1–12: Why did Jesus send them out two by two? (Note Eccl. 4:9–12.) What relationship is there between v. 2 and the verses that follow? What are some parallels between Mt. 10 and Luke 10 that possibly highlight key guidelines for missionary work?

Mt. 28:18–20: The base for the great commission is Christ's authority (v. 18). How do we come to have that base for our ministry? What is the key imperative of the passage? (*Answer: 'make disciples'. 'Go' in the Greek is a participle — 'going' — not an imperative.*) Of what importance is this key imperative? In what ways does the role of the church surface in these verses?

John 17:18–21: How did the Father send the Son (v. 18)? (Cf. Phil. 2:5–8.) And how does this relate to how the Son sends us? What relationship is there between the sending of v. 18 and the unity of v. 21? Missions have commonly extended, and often deepened, the divisions of their home countries overseas. How might missions better express unity? What might v. 18 have to do with missionary work?

Acts 2:42,43: What was the apostle's role in founding the first church? To what four things did the early church devote itself? Of what importance are these for the life of a missionary? For the life of a church?

Acts 6:1–4: Did the apostles follow the model of the 'orchestral' pastor who does everything (plays all the instruments)? Why not?

Why was it so important that the apostles devote themselves to prayer? And to the ministry of the Word?

Acts 11:19–26: Would the believers of vv. 19–21 be called missionaries in the same sense as Barnabas? In what way was their vocation or calling different? Which of Barnabas's characteristics would be important for a missionary today?

Acts 13:1–4: Why did the Holy Spirit set aside some of the best leaders of the church instead of young people or secondary leaders? Paul and Barnabas worked for years as committed members of a local church before becoming leaders of a new church at Antioch; this then served as the base for their calling into a broad extralocal ministry here in this passage. What are some advantages of this form of training for missionary work?

Acts 13:44–52: How important was it to have a clear call from God (v. 47) when opposition arose? What strategies for dealing with opposition surface from this passage?

Acts 14:21–23: What functions do we see here that a missionary team should fulfill? (*Nearly every verb indicates an important function.*)

Acts 14:26–28: Why was the Antioch church so important to Paul and Barnabas? How important is it for missionaries to have a home church and be able genuinely to settle in there between trips or terms of service?

Acts 15:1,2,22–35: How important was it to have the Jerusalem Council to whom to appeal? How did the council ensure that their decision would be communicated accurately and effectively? Why was this so important? What lessons are there here for missionaries today?

Acts 15:36–41: Why was it important to return to visit the cities where they had been before? Why was it important to go as a team? We never hear again of Barnabas. Was he in error in taking John Mark? (*Look at his career thereafter. 13 years later: Col. 4:10 and Philemon 24; four years later yet: II Tim. 4:10,11; and as a final outcome, the first written Gospel on which Matthew and Luke based their work!*)

Acts 16:1–5: What model of missionary training do we see here? Given the Jerusalem council's decision, why did Paul circumcize Timothy? What impact might this have had on the missionary work?

Acts 16:6–10: Why did the Holy Spirit prohibit them from speaking God's Word (vv. 6,7)? How important was it to be obedient even though they had to abandon good plans? What implications are there here for how missionary teams should work today?

Acts 18:1–5: How important is it to be able to earn a living in another country? (Cf. Acts 20:33–35). Of what importance was the coming of Paul's team — Silas and Timothy? (*Note II Cor. 2:12,13 regarding the importance Paul put on working in a team context.*) Of what importance was it to begin their ministry in the synagogue? Is there a comparable centre or institution today that might be strategic in beginning missionary work.

Acts 19:8–12: In this passage what are we seeing as some strategic repetitions in how Paul did missionary work? What does this suggest for us today?

Acts 20:3–6; Col. 4:7–14: What does this tell us about Paul's team? Was its composition fixed or flexible? Was it large or small? From one place or international? All together with the leader, or able to function as one even when separate? Did they establish a centre of operations, or were they itinerant? (*In some cases the answers to these questions is 'Both'!*)

Acts 20:17–32: What does this tell us about the character of a missionary? About his vision? His heart? His values? His role?

I Cor. 3:6–11: Does one person do all the missionary work? What happens when one tries to build a great building with a master architect (v. 10)? What happens when one builds without a foundation? How much good are good foundations if no one builds on them?

Eph. 4:11–13; I Cor. 12:28–31: The word 'missionary' comes from the Latin translation of the Greek word 'apostle', but many have lost sight of the original root word. What do these passages indicate about the apostolic function? Is there anything in these passages that might indicate that the gift of apostle or of prophet has passed away? What problems might arise from ignoring these two foundational giftings (cf. Eph. 2:20; 3:5)?

I Thess. 1:1–8: Look at v. 2,3 — is this kind of praying *common* or *unusual* for the apostle Paul, regarding the churches and workers he has raised up? In what ways did their Gospel go beyond words (v. 5)? What difference did it make (vv. 6–8)? (*Answer: Paul's ways were* *imitated by the Thessalonians who then became examples for whole regions!*)

I Thess. 2:5–12: What did the apostolic team *not* do (vv. 5,6,9)? Why was it important to Paul not to depend on a new work for financial support? How much of their lives, if it could be measured, did the team give to the Thessalonians? What implications are there here for missionary work today?

II Tim. 2:2: How many generations of learning are included in this verse? (*Answer: four.*) Why is this so important to missionary work? Is there any other missionary activity that is more important than discipling and leadership formation? Of what significance is 'the presence of many witnesses'? (*Possibly: accountability . . . support . . . corporateness . . .*)

Titus 1:4,5: Here we see apostolic or missionary work in an area where churches already exist. What qualities does one need to be able to 'set in order what remains'? (*Some ideas are: be able to identify what is out of order; visualize how it should be; understand the steps to get it to what it should be; motivate others in taking those steps.*) Remodelling can often be harder than constructing a house from scratch. What remodelling lessons might apply to setting in order what remains? Of what importance in this process is the appointing of elders in every city, according to Paul's directions?

> Good Scriptures for further study which are not listed above include: Ps. 96:3,10,13; Jonah 3:1–9; Mt. 24:14; Jn. 1:14,18; I Cor. 9:1–12; II Cor. 7:5–7; 10:6,8,12–16; II Tim. 4:1–5.

CHAPTER TWELVE: BIBLE STUDY OUTLINE

WHAT DO THESE PASSAGES TELL US ABOUT
SOCIAL RESPONSIBILITY?

> *Remember to review the leader's instructions on page 219 before going ahead with the study.*

Deut. 15:7–11: What kind of testimony would this be to the surrounding nations? What value does the year of remission have in strengthening brotherhood? In what ways does God stress the importance of heart attitudes and motives?

Neh. 5:1–13: Given the people's need, did Nehemiah set up a welfare system? (*Answer: no, land reform for self-help independence.*) Why was Nehemiah so angry? How did Nehemiah ensure the participation of the rich in the land reform?

Job 29:11–17: Why does God put a special emphasis on caring for the widows and orphans (cf. James 1:27)? Is it possible to ignore the needy and stil be clothed in righteousness and justice? How could one be 'eyes to the blind and feet to the lame'?

Prov. 14:31: (Read this together with Prov. 19:17; 21:13; 28:27.) Why might we care for the poor and needy? How does an oppressor reproach or rebuke God? How is graciousness to the needy a way of honouring God?

Is. 1:10–18: How devout were the people whom God addresses here? (*Answer: very!*) Why is God so upset with those who worship him (cf. Ezek. 16:43)? What is the relationship between vv. 16, 17 and verse 18?

Is. 58:1–12: Is personal righteousness (vv. 2, 3a, 5) sufficient? Why or why not? What are the results of corporate or societal righteousness? In v. 12, why are the corporate and societally righteous people referred to as being the rebuilders of the age-old foundations and repairers of the breach?

Jer. 22:13–16: In v. 13, how might we 'build our houses' without righteousness and justice? *With* righteousness and justice? In v. 16, how does *pleading the cause of the afflicted and needy* equal *knowing God*?

Mt. 4:23,24: Why is it that *proclaiming the gospel of the Kingdom* and *healing* so often go hand in hand in the life of Christ and in the early church? What evangelistic function does healing have?

Mt. 5:13–16: Why does Christ call his followers the salt of the earth? Why does he call his followers the light of the world? How does this fit with the fact that *he* is the Light of the World (John 8:12)? How does 'being salt and light' relate to evangelism?

Mt. 5:38–48: Is it sufficient to do good works or engage in social action for other church members? Why or why not? V. 48 says the Father is to be our standard. In what sense is the Father's mercy, grace and love unconditionally available to all people? In what sense is his mercy, grace and love conditional on people's accepting him as Lord and Saviour? Do your answers to these two questions tell us anything about the relationship between social responsibility and evangelism?

Lk. 4:16–21: It is easy to spiritualize vv. 18 and 19. What basis is there for thinking that Christ had *physically* as well as *spiritually* poor and hurting people in mind? (*Note: the 'favourable year of the Lord' probably refers to the jubilee year of Lev. 25:10–28.*) How important was the Spirit's presence and anointing for accomplishing the rest of vv. 18 and 19? Why might vv. 18 and 19 be considered to pertain to the Church today?

Mk. 6:30–44: How did Christ respond to the interruption to his retreat plans (vv. 31,32)? (*Answer: he went the first mile (v. 34) and then the second (vv. 35ff).*) How do you and I respond to 'interruptions'?! Why did Christ respond to the crowd's needs? (*Answer: v. 34 — compassion.*) What might have limited or undermined the compassion of the disciples, so that they would be more interested in getting rid of the crowd than in ministering to them?

Mt. 25:31–46: Why does Christ say that the sheep are distinguished from the goats by their service to the needy and destitute? How it it that when we express physical care for the least important person, Christ says we have done this for him? Does this passage refer *only* to individual care and service of the needy, or does it refer *also* to corporate (church or societal) care of the poor and needy? (Note v. 32 *re* the nations).

Lk. 10:25–37: Can we fulfill either of the two great commandments without the other? Who is our neighbour? Just fellow Christians? The Jewish victim was pretty far separated from the Samaritan culturally. Who might be the Jewish victim for us? What reasons (excuses?) do we often give for not attending the poor and hurting who cross our path from time to time (unless we successfully avoid them)?

Acts 6:1–7: With whom did the church's social responsibility begin? (*Answer: with widows.*) Why might this be important? Why was it important for the apostles to delegate this responsibility? Of what significance is it that most of the seven deacons were of the complaining party, the Hellenistic Jews?

II Cor. 5:17–21: 'The old order has gone and a new order has already begun' (NEB, v. 17). In terms of poverty, needs and justice, what might characterize this new order? What would be a synonym for reconciling? (*Perhaps: 'harmonizing'*.) Is reconciling or harmonizing the world to Christ just a spiritual matter? In v. 20, is Paul's petition to be reconciled to God directed to Christians or nonchristians? (*Answer: Christians*.)

II Cor. 9:8,9: In v. 8, is Paul exaggerating in using four superlatives ('all' and 'every') in one sentence? What relationship is there between v. 8 and v. 9? In v. 9, what does it mean to 'scatter abroad'?

Gal. 6:9,10: V. 9 — what will we reap in due time? (*Answer: it depends on what we sow — a spiritualized Gospel . . .?*) V. 10 — why would preference be given to the household of faith? What happens if our doing good does not extend beyond the church?

I Tim. 5:9–13: If the church is going to provide regular assistance to a needy person, which of the qualities listed here are especially important? What might a church be losing by not being committed to supporting this kind of widow? What kind of testimony to the world might this practice give?

James 2:15–17 and I John 3:16–18: Why is it important to meet a brother's physical needs? What elements in our faith compel us to meet the needs of others? In what ways can we lay down our lives for others?

CHAPTER THIRTEEN: BIBLE STUDY OUTLINE

WHAT DO THESE PASSAGES TELL US ABOUT SPIRITUAL WARFARE?

Remember to review the leader's instructions on page 219 before going ahead with the study.

Ex. 17:8–13: What would have happened to Israel without Moses?

What would have happened to Moses without Aaron and Hur? Why does Satan particularly attack leaders? What can we do to uphold and strengthen our leaders?

I Sam. 17:45–51: What was David's principal weapon? (*Not the sling, but his confidence in the Lord!*) What does David's example suggest about how we might meet the 'giants' who come our way? Which of David's qualities are especially helpful in spiritual warfare?

Job 1:6–22: What does this tell us about Satan? What does this tell us about how to respond to his attacks or to inexplicable affliction? What does this tell us about God?

Is. 14:12–17: What was the essence of Satan's sin? (*Answer: pride — 'I will . . .' repeated five times.*) How does this relate to the essence of Adam and Eve's sin? (*They too wanted to make themselves like the Most High, in knowing the difference between good and evil . . .*)

Dan. 10:2–13,20,21; 12:1: What effect did Daniel's prayer and fasting have? What impeded the Lord's answer? What do these passages tell us about angels? What does this say to us about persisting in prayer when our prayers are not answered quickly?

Mt. 4:1–11: What was Jesus' main weapon? (*Answer: the Scriptures.*) What were Satan's tactics? What is the essence of all temptations? (*Something that elevates us and diminishes God.*) When we realize we are being tempted, what should we do?

Mt. 4:23,24: This is Jesus' job description, the pattern of his ministry. In what ways was Jesus confronting the kingdom of this world?

Mt. 8:16,17: Is the quote from Is. 53 referring to spiritual infirmities and diseases? (*Here it is applied to physical problems!*) What are the implications of Jesus bearing not only our sins on the cross, but also our sicknesses? Did Jesus get into lengthy conversations with evil spirits? (*Answer: no, he cast them out without a word!*)

Mt. 12:24–29: Of what significance is division in the church? Has Jesus bound the strong man? In what way did Christ plunder Satan's house? In what way are we to plunder Satan's house?

Mt. 12:43–45: How can deliverance be lasting? (*Possibilities: through* *the filling of the Spirit . . . through good pastoral care to overcome old habits and establish new ones . . .)*

Mt. 16:16–19; 18:18: What is the rock that hell cannot overcome? *(The confession of who Christ is, and the recognition of his presence.)* What might be the keys of the kingdom? What does it mean to bind and to loose? *(These are rabbinical terms meaning 'to decide with authority.)* To whom is this authority given? *(Answer: Peter, in Mt. 16:19 where 'you' is singular; the church, in Mt. 18:18 where 'you' is plural and follows a passage speaking about the church.)*

Mt. 17:14–21: Why is faith so important? This kind of faith is different from saving faith, sanctifying faith, or even perhaps visionary faith. What kind of faith is this? How do we acquire this kind of faith?

Lk. 10:17–21: On what should our joy be based? Why? Why were the disciples effective in casting out demons? What are 'these things' in v. 21 that have been revealed to babes? Do we qualify as babes (v. 21) to whom these things have been revealed?

Lk. 22:31–34: What does it mean to be sifted like wheat? Did Jesus' prayer make a difference in Peter's life? When you see someone being sifted like wheat, what can you do? If our faith does not fail when we are sifted, what is the result? *(Answer: we come out stronger than ever, in a position to strengthen our brothers.)*

Rom. 8:31–39: What aspects of spiritual warfare are brought out here? *(Opposition, accusation, condemnation, intercession, separation or alienation, overwhelmingly conquering . . .)* Why do many of us 'play it safe', not acting with, or expressing, great confidence in the Lord? What do we lose by 'playing it safe'? We like the sound of being overwhelming conquerors; how do we get to that point? *(Answer: by going through such things as those listed in vv. 35;39!)*

I Cor. 15:24–26, 54–58: Why is death the ultimate enemy? Given Christ's victory over death, what is to be our attitude in the face of death?

II Cor. 10:2–6: What does it mean to regard someone according to the flesh (v. 2)? How would we regard people according to the spirit? What might be the weapons of our warfare that Paul refers to in v. 4? What is a fortress or stronghold? How is one built? How is one destroyed?

Eph. 4:25–27: How does falsehood (v. 25) give the devil a foothold? (*Answer: much worse than the specific lie, trust in one's word is undermined . . .*) How does letting the sun go down on our anger give the devil a foothold? (*Answer: the door is opened to bitterness . . . to negative thinking and talking about another . . . to losing the habit of keeping short accounts . . .*) What does Satan do with a foothold over time? (*Tries to develop it into a stronghold.*)

Eph. 6:10–18: Why is it so critical to be strong in the Lord? Why is the call here to stand firm rather than to advance? Are we to oppose evil people? (*Answer: if we can make the distinction, we should oppose not the people, but what they do. They are not the enemy. They are deceived, trapped in the Enemy's service, and need release.*) How do we put on the full armour of God? Briefly, what kind of attack is each piece of armour made to withstand? (*Consider the opposite of each piece of armour . . .*)

James 4:4–10: How do we befriend *people* in the world, walking closely with them, and yet be sure to avoid befriending the world? How do we resist the devil (vv. 7–10)?

I Pet. 5:5–9: How does lack of submission (v. 5) make us vulnerable to the devil? How does pride (vv. 5,6) make us vulnerable to the devil? How does anxiety (v. 7) make us vulnerable? Why do we need to be on the alert? (*Answer: because the devil will take advantage of any weakness he can, including our lack of alertness!*) How can we rise above all these points of vulnerability? Why has God permitted us to have an adversary . . . especially such a powerful one?

I John 2:12–17: Why does John link young men with overcoming the evil one? Do you think he is speaking about young men spiritually or chronologically? How is the evil one overcome? (*Answer: v. 14 — by the word of God abiding in us.*) What is the lust of the flesh? (*Answer: letting bodily desires control us — sex, hunger, sleep . . .*) What is the lust of the eyes? (*The world's values — beauty, brawn, bucks, brains . . .*) What is the boastful pride of life? (*Fame, success, making plans for your life without taking God into consideration (Cf. James 4:13–16).*)

I John 3:6–10: Why is the ongoing conscious practice of sin impossible for the believer? What is the opposite of practising sin? (*Answer: practising righteousness!*) Can a child of God be neutral, neither given to sin nor to righteousness? (*No, v. 10.*) Why did Jesus come (v. 8)?

I John 4:1–4; 5:4–5: Why is truly understanding and knowing Christ so critical to overcoming Satan? Is Jesus' victory over the world past, present, or future? (*Answer: all three. The decisive battle ('D-day') is past. The victorious skirmishes on the part of Christ in us are present. The final victory to bind Satan eternally is still future.*)

Jude 4,8–13,16,19–25: Why should we not confront Satan and rebuke him? (*Answer: we are tangling with someone bigger than we can handle!*) Ungodly people are, in many places, church members. What qualities should we especially avoid, not to allow ourselves to fall into being the Enemy's instruments? (*A good list would be: making ourselves the final word (vv. 8–11), wandering without roots and commitments (vv. 12–13), criticizing (v. 16), and causing divisions (v. 19).*) How should we relate to people who are evidencing some of these characteristics? (Vv. 20–23).

Rev. 12:7–12: Which of Satan's functions are highlighted here? What characterizes overcomers? What is the word of our testimony? Is the blood of the Lord sufficient by itself for victory? (*Answer: it is indispensable, but also requires our doing our part.*)

HOW TO FIND SOURCES OF HELP

THIS WILL HELP YOU WITH *STEP E*
OF THE PLANNING PROCESS (SEE P. 20)

After completing your *action plan* for any of the thirteen areas of renewal, you have to decide upon the *resources* you need in order to complete the plan. As you do this, you may find some suggestions from the following lists helpful to you. Mark any of these resources which you think may be useful.

RESOURCES FOR CHAPTER ONE (THE KINGDOM OF GOD)

a. Key books or articles

1) Barclay, William; *The King and the Kingdom*, Westminster Press, Philadelphia, PA, 1968, 211 pages. Easy to understand, challeng-

ing, reviews God's intention of theocracy and its rise and fall from
O.T. times to Christ; discussion questions after each of 30
chapters; historical and devotional. (Published in Great Britain
by St. Andrew's Press.)

2) Jones, E. Stanley; *The Unshakable Kingdom and the Unchanging
Person*, Abingdon Press, NY, 1972, 301 pages. Easy to understand, deep, moving, challenging, very biblical, illustrations from
a number of countries, detailed outline and a beautiful balance
between devotion to Christ as a person and devotion to his
Kingdom.

3) Kuzmič, Peter; 'The Church and the Kingdom of God,' pp. 49–
81 of *The Local Church: God's Agent of Change*, (Wheaton '83
papers), Paternoster Press, Exeter, England, 1986, 299 pages.
Superb, succinct summary of Christ's vision. Theological, yet
readable. Reflects a broad grasp of Protestant writing on the
Kingdom, both historical and contemporary, well footnoted;
analyzes and challenges present evangelical understanding of the
Kingdom.

4) Ladd, George Eldon; *The Presence of the Future*, William B.
Eerdmans Publ. Co., Grand Rapids, MI, 1974. The classic work
regarding the Kingdom (published under another title in 1964).
He stimulates and challenges evangelicals' perspective of the
Kingdom. Ladd's writings are the starting point for most writing
and thinking on the Kingdom since. (Published in Great Britain
as *The Gospel of the Kingdom* by Paternoster Press.)

**b. A few model movements or denominations intentionally
expressing and actively extending the Kingdom of God (among
many more which could be listed!).**

1) Gospel Outreach (headed by Jim Durkin), PO Box Z, Eureka, CA
95501, USA. Phone: 707/445–2135. (Primarily on the west coast of
the USA, a focus on Hispanic ministries, and work in Guatemala,
Nicaragua, Ecuador, Brazil, England, West Germany and Italy.)

2) Vineyard Ministries Int'l (headed by John Wimber), PO Box
1359, Placentia, CA, 92670, USA. Phone: 714/996–4340. (Primarily
in the USA.)

3) Youth With a Mission (YWAM, headed by Loren Cunningham),
PO Box YWAM, Tyler, TX 75710, USA. Phone: 214/597–1171. (A
missions-oriented parachurch organization with approximately
ninety permanent bases or teams in most countries around the
world.) See page 00 for British address.

RESOURCES FOR CHAPTER TWO
(PRAYER AND DEVOTIONAL LIFE)

a. Billheimer, Paul E.; *Destined for the Throne*, Christian Literature Crusade, Fort Washington, Pa 19034, USA, 1975, 140 pages. Chapters on God's eternal purposes for the church, Christ's delegating authority to the church to carry out these purposes and the role of prayer in accomplishing those purposes. Inspiring and practical. (Published in Britain by Christian Literature Crusade.)

b. Bounds, E.M.; *The Power of Prayer*, Zondervan, Grand Rapids, MI, 49506, USA, 1962, 87 pages. Twenty chapters; special focus clarifying the role of prayer in making preaching powerful. Inspiring and challenging. (Available in Britain from Send The Light Trust, Bromley, Kent.)

c. Bryant, David; 'Concepts of Prayer'. For more information write him at InterVarsity Missions, 233 Langdon, Madison, WI 53703, USA. He works around the world as the Lausanne Senior Associate for Prayer, working with local committees to establish urban strategies for prayer mobilization. (In Britain contact John Earwicker, Evangelical Alliance, Whitefield House, 186 Kennington Park Rd., London SE11 4BT.)

d. Change the World School of Prayer (headed by Dick Eastman), PO Box 5838, Mission Hills, CA 91345, USA. Phone: 213/341–7870. Superb seminar, manual and books for mobilizing a congregation in ongoing prayer. Excellent sermon outlines for preachers.

e. Foster, Richard J.; *Celebration of Discipline (The Path to Spiritual Growth)*, Harper & Row, New York, NY 10022, USA, 179 pages. (Published in Britain by Hodder and Stoughton.) Deeply insightful and practical sections on:
— inward disciplines (meditation, prayer, fasting and study)
— outward disciplines (simplicity, solitude, submission and service)
— corporate disciplines (confession, worship, guidance and celebration).

f. Yocum, Bruce; *Prophecy (Exercising the Prophetic Gifts of the Spirit in the Church Today)*, Servant Books, Box 8617, Ann Arbor, MI 48107, USA, 148 pages. Part one regarding the prophet's role in the church gives a historical and biblical perspective; part two gives practical guidelines for using the gift without abusing it. 'Must' reading for anyone with the gift of prophecy, or anyone overseeing such a person. (Available in Britain from Redemptorist Book Service, Chawton, Alton, Hants., GU34 3HQ.) An extra resource available in Britain is the magazine *Prophecy Today*, edited by Dr. Clifford Hill, issues monthly from 64 Temple St., Rugby CV21 3TP (administrative office). Clifford Hill has also written *A Prophetic People* (Fount), a study of the church's prophetic role.

RESOURCES FOR CHAPTER THREE (CORPORATE WORSHIP)

a. Liturgical worship sources include:
— *The Book of Common Prayer*, as used by the Episcopal Church (The Seabury Press, New York, 1979, 1001 pages). Refined and updated from its predecessor (1789). It includes a variety of liturgies, administration of the sacraments, other rites and ceremonies of the church, the Psalms, a catechism, historical documents of the church, the church calendar and the lectionary. (In Britain editions are published by Oxford University Press and Canterbury Press.)
— Howard, Thomas; *The Liturgy Explained*, Morehouse-Barlow Co., 78 Danbury Road, Wilton, CONN 06897, USA, 1981, 48 pages. Outstanding simple explanation of the Episcopal liturgy, giving the meaning of each step and ritual throughout. (A British partial equivalent might be William Purcell, *A Communicant's Manual*, published by Mowbray.)
— *Celebration* (A Creative Worship Service), PO Box 281, Kansas City, MO 64141. This weekly newsletter provides Scripture commentary on the Sunday readings, liturgical news, model homilies, planning tips, bulletin art, children's liturgy, music suggestions, general intercessions, prayer suggestions, ministry ideas and book reviews. (In Great Britain teaching and worship ideas for church life are available from Scripture Union, 130 City Rd., London EC1V 2NJ.)
b. Classics on knowing God better include:
— Packer, J. I.; *Knowing God*, InterVarsity Press, Downers Grove, IL 60515, USA, 1973, 256 pages. Six chapters on knowing God followed by eleven on various attributes of God, concluding with five chapters personalizing this for the children of God. (Published in Britain by Hodder and Stoughton.)
— Tozer, A. W.; *The Knowledge of the Holy*, Harper & Row Publ., 10 East 53rd St., New York, NY 10022, USA, 1961, 128 pages. Similar format as Packer with nineteen chapters on various attributes of God. (Published in Britain by Send The Light Trust, Bromley, Kent.)

— Brother Lawrence, *The Practice of the Presence of God*, Fleming H. Revell Co., Old Tappan, NY 07675, USA, 1958, 63 pages. The simple wisdom of a 17th century French Carmelite who felt the constant companionship of God in his every-day work. (Published in Britain by Hodder and Stoughton.)

c. Webber, Robert E.; *Common Roots (A Call to Evangelical Maturity)* (1978), *Worship Old and New* (1982), and *Worship is a Verb* (1985) published by Zondervan, Grand Rapids, MI 49506, USA. A challenging call to learn from the historic traditions of the church. Keen insights into the meaning and the form of worship. The last book includes a study guide for church leaders and worship committees.

Most Zondervan titles are available in Britain from B. McCall Barbour, George IV Bridge, Edinburgh, Scotland. Alternatively, two good British books on the nature of worship are *Worship* by Graham Kendrick (Kingsway) and *Hallelujah!* by Herbert Carson (Evangelical Press).

RESOURCES FOR CHAPTER FOUR (STEWARDSHIP)

a. Burkett, Larry; *Your Finances in Changing Times (God's Principles for Managing Money)*, Campus Crusade for Christ, Inc. Arrowhead Springs, San Bernardino, CA 92414, USA, 1975, 202 pages. Very practical and very biblical. Cuts across materialism, selfishness and poor financial management. Burkett has also put out a 117 page Bible study workbook on the same subject. (Campus Crusade titles are distributed in Great Britain by Scripture Press, Amersham, Bucks.)

b. DeMoss, Arthur S.; 'God's Secret of Success,' available from Mrs. Arthur DeMoss, 'Laurier', Bryn Mawr, PA 19010, USA, 22 pages. A simple practical booklet explaining how we can give God the first place in everything.

c. Eller, Vernard; *The Simple Life (The Christian Stance Toward Possessions)*, W. B. Eerdmans Publ. Co., 265 Jefferson Ave S.E., Grand Rapids, MI 49502, USA, 1973, 122 pages. Beautiful parables drawn from Kierkegaard and expounding on Mt. 6:33. Delightful view of the simple life as joyous freedom rather than anxious scrupulosity. Radical, yet liberating rather than guilt-producing. (Available in Britain from Paternoster Press.)

d. White, John; *The Golden Cow (Materialism in the Twentieth-Century Church)*, InterVarsity Press, Downers Grove, IL 60515, USA, 1979, 175 pages. Tough prophetic writing regarding the high

priority of church buildings and other ways churches use their
money. Hosea and Rev. 2,3 are used to illustrate the Church's
deep trouble. (Published in Britain by Send The Light Trust.)
e. Longacre, Dors Janzen; *Living More-with-Less*, Herald Press,
Scottdale, PA 15683, USA, 1980, 295 pages. Following on her
popular *More-with-Less Cookbook*, she shares a wealth of practical
suggestions from the worldwide experiences of Mennonites.
Chapters on money, clothing, homes, homekeeping, transpor-
tation and travel, celebrations, recreation, meetinghouses, eating
together, and strengthening each other are filled with personal
testimonies and concrete models. (The *Cookbook* is published in
Britain by Lion Publishing, but *Living More-with-Less* is no
longer in print. Three other titles available in Britain are:
Coffey, Ian; *Pennies from Heaven*, Kingsway — on the use of
wealth;
Dammers, Horace; *A Christian Lifestyle*, Hodder and Stoughton
— on living as stewards of God's resources;
Hartman, Jack, *Trusting God with your Money*, Marshall's — on
finances and faith.)

RESOURCES FOR CHAPTER FIVE
(TEACHING AND STUDY OF THE WORD)

a. Marlowe, Monroe; and Reed, Bobbie; *Creative Bible Learning for
Adults* (Int'l Center for Learning, Teacher's/Leader's Handbook), PO Box 1650, Glendale, CA 91209, USA, 1977, 192 pages.
Very well written, easy to read, with especially good chapter on
principles of adult learning (lists 12 characteristics of adult
learners and 9 ways to motivate adults to learn). More good
chapters on the learning process, using Bible learning activities,
conducting effective discussions, and the ministry of caring. Each
chapter has footnotes and discussion questions. 4-page bibliography. (An excellent British alternative is Anton Baumohl's
Making Adult Disciples, published by Scripture Union.)
b. Nee, Watchman; *The Release of the Spirit*, available from
Ministry of Life, PO4 Box 74, Route 2, Cloverdale, IND
46120, USA, 94 pages. Written from a Chinese background. An
excellent and life-changing perspective on how to see the Spirit
released in and through us. Applicable to teaching the Word as
well as any other ministry. (Published in Britain by New Wine
Press. For a good criticism of Nee's theology, see J. Barrs and
R. Macaulay, *Christianity with a Human Face*, published by IVP.)
c. Nyquist, James F.; *Leading Bible Discussions*, InterVarsity Press,

Downers Grove, IL 60515, USA, 1967, 59 pages. Practical, field-tested guide for leaders in preparing, leading and evaluating Bible studies. An appendix lists 20 small group Bible study guides put out by IVP.

d. Patterson, George; *Obedience-Oriented Education*, 5140 NE 34th Ave., Portland, OREGON 97211, USA, 1976, 35 pages. Outstanding succinct work based on missionary experience in Honduras. Very practical field-tested eldership training through obedience-orient- ation rather than information-orientation. Classic. A must for every trainer of church leaders (i.e. every pastor!).

e. Richards, Lawrence; *Creative Bible Study*, Zondervan, Grand Rapids, MI 49506, USA, 1971, 244 pages. 19 chapters, each concluding with exercises for applying that chapter. Focus on good learning/teaching methods, heart attitude and grasping biblical content. Excellent!

f. Walk Thru the Bible Ministries (headed by Bruce Wilkinson), 61 Perimeter Park N.E., Atlanta, GA 30341, USA. Phone: 404/458–9300 or toll free 800–554–9300. Features a one day O.T. survey, a one day N.T. survey, and a one day personal Bible study seminar. Creative teaching methods allow people to retain the complete survey in their memory. Over 500 seminars in North America, other English-speaking countries and Spain each year.

Some of these resources may be difficult to obtain in Britain. If so, alternatives could be:

The Navigators, *How to Lead Small Group Bible Studies* (available from Scripture Press, Amersham, Bucks.) — a simple but comprehensive approach;

Hestenes, Roberta; *Using the Bible in Groups*, Bible Society — an alternative set of methods;

Mallison, John; *Building Small Groups*, Scripture Union and *Creative Ideas for Small Groups*, Scripture Union — astonishingly detailed collection of ideas for healthy group study.

The staff of the Bible colleges will often give help to churches in designing their teaching and study programmes. Contact, for instance, The Bursar, Moorlands Bible College, Sopley, Christchurch, Hants.

RESOURCES FOR CHAPTER SIX
(DISCIPLING AND PASTORAL CARE)

a. Key books or articles

1) Coleman, Robert E.; *The Master Plan of Evangelism*, Fleming H.

Revell Co., Old Tappan, NY, USA, 1964, 126 pages. A classic.
Chapters on selection, association, consecration, impartation,
demonstration, delegation, supervision and reproduction. Very
practical. (An older classic more readily available in Britain is
Bruce, A.T.; *The Training of the Twelve*, distributed by Send The
Light Trust, Bromley, Kent.)

2) Henrichsen, Walter A.; *Disciples are Made — not Born (Making
   Disciples out of Christians)*, Scripture Press Publ., PO Box 1825,
   Wheaton, IL 60187, USA, 1974, 160 pages. Drawing from the
   author's experience of work with the Navigators, a call to discipling relationships and guidelines for discipling.

3) Keller, Phillip; *A Shepherd Looks at Psalm 23*, World Wide
   Publ., 1303 Hennepin Ave., Minneapolis, MIN 55403, USA,
   1970, 142 pages. Twelve chapters on each phrase of Psalm 23;
   shares keen insights from actual sheep-herding.

4) Kuhne, Gary W.; *The Dynamics of Discipleship Training (Being
   and Producing Spiritual Leaders)*, Zondervan Publ., Grand Rapids
   MI 49506, USA, 1974, 162 pages. Drawing from lessons learnt in
   Kuhne's work with Campus Crusade for Christ, the book
   includes chapters on the vision of disciple-making, 'life trans-
   ference' and the way to develop a disciplined disciple, a
   discerning disciple, an organized disciple, a biblical disciple, the
   relationship of fellowship to discipleship training and the way to
   structure your discipling ministry.

5) Nee, Watchman; *Spiritual Authority*, available from Christian
   Fellowship Publ. Inc., Box 1021, Manassas, VA 22110, USA 1972,
   191 pages. Insights from a Chinese background. Theologically,
   the 'heavyweight' of the books listed here. Eleven chapters on a
   biblical perspective of authority and nine chapters on requirements for functioning well as God's delegated authority. (Available in Britain through Christian Literature Crusade.)

6) Sanders, J. Oswald; *Spiritual Leadership*, Moody Press, Chicago,
   IL, USA, 1967, 160 pages. Outstanding classic work on being a
   leader. A 'must' for every aspiring leader to read.
   If some of these titles prove unavailable in Britain, alternatives
   could be:
   Ortiz, Juan Carlos; *Disciple*, Marshall's — a reflection on the
   nature of genuine discipleship, based on Ortiz' experience as a
   church leader in Argentina;
   Watson, David; *Discipleship*, Hodder and Stoughton — a detailed
   guide to the various dimensions of discipleship, including a guide
   to helping new Christians.

b. A few model movements intentionally discipling or extending pastoral care (among many more which could be listed!).

1) Campus Crusade (headed by Bill Bright), Arrowhead Springs, San Bernardino, CA 92414, USA. Phone: 714/886–5224. Parachurch youth and university ministry with offices in most countries. Many discipleship publications. (In Britain: 103 Friar St., Reading, Berks., RG1 1EP).

2) Center for Pastoral Renewal (headed by John Blattner), PO Box 8617, Ann Arbor, MI 48107, USA. Phone: 313/761–8505. Annually sponsors an 'Allies for Faith and Renewal Conference' for leaders of Protestant, Orthodox, and Catholic renewal work. Monthly publication of *Pastoral Renewal*, a practically oriented 16–page journal for pastors.

3) Churches Alive (Growing by Discipling) (headed by Howard Ball), PO Box 3800, San Bernardino, CA 92413, USA. Phone; 714/886–5361. Around North America, 7 European countries, Japan and India. Combines the best of Campus Crusade, Navigators and Evangelism Explosion materials and programmes. Goes beyond any other resource listed here in offering a consultant service for guiding a church into implementing a well-rounded discipleship programme. (Some help in Britain is available from the Church Programmes Dept of Bible Society, Westlea, Swindon, Wilts; and the British Church Growth Association, 59 Warrington Rd., Harrow HA1 1SZ.)

4) InterVarsity Christian Fellowship (headed by Gordon MacDonald), 233 Langdon St., Madison, WI 53703, USA. Phone: 608/257–0263. Parachurch university ministry with fellowships in most countries. Excellent training materials for campus leaders and staff members. (In Britain: Universities and Colleges Christian Fellowship, 38 de Montfort St., Leicester LE1 7GP.)

5) Navigators (headed by Lorne Sanny), PO Box 6000, Colorado Springs, CO 80934, USA. Phone: 303/598–1212. Begun as a parachurch organization, it has done a good job of adapting its discipleship materials for the local church. (In Britain: Tregaron House, 27 High St., New Malden, Surrey KT3 4BY.)

6) Youth With a Mission (often called 'YWAM' and headed by Loren Cunningham), PO Box YWAM, Tyler, TX 75710, USA. Phone: 214/597–1171. A missions–oriented parachurch organization with approximately ninety permanent bases or teams in countries around the world. Offers a 5–month discipleship training school in various countries. (In Britain: 22 King St., Paisley, Renfrewshire, Scotland, PA1 2PN.)

RESOURCES FOR CHAPTER SEVEN
(CHRISTIAN COMMUNITY LIFE)

a. Cho, Paul Yonggi; with Harold Hostetler; *Successful Home Cell Groups*, Logos International, Plainfield, NJ 07060, 1981, USA, 176 pages. Home cell groups bring revival, every member participation, and church growth. Drawing on personal experience, Cho has excellent chapters on problems he found in developing cell groups, how he overcame them, using groups for evangelism and how to begin home cell groups. Very practical! (Distributed in Britain by Anfield Music Ltd., 201 Monument Rd., Edgbaston, Birmingham B16 8UU.)

b. Clark, Stephen (ed.); *Patterns of Christian Community (A Statement of Community Order)*, Servant Publ., PO Box 8617, Ann Arbor, MI 48107, USA, 1984, 86 pages. Written from practical experience, excellent chapters on basic commitment, functioning as a Body, elders, peace and discipline, government and personal direction, unity and disagreement and patterns of life. (Available in Britain from Redemptorist Publications Book Service, Chawton, Alton, Hants., GU34 3HQ.)

c. *Commonlife (Concerning Christian Community and Renewal)*, Grace Haven Ministry Center, Route 10, Woodville Road, Mansfield, Ohio 44903. Excellent practical quarterly journal focusing on one area of renewal each issue (such as one of the chapters of this manual). Articles drawn from churches committed to the practice of Christian community. (No precise British equivalent exists, but you might like to investigate *Renewal*, monthly from 6 The White House, Beacon Rd., Crowborough, East Sussex, TN6 1AB.)

d. Gish, Arthur G.; *Living in Christian Community*, Herald Press, Scottdale, PA, 15683, 1979, 379 pages. Deeply insightful and challenging. Chapters on community as faithful, sharing, discerning, discipling, voluntary (membership), organized, worshipping, nonconforming and witnessing. Footnotes, Bibliography, Indexes.

e. Harville, Sue; *Reciprocal Living (A Biblical Answer to the Fellowship Crisis)*, Worldteam, PO Box 343038, Coral Gables, FL 33134, USA, 1976. Outstanding careful study of all the one anothers of the New Testament, using the Greek and providing study/ teaching helps.
   (An alternative available in Britain is Getz, Gene; *Building Up One Another*, distributed by Scripture Press, Amersham, Bucks.)

f. Jackson, Dave & Neta; *Living Together in a World Falling Apart (A Handbook on Christian Community)*, Creation House, 499

Gundersen Drive, Carol Stream, IL 60188, USA, 1974, 304 pages. Drawing from their practical experience at Reba Place. Excellent frank discussion of the ins and outs of extended households and communal-type living. Closes with describing selected Christian communities, annotated bibliography. (More easily available in Britain is Banks, Robert and Julia, *The Home Church*, distributed by Lion Publishing.)

g. O'Connor, Elizabeth; *Call to Commitment*, Harper & Row Publ., 10 East 53rd St., New York, NY 10022, USA, 1963, 205 pages. The exciting story of the renowned Church of the Savior in Washington, D.C. in its development of community and mission groups. Deeply challenging.

h. McBride, Neal; *The Adult Class; Caring for Each Other*, Int'l Center for Learning, PO Box 1650, Glendale, CA, 91209, 1977, 31 pages. Excellent on starting or strengthening caring groups; summarized as a chapter in *Creative Bible Learning for Adults*, pp. 169–181, also published by ICL. (In Britain, a partial alternative might be Bigelow, Jim; *Love has Come Again*, published by Marshalls; or Copley, Derek and Nancy; *Building with Bananas*, from Paternoster Press.)

i. Reba Place Fellowship, (headed by Virgil Vogt) 620 Madison, Evanston, IL 60202; Phone: 312/869–0660. Outstanding Christian community of long standing, has worked through very practically many of the challenges of Christian community. Mennonite tradition. (In Britain, contact Post Green Community Trust, 56 Dorchester Rd., Lytchett Minster, Poole, Dorset, BH16 6JE. Not Mennonite.)

j. *Sojourners* (An Independent Christian Monthly), PO Box 29272, Washington, DC 20017, USA, Phone: 202/636–3637. A radical magazine that grows out of a radical Christian community (previously called Post-American). Strongly committed to justice, peace and political conscience. Never fails to be provocative, challenging, disturbing. Excellent monthly bibliographies on topics related to the chapter titles of this manual as well as various political issues like liberation, feminism, economics and third-world development.

k. Snyder, Howard; *The Community of the King*, InterVarsity Press, Downers Grove, IL 60515, USA, 1978, 215 pages. Easy to read, excellent introduction to Kingdom community with three main sections: perceiving the Kingdom, understanding the Kingdom community, and embodying the Kingdom community. Especially good insights into leadership gifts, church structures and unity. Very helpful outline. Footnotes, bibliography, text index

and Scripture index. (Distributed in Britain by Send the Light
Trust, Bromley, Kent.)
1. Vanier, Jean; *Community & Growth (Our Pilgrimage Together)*,
Griffin Press Limited, 461 King Street West, Toronto M5V 1K7,
Canada, 1979, 214 pages. Deep insights from community life in
France about unity, covenant, growth, nourishment, authority
and gifts, welcoming new people, meetings, every day life and
celebrations. (Distributed in Britain by Darton, Longman and
Todd.)

RESOURCES FOR CHAPTER EIGHT
(MINISTRY, SPIRITUAL GIFTS)

a. Clinton, Bobby; *Spiritual Gifts*, Horizon House Publishers,
Beaver Lodge, Alberta, Canada, 1975, 152 pages. Extremely well
organized and detailed explanation of each of the gifts with
careful attention to the Greek; filled with practical helps for
discovering gifts and guidelines for developing specific gifts.
b. Cosby, Gordon; *Handbook for Mission Gifts*, available from The
Potter's House, 1658 Columbia Road, N.W., Washington, DC
20009, USA, 1974, 182 pages. After giving a history of Church of
the Savior which Cosby pastors, chapters focus on creating
mission groups, a structure to facilitate them, sermons to
encourage them and case studies of how people have found their
calling or mission through Church of the Savior. Also a useful
annotated bibliography.
c. Haney, David: *The Idea of the Laity*, Zondervan Publ. House,
Grand Rapids MI 49506, USA, 1973, 188 pages. Very practical and
challenging; focuses on mobilizing the laity, bringing the
Kingdom to every area of our lives. Written as a group-study
guide, each chapter begins with a Bible study passage and
concludes with discussion questions and exercises. Shares how
small groups work in his church.
d. Howard, David; *By the Power of the Holy Spirit*, InterVarsity
Press, Downers Grove, IL 60515, 1973, 172 pages. Good chapters
on the various functions of the Spirit: baptizing, infilling,
empowering, sending (for missions), unifying, gifting and
helping us to walk well. A special focus on the issue of tongues,
affirming them for today, and noting biblical guidelines for their
usage.
e. O'Connor, Elizabeth; *Eighth Day of Creation (Gifts and Creativity)*,
Word Books Publ., Waco, Texas USA, 1971, 115 pages. Drawn
from the Church of the Savior; practical; challenging encouragement for discovering gifts, pursuing callings and forming mission

groups. Helpful exercises. A long appendix of stimulating quotes for reflection. See also O'Connor's *Call to Commitment* and *Journey Inward Journey Outward* (Both Harper and Row).

f. Snyder, Howard; *The Problem of Wineskins*, InterVarsity Press, Downers Grove, IL 60515, 1975, 214 pages. Examines the old wineskins of church buildings and super-pastors; highlights the Spirit's role and biblical structures for renewal, particularly gifts and small groups. Reviews church structures throughout history. (In Britain, see Snyder's book *New Wineskins*, published by Marshall's.)

g. Robinson, James; *New Growth (What the Holy Spirit wants to do for you)*, Tyndale House Publ., Wheaton, IL 60187, USA, 1978, 109 pages. Good chapters on the Holy Spirit, his baptism, fullness, fruit and gifts. Explains and describes the differences between motivational, ministerial and manifestational gifts. These same categories are taught by many others including Bill Gothard.

h. Stedman, Ray; *Body Life (The Church Comes Alive)*, Regal Books Division, Glendale, CA 91209, USA, 1972, 149 pages. Carefully explains Eph. 4. with a chapter given to each phrase of v. 12, concluding with an explanation of how this teaching has transformed his church.

Many of these books are not easy to find in Britain (although Zondervan books are imported by M. McCall Barbour, George IV Bridge, Edinburgh, and Word Books are distributed by Word (UK) Ltd., Milton Keynes). More accessible may be:

Calver, Clive; *The Holy Spirit*, SU — a careful short guide to the Spirit's ministry;

Green, Michael; *I Believe in the Holy Spirit*, Hodder and Stoughton — an overall survey of the doctrine and operations of the Holy Spirit;

Packer, J. I.; *Keep in Step With the Spirit*, Hodder and Stoughton — a thorough analysis of the main theological positions Christians have adopted towards the work of the Holy Spirit, and an exposition of the Scriptural statements;

Wagner, Peter; *Your Spiritual Gifts Can Help Your Church Grow*, Gospel Light/Regal Books — how to find and develop your spiritual gifts.

RESOURCES FOR CHAPTER NINE (FAMILY LIFE)

a. Christenson, Larry; *The Christian Family*, Bethany Fellowship, 6820 Auto Club Road, Mineapolis, MN 55438, USA, 1970, 216

pages. Outstanding biblical and practical focus on 1) God's order for the family and, 2) practising the presence of Jesus in the family. Study guide available for groups. Also available in cassette form.
(In Britain, available from Nova Distribution Ltd., 29 Milber Industrial Estate, Newton Abbot, Devon.)

b. Dobson, James; *Dare to Discipline*, Tyndale House Publ., 336 Gundersen Drive, Wheaton, IL 60187, USA, 1970, 198 pages. Classic in the field. Written for parents and teachers. Focuses on healthy consistent discipline and teaching respect and responsibility to children. (In Britain the book is published by Kingsway.) Also by Dobson is another excellent book, *Hide or Seek, Self-Esteem for the Child* (Fleming H. Revell Co., 1974). (British publisher: Hodder and Stoughton.)

c. Elliot, Elisabeth; *The Mark of a Man*, Fleming H. Revell Co., Old Tappan, NJ, 1981, 176 pages; and, *Let Me Be a Woman*, Tyndale House Publ., Wheaton, IL 60187, 1976, 190 pages. Strong well-written thinking rewarding the mystery of masculinity and femininity. Excellent for building manliness and womanliness respectively. (In Britain the first title is published by Hodder and Stoughton; the second is no longer available.)
Other books available in Britain, on the subject of feminine identity, include:
Evans, Mary; *Woman in the Bible*, Paternoster Press — an exhaustive survey of the Scriptural evidence;
Langley, Myrtle; *Equal Woman*, Marshall's — which includes a historical analysis of the church's pronouncements about femininity;
Storkey, Elaine; *What's Right With Feminism?*, SPCK — a survey of contemporary ideas and a Biblical critique.

d. *Fathergram* started by Charles Simpson, available from PO Box Z, Mobile, Alabama 36616. Free subscription (contributions encouraged). Monthly four-page newsletter for fathers. Designed for the busy father, full of practical tips and biblical insights. Books, tapes, programmes and other resources are regularly reviewed.

e. Gaither, Gloria and Dobson, Shirley; *Let's Make a Memory*, Word Books, Waco, Texas, 1983, USA, 223 pages. Great ideas for building family traditions and togetherness arranged in sections under holidays, seasons, places and people. Draws on the experience of well-known Christians. Extensive bibliography.

f. Heidebrecht, Paul and Rohrback, Jerry; *Fathering a Son*, Moody Bible Institute, Chicago, IL, USA, 1979, 200 pages. Focuses on how to teach children independence, security, self-discipline, spiritual growth, sexual understanding and preparation for adult living. Very practical. Appendix of parent handbooks and children's literature. (Distributed in Britain by Scripture Press, Amersham, Bucks.)

g. LaHaye, Tim and Beverly; *The Act of Marriage (The Beauty of Sexual Love)*, Zondervan Publ. House, Grand Rapids, MI 49506, USA, 1976, 294 pages. Excellent, frank and practical. Shares male and female perspectives on lovemaking and helping one's partner enjoy lovemaking; gives good family planning advice. Bibliography. (Published in Britain by Marshall's.)

h. MacDonald, Gail; *High Call, High Privilege*, Tyndale House Publ., Wheaton, IL 60187, USA, 234 pages. A pastor's wife shares the joy and fulfillment she has found in her five major roles: daughter of God, woman, wife, mother and leader. Excellent appendix on hospitality. Extensive bibliography ordered by topics.

i. Schaeffer, Edith; *What is a Family?*, Fleming H. Revell Co., Old Tappan, NJ, 1975, 255 pages. Eleven chapters vividly highlight the many life-giving functions of a family such as the birthplace of creativity, a formation centre for human relationships, a shelter in the time of storm, an economic unit, an educational control and a museum of memories. (Published in Britain by Highland Books.)

RESOURCES FOR CHAPTER TEN (LOCAL EVANGELISM)

a. Aldrich, Joseph C.; *Life-Style Evangelism (Crossing Traditional Boundaries to Reach the Unbelieving World)*, Multnomah Press, Portland, OR 97266, USA, 1981, 246 pages. Focuses on evangelism as sharing an attractive beautiful way of life, church based evangelism and neighbourhood evangelism. Excellent book filled with practical illustrations. Scripture index and subject index. (Published in Britain by Marshall's.)

b. Chantry, Walter J.; *Today's Gospel, Authentic or Synthetic?* The Banner of Truth Trust, London, 1970. Challenging discussion of the rich young ruler, indicating that much of today's gospel presentations are not 'authentic'. Outlines key points to have an authentic 'gospel'.

c. Kennedy, James D.; *Evangelism Explosion (The Coral Ridge Program for Lay Witness)*, Fort Lauderdale, FL, USA, 1970. Outstanding training manual for mobilizing people in evangelism. Readily transferable techniques. Excellent well-proven training methods. Teaches people to share their faith, give their testimony, handle objections, illustrate the Gospel meaningfully for nonchristians — all through practical experiences of witnessing to people with someone who already knows how to do it well. (For information about Evangelism Explosion in Britain, contact Evangelism Explosion (UK), 228 Shirley Rd., Southampton, SO1 3HR.)

Other useful books available in Britain include:
Jim Petersen, , *Evangelism as a Lifestyle* (Navpress, available through Scripture Press, Amersham, Bucks.) — a challenging analysis of how much evangelism misses its target by being directed at the already-Christianized rather than the real world;
Rebecca Manley Pippert, *Out of the Salt Shaker* (IVP) — explanations of, and remedies for, the reluctance Christians often feel about being involved in evangelism;
David Watson, *I Believe in Evangelism* (Hodder and Stoughton) — magnificently comprehensive doctrinal outline which succeeds also in being extremely practical.

---

d. Good books on church growth principles include Wagner, Peter: *Strategies for Growth*, MARC Europe; Gibbs, Eddie: *I Believe in Church Growth* (Hodder in Great Britain, Eerdmans in USA); McGavran, Donald, and Arn, Win: *How to Grow a Church*, Gospel Light; Pointer, Roy: *Why Do Churches Grow?*, Marshall's.

RESOURCES FOR CHAPTER ELEVEN (MISSION STRATEGY)

a. Missionary methodology

1) Allen, Roland; *Missionary Methods: St. Paul's or Ours?*, Eerdmans Publ. Co., Grand Rapids, MI, 1962, 189 pages. Based on missionary work in the early 20th century, this book and his others challenge much of contemporary missions thinking. (Distributed in Britain by Paternoster Press.)
2) Journals: *Evangelical Missions Quarterly*, published quarterly by Evangelical Missions Information Service, Inc., Box 794, Wheaton, IL 60187 (practically oriented); and, *Missiology*, (Continuing Practical Anthropology), published quarterly by the American Society of Missiology, 135 N. Oakland Ave., Pasadena, CA 91101 (a little more scholarly).

3) Hesselgrave, David J.; *Planting Churches Cross-Culturally (A Guide for Home and Foreign Missions)*, Baker Book House, Grand Rapids, MI 49506, USA, 1980, 462 pages. Outstanding explanation of a ten-phase Pauline church planting cycle drawn from Acts 13ff. Extensive bibliography, subject index and Scripture index.

4) Kornfield, David E.; 'Apostles are for Today,' *Global Prayer Digest*, PO Box WEF, Wheaton, IL 60189, USA, November, 1985, 5 pages. Deals with biblical basis, historical basis, and pragmatic basis for a church-planting gift/calling. More extensive 15 page paper available from the author.

5) Mayers, Marvin K.; *Christianity Confronts Culture (A Strategy for Cross-Cultural Evangelism)*, Zondervan, Grand Rapids, MI 49506, USA, 1974, 348 pages. This, or something like it, is a must for all missionaries. Major sections focus on 1) acceptance of the person (chapters on trust, self-acceptance, accepting others, mutual respect), 2) what makes cultural groups hold together and function, 3) fitting into other cultures, 4) effective ministry, and 5) case studies in biculturalism illustrating almost every chapter. Each chapter includes discussion questions and group activities or exercises. Bibliography and index.

6) Mellis, Charles J.; *Committed Communities (Fresh Streams for World Missions)*, William Carey Library, 533 Hermosa Street, South Pasadena, CA 91030, 1976, 138 pages. Outstanding study of the structures that God has used in mission work through the centuries. Describes a half dozen present-day missions movements that follow the historical method of committed communities.

In Britain, foreign books on mission methodology are sometimes available by import; two sources of information are:

British Church Growth Association, 59 Warrington Rd., Harrow HA1 1SZ; and Evangelical Missionary Alliance, 186 Kennington Park Road, London, SE11 4BT.

b. Mobilizing the local church in missions

The Association of Church Missions Committees, PO Box ACMC, Wheaton, IL 60189, USA (Phone 312/260–1660). Excellent tools, staff and conferences for helping a church's mission committee. (In Britain, contact the Evangelical Missionary Alliance — see preceding paragraph.)

c. Prayer resources

World Evangelical Fellowship's *Evangelical World*, PO Box WEF, Wheaton, IL 60189 (a small magazine that features news of missions and provides a prayer guide for unreached peoples); and *The Church Around the World*, PO Box 1911, Marion, OH 43302 (a monthly news bulletin to distribute to church members).

Patrick Johnstone's book *Operation World* (Send The Light Trust, Bromley, Kent, and PO Box 28, Waynesboro, GA 30830, USA) offers statistics and thumbnail sketches illustrating the spiritual state of every country in the world.

d. Preparation for missions:

1) Brewster, Thomas & Brewster, Elizabeth; *LAMP, Language Acquisition Made Practical (A Comprehensive 'How-to' Book for Learning Any Language)*, Lingua House, 915 West Jackson, Colorado Springs, CO 80907, USA, 395 pages. Based on cultural immersion. Excellent!
2) Missionary Internship, PO Box 457, Farmington, MI 48024, USA. Phone: 313/474–9110. Outstanding training programme, used by many missions to help in orienting prospective missionaries.

e. Study Centers:

Study programmes in missiology can be found at many Christian graduate schools. In addition to this, schools or centers that focus on missions include:

1) Four North American Centers for World Mission (for further information write to the U.S. Center for World Mission, 1605 Elizabeth St., Pasadena, CA 91104, USA or call 818/797–1111).
2) The Overseas Ministry Study Center, PO Box 2057, Ventnor, NJ 08406, USA. Phone: 609/823–6671. Focuses on continuing education for missionaries.
3) Missions Advance Research and Communication Center (MARC, a ministry of World Vision Int'l, 919 West Huntington Drive, Monrovia, CA 91016. Statistics on the church and missions worldwide. (British address: MARC Europe, Cosmos House, 6 Homesdale Rd., Bromley, Kent, BR2 9EX.)
4) The Lausanne Committee for World Evangelization (LCWE), PO Box 2308, Charlotte, NC 28211. An interdenominational, international movement encouraging missions and churches in evangelization worldwide.

(In Britain, All Nations Christian College, Easneye, Ware, Herts., SG12 8LX, has a special emphasis on preparing students for missionary service. There are several short-term schemes to give Christians a 'taste' of missionary service, perhaps as a prelude to full-time activity; organisers include:

Horizons, Glanmor Rd., Llanelli, Dyfed, Wales, SA15 2LU; and

Operation Mobilisation, The Quinta, Weston Rhyn, Oswestry, Shropshire, SY1 07L.
A mission study centre specializing in the Muslim world is run by People International, PO Box 26, Tunbridge Wells, Kent, TN1 1AA — who also supply information and training for churches.)

RESOURCES FOR CHAPTER TWELVE (SOCIAL ACTION)

a. *Development Training for Practitioners* (Second Edition), edited by Bryant Myers, available from World Vision Int'l, 919 W. Huntington Drive, Monrovia, CA 91016. Addresses and descriptions of 26 agencies, at least half of which are evangelical and a third of which are in the Third World. World Vision has offices in most developing countries and an excellent quarterly development journal called *Together*. Some agencies with outstanding training programmes that were overlooked in Myer's book follow:
   1) Food for the Hungry (headed by Tetsunao Yamamori); information on their simulated third world villages as training settings can be obtained from 7729 E. Greenway Road, Scottsdale, AZ 85260.
   2) Harvest (headed by Bob Moffitt), 3080 N. Civic Center Plaza, Suite 10, Scottsdale, AR 85251, USA; phone 602/945–2300. Specializes in partnering specific U.S. churches with specific Third World churches. Uses Lk. 2:52 as the basis for a four-pronged development process.
   3) World Relief (headed by Jerry Ballard), PO Box WRC, Wheaton, IL 60187, USA; phone 312/665–0235. Works through the national alliances of evangelicals around the world. Excellent one-week training course for community development facilitators (in Spanish and English).
b. Dorr, Donal; *Option for the Poor (A Hundred Years of Vatican Social Teaching)*, Orbis Books, Maryknoll, NY 10545, USA, 1983, 328 pages. An evangelical reading this can see how far we have come in the social action pilgrimage the Catholics have made to date and where we may be heading! Fascinating and insightful.
c. Cizik, Richard (ed.); *The High Cost of Indifference*, Regal Books, Gospel Light Publications, 2300 Knoll Drive, Ventura, CA 93003. Evangelical experts on each of these issues clarify them and give positive practical steps for working to solve the problems: nuclear arms, media bias, educational values, pornography, abortion, poverty, religious freedom, crime and prison reform.
d. Perkins, John; *With Justice for All*, Regal Books, Ventura, CA

93006, 1982, 211 pages. Following his earlier book *Let Justice Roll Down*. Highlights key principles learned through twenty years of church involvement in overcoming poverty and racism. Three major sections focus on relocation, reconciliation and redistribution. Radically biblical!

e. National Integrity Forum, PO Box 81150, Mobile, Alabama, 36608, USA. Puts out a monthly newsletter focusing on a biblical perspective on current public issues. Its objectives include informing and educating Christians about issues especially relevant to them, working toward the passing of sound legislation, and developing a prophetic standard and model of God's ways. Francis Schaeffer, John Whitehead and R.J. Rushdoony particularly express the Forum's values and perspectives.

f. Samuel, V., and Sugden, C. (eds), *The Church in Response to Human Need*, Eerdmans Publ. Co. (see following item), 1987, 268 pages. Compendium of key articles on social involvement written for the Wheaton '83 conference on the church, and the Wheaton '83 Statement, 'Transformation: The Church in Response to Human Need'. (Published in Britain by Regnum Books.)

g. Scott, Waldron; *Bring Forth Justice*, Eerdmans Publ. Co., 255 Jefferson Ave. S.E., Grand Rapids, MI4 49503, USA, 1980, 318 pages. Examines mission both historically and biblically, then offers constructive criticism and practical suggestions for how to blend mission, disciple-making and social justice. Theologically sound, yet very provocative! (Published in Britain by Marshall's.)

h. *Sojourners* (An Independent Christian Monthly), PO Box 29272, Washington, DC 20017, USA; Phone: 202/636–3637. A radical magazine that grows out of a radical Christian community. Strongly committed to justice, peace and political conscience. Never fails to be provocative, challenging, disturbing. Excellent monthly bibliographies on various political issues such as liberation, feminism, economics and third-world development.

In Britain, the following bodies can supply useful information and research findings, or training courses of different kinds:

Jubilee Centre, 114 Barton Rd., Cambridge, CB3 9LH;

London Institute for Contemporary Christianity, St. Peter's Church, Vere St., London W1M 9HP;

Shaftesbury Project, 79 Maid Marian Way, Nottingham, NG1 6AE.

RESOURCES FOR CHAPTER THIRTEEN (SPIRITUAL WARFARE)

a. Basham, Don; *Can A Christian have a Demon?*, Whitaker House, 504 Laurel Drive, Monroeville, PA 15146, USA, 1971, 94 pages.

Examines the arguments against Christians being demonized, examines Scripture, concludes that Christians can experience demonic affliction. Guidelines for deliverance. Many practical experiences and testimonies.

b. Bubeck, Mark I.; *The Adversary (The Christian Versus Demon Activity)*, Moody Press, Chicago, IL 60610, USA, 1975, 160 pages. Topics include a biblical perspective of warfare, the flesh, the world, the Sword of the Spirit, aggressive prayer, bold confrontation, facing Satan's kingdom, hindrances to revival, tools for warfare, being unafraid, warfare through oneness. Excellent examples of warfare prayers! Very practical, bibliography. The sequel, *Overcoming the Adversary*, deals with each element of the 'armour' in Eph. 6.

c. Lahaye, Tim; *How to Win Over Depression*, Zondervan Publishing House, Grand Rapids, MI 49506, USA, 1974. Writes of the causes and cures for depression. Gives guidelines for avoiding or preventing depression; outlines how to help a depressed friend. (A British alternative title could by Myra Chave Jones; *Coping with Depression*, published by Lion.)

d. Seamands, David; *Healing for Damaged Emotions*, Victor Press, Division of Scripture Press, Wheaton, IL, 60187, 1981. (Victor books are distributed in Britain by Scripture Press, Amersham, Bucks. Or a British alternative title could be Derek Copley and Mary Austin; *My Chains Fell Off*, Paternoster Press.)

e. Wilson, James I.; *The Principles of War (A Strategy for Group and Personal Evangelism)*, Wallace Press, Chicago, IL 60610, USA, 1967, 68 pages. A superb paperback from a military perspective discussing the warfare principles of objective, offensive, concentration, mobility, security, surprise, cooperation, communication, economy of force, pursuit and obedience.

f. Wimber, John; with Springer, Kevin; *Power Evangelism*, Harper and Row Publications, 10 East 53rd Street, New York, NY 10022, USA. (Together with its companion title *Power Healing*, this book is published in Britain by Hodder and Stoughton.) Explains both biblically and practically how the Kingdom of God is made real; stresses that people need to come under the power of the Gospel as well as hear its truth. A compelling presentation of signs and wonders today, a serious study of Scripture, valuable appendices supporting his thesis drawn from church history. More information on his movement and teaching is available from Vineyard Ministries International, PO Box 1359, Placentia, CA 92670, USA; phone 714/996–4340. (A more cautious perspective than Wimber's, available in Britain, is Donald Bridge's *Signs and Wonders*, published by IVP. Colin Brown's *Miracles and the Critical Mind*, and his shorter *That You May Believe: Miracles*

Then and Now, are both published by Paternoster Press in Britain
and Eerdmans in USA.)
Other useful resources available in Britain include:
Green, Michael; *I Believe in Satan's Downfall*, Hodder and
Stoughton — a doctrinal survey which includes valuable practical
ideas about ministering in a context of spiritual warfare; and
Twelftree, Graham; *Christ Triumphant*, Hodder and Stoughton —
an examination of the need for exorcism today.

HOW TO END THE PLANNING PROCESS
IN WORSHIP

> THIS WILL HELP YOU WITH THE
> CONCLUSION OF *STEP E* OF THE
> PLANNING PROCESS (SEE P. 22)

CHAPTER ONE (THE KINGDOM OF GOD)

Our Father in Heaven, may Your holy name be honoured. May
Your Kingdom come in and through us; Your will be done in our
midst — as it is in Heaven! To You who sit on the throne be blessing
and honour and glory and dominion now and forever. Amen.

Come, Thou Almighty King

Come, Thou Almighty King,
    Help us Thy name to sing,
Help us to praise;
    Father, all glorious,
O'er all victorious,
    Come, and reign over us,
Ancient of Days.

Come, Thou Incarnate Word,
    Gird on Thy mighty sword,
Our prayer attend.
    Come, and Thy people bless,
And give Thy word success;
    Spirit of holiness,
On us descend.

Come, Holy Comforter,
    Thy sacred witness bear
In this glad hour:
    Thou who almighty art,
Now rule in every heart,
    Never from us depart,
Spirit of power.

To Thee, great One in Three,
    The highest praises be,
Hence evermore!
    Thy sovereign majesty
May we in glory see,
    And to eternity
Love and adore.

                (*Anon.*)

CHAPTER TWO (PRAYER AND DEVOTIONAL LIFE)

May the Lord fill you with the confidence that he is changing the world through your prayers. May his power be poured out on you as never before! To him be all the honour and glory, wisdom and power for all he's done and all he's intending to do!

Speak, Lord, in the Stillness

Speak, Lord, in the stillness
    While I wait on Thee;
Hushed my heart to listen
    In expectancy.

Speak, O blessed Master,
    In this quiet hour,
Let me see Thy face, Lord,
    Feel Thy tough of power.

For the words Thou speakest,
    'They are life' indeed;
Living Bread from Heaven,
    Now my spirit feed!

All to Thee is yielded,
    I am not my own;
Blissful, glad surrender,
    I am Thine alone.

Fill me with the knowledge
Of Thy glorious will;
All Thine own good pleasure
In my life fulfill.

(*E. May Grimes*)

CHAPTER THREE (CORPORATE WORSHIP)

Lord Jesus Christ, Head of the Church, with real sadness we confess to having a spirit of independence from You. We have attempted to do so much of Your work in our own strength. We repent of the lack of adoration in our personal devotional times and in our corporate worship services. We also repent of thinking that our primary function is, like Martha, to rush about in Your work rather than, like Mary, to sit at Your feet. We confess that we quickly and easily forget that we were created for the purpose of glorifying and enjoying You forever. We cry out to you to renew our adoration and help us have a continually growing concept of You, O High and Lofty One who inhabit Eternity.

Lord, we lift our hearts to You in the *Te Deum* with which your saints have praised You down through the centuries.

We praise Thee, O God:
We acknowledge Thee to be the Lord.
All the earth doth worship Thee, the Father everlasting.
To Thee all angels cry aloud; the heavens and all the powers therein.
To Thee cherubim and seraphim continually do cry;
Holy, Holy, Holy, Lord God of Sabaoth.
Heaven and earth are full of the majesty of Thy glory.
The glorious company of the apostles praise Thee.
The goodly fellowship of the prophets praise Thee.
The noble army of martyrs praise Thee.
The holy Church, throughout all the world, doth acknowlege Thee,
The Father of an infinite majesty
Thine adorable, true, and only Son;
Also the Holy Spirit, the Comforter . . .
Day by day we magnify Thee;
And we worship Thy name ever, world without end . . .
Amen.

CHAPTER FOUR (STEWARDSHIP)

We acknowledge, O Lord, that there is so little in us that is lovable. So often we are not lovely in our thoughts, in our words, or in our deeds. And yet Thou dost love us still, with a love that neither ebbs nor flows, a love that does not grow weary, but is constant — year after year, age after age.

O God, may our hearts be opened to that love today. With bright skies above us, the fields and woods and gardens bursting with new life and beauty, how can we fail to respond? With the clear notes of bird songs challenging us to praise, with every lowly shrub and blooking tree catching new life and beauty, our hearts indeed would proclaim Thee Lord, and we would invite Thee to reign over us truly Thine own. May Thy healing love invade our inmost hearts, healing sorrow, pain, frustration, defeat, and despair.

May this day create within us a love for Thee of stronger stuff than vague sentimentality — a love which seeks to know Thy will and do it. So grant that this day of hallowed remembrance may be the beginning of a new way of life for each of us, a new kind of living that shall be the best answer to the confusion and to the challenge of evil in our day. This we ask in Jesus' name. Amen.

Peter Marshall

When I Survey the Wondrous Cross

When I survey the wondrous cross
    On which the Prince of glory died
My richest gain I count but loss,
    And pour contempt on all my pride.

Forbid it, Lord, that I should boast,
    Save in the death of Christ my God;
All the vain things that charm me most,
    I sacrifice them to His blood.

See, from His head, His hands, His feet,
    Sorrow and love flow mingled down:
Did e'er such love and sorrow meet,
    Or thorns compose so rich a crown?

Were the whole realm of nature mine,
    That were an offering far too small;
Love so amazing, so divine,
    Demands my soul, my life, my all.

(Isaac Watts)

CHAPTER FIVE (TEACHING AND STUDY OF THE WORD)

We thank You, Lord, for the power of Your Word to affect our lives — to challenge our deepest emotions, kindle our enthusiasm to a blaze, soothe us with the calm of Your presence, humble us and teach us Your wisdom. And we are conscious that Your Word is worthless to us unless that same Holy Spirit who inspired it and has safeguarded it through the centuries will also illumine our hearts and minds so that in Your Word we detect Your voice.

Break Thou the Bread of Life

Break Thou the bread of life,
    Dear Lord, to me,
As Thou didst break the loaves
    Beside the sea;
Beyond the sacred page
    I seek Thee, Lord;
My spirit pants for Thee,
    O living Word.

Bless Thou the truth, dear Lord,
    To me, to me,
As Thou didst bless the bread
    By Galilee;
Then shall all bondage cease,
    All fetters fall:
And I shall find my peace,
    My all in all.

Thou art the bread of life,
    O Lord, to me;
Thy holy Word the truth
    That saveth me;
Give me to eat and live
    With Thee above;
Teach me to love Thy truth,
    For Thou art love.

O send Thy Spirit, Lord,
    Now unto me,
That He may touch my eyes
    And make me see;
Show me the truth concealed
    Within Thy Word,
For in Thy book revealed
    I see Thee, Lord.

(*Mary A. Lathbury with Alexander Groves*)

CHAPTER SIX (DISCIPLING AND PASTORAL CARE)

Lord, we marvel yet again that You took on flesh and blood and
became like us. Praise be to You for sharing Your very life and grace
with us in human form. Thank You for the gift of Your Spirit
inhabiting us and inhabiting those whom You have anointed and
gifted to be our leaders. Thank You, Lord, for Your pastoral care for
us. Thank You for expressing Your pastoral care through the leaders
You give us. Bless You, Lord, for understanding us so well. We
bless You for showing us Your love and serving leadership in
tangible flesh and blood ways. We marvel that You honour our
humanity so much. Thank You for the example You gave us, while
here on earth, of laying down our lives for one another.
O Great Shepherd of the sheep, we offer ourselves once again to
You. We offer ourselves not in some abstract spiritualized way, but
in committing ourselves to obey our leaders and submit to them as
they do to You. Help us to see You in them and to follow You truly.
Lord, strengthen them as they watch over our souls. Give them
grace to lead as You lead. We would follow them in such a way as to
bring them and You great joy. When they give an accounting for us
it may be with thanksgiving rather than sorrow. In Jesus' name,
Amen.

CHAPTER SEVEN (CHRISTIAN COMMUNITY LIFE)

Lord Jesus, we recognize that only You can help us to overcome our
selfishness and our differences with one another. We desperately
need You to bring us into being Your community. Please hear our
heart cry and lead us into an interdependent way of life. Lord, you
have given us the desire to live in community; now we pray, give us
the grace to do so and the wisdom to know how to grow in that
direction. Lord, we ask this not for our sakes, but for Yours. May
Your name be glorified. May You be exalted! May the beauty and
joy of Your unity be so evident in us that people are drawn into Your
life. In Jesus' Name. Amen.

CHAPTER EIGHT (MINISTRY, SPIRITUAL GIFTS)

There's a gift of God in me that his Spirit wants to free
    For his use in blessing others with his grace.
And the gift he gave to me, he gave to others differently
    Each to serve the other with a special grace.

So together we may know every blessing he bestows,
But we need each other's portion of the grace.
Lord, take my gift and make it free,
let your blessing flow through me;
Use my portion in the fulness of your grace.

(May be sung to the tune of 'Five hundred miles')

CHAPTER NINE (FAMILY LIFE)

O give us homes built firm upon the Saviour,
Where Christ is Head and Counsellor and Guide;
Where every child is taught his love and favour
And gives his heart to Christ, the crucified:
How sweet to know that though his footsteps waver
His faithful Lord is walking by his side!

O give us homes with godly fathers, mothers,
Who always place their hope and trust in him;
Whose tender patience turmoil never bothers,
Whose calm and courage trouble cannot dim;
A home where each finds joy in serving others,
And love still shines, the days be dark and grim.

O Lord, our God, our homes are Thine forever!
We trust to Thee their problems, toil and care;
Their bonds of love no enemy can sever
If Thou art always Lord and Master there:
Be Thou the centre of our least endeavour
Be Thou our Guest, our hearts and homes to share.
Amen.

Barbara B. Hart
(Can be sung to the tune of 'Finlandia')

A Christian Home

O give us homes built firm upon the Saviour,
Where Christ is Head and Counsellor and Guide;
Where every child is taught His love and favour
And gives his heart to Christ, the crucified:
How sweet to know that though his footsteps waver
His faithful Lord is walking by his side!

O give us homes with godly fathers, mothers.
　Who always place their hope and trust in Him;
Whose tender patience turmoil never bothers
　Whose calm and courage trouble cannot dim;
A home where each finds joy in serving others,
　And love still shines, though days be dark and grim.

O Lord, our God, our homes are Thine forever!
　We trust to Thee their problems, toil and care;
Their bonds of love no enemy can sever
　If Thou art always Lord and Master there:
Be Thou the centre of our least endeavour
　Be Thou our guest, our hearts and homes to share.

(Barbara B. Hart)

CHAPTER TEN (LOCAL EVANGELISM)

We confess, Lord of the harvest, that we have often been lethargic and cold in our concern for the those who do not know you. We hear You anew now telling us 'The harvest is plentiful, but the workers are few.' With tears over having grieved your Spirit, we beseech You to send out workers into Your harvest. We are fully aware that You are likely to answer our cry through burdening us further for the unsaved. We open our hearts to You that You might teach us to feel Your love, compassion and pain at the lostness of those around us. Open our eyes to see how distressed and downcast people are. And open our ears to hear the loneliness, despair, and cries for help that we have become accustomed to ignoring.

Lord, oh Lord, change our lives as only You can. Take us beyond feeling badly over our faithlessness, to a new way of life. We recognize we have let you down; but more than that, we repent of our old ways of thinking and living. Melt us. Mould us. Fill us. Use us. Change whatever You need to in us, we pray, that we might see people regularly coming into Your kingdom. In Jesus' name, Amen!

CHAPTER ELEVEN (MISSION STRATEGY)

Like Isaiah, we dwell in a world filled with darkness, death and distress. Yet we see You seated on a throne, high and exalted, and the train of Your robe fills the temple. We see the seraphim surrounding you in glorious praise, crying, 'Holy, holy, holy is the

Lord Almighty; the whole earth is full of Your glory!' And we realize anew that we are ruined; we are unclean and unworthy and apart from You, rightly damned. But we have been touched by the Master's hand, redeemed and cleansed by his blood. Our guilt is taken away and our sin atoned for.

Now we can hear what we did not hear before. We hear Your voice saying 'Whom shall I send? And who will go for us?' And we each answer 'Lord, here am I. Send me!'

Lord, we are all available for Your missionary work. We do not know in Your sovereign will who among us You may choose to send. But we say from our hearts, 'Speak, Lord, for Thy servant heareth.' Whether we are called to go or called to support those who go, we rejoice. We rejoice because we look forward in eager anticipation to gathering at Your glorious throne. There we will join the great multitude whom no one can count, from every nation, tribe, people and language. Wearing white robes and holding palm branches in our hands, we will cry out 'Salvation belongs to our God, who sits on the throne, and to the Lamb.' We will raise our hands — black, yellow, red, white and brown — and shout, 'To You belongs all authority and power, every status and domain! To You be all honour and glory, now and forever, Amen!'

CHAPTER TWELVE (SOCIAL ACTION)

Lord, let our hearts be broken with whatever breaks Your heart. We have closed our eyes and ears too long to the cires of the poor. Oh merciful God, forgive us! Forgive us for what we have done and even more for what we have failed to do. Be gracious to us; let us hear and see where we have previously been deaf and blind.

Lord, we want to know You. We want to know the fellowship of Your sufferings and be conformed to Your death. Show us how to be emptied of ourselves in becoming one with those who need You. Let our hands be Your hands, serving in Your stead. May Your justice roll down like water and Your mercy lift the burdens of the hurting. May our hands be hands of healing, changing lives through Your power. May Your Kingdom come, Your will be done on earth — through us — as it is in heaven.

Then will the poor exalt You and the oppressed raise his head once more! The fatherless and the widow will praise Your name! For You are their champion. You are not a man that You would forget them. Great is the Lord and greatly to be praised. Righteousness and mercy have met; justice and loving kindness are here. Your throne and Your kingdom will never be shaken. All glory and honour be to You, both now and forever, amen and amen!

CHAPTER THIRTEEN (SPIRITUAL WARFARE)

A mighty fortress is our God, a bulwark never failing;
Our helper He, amid the flood of mortal ills prevailing.
For still our ancient foe doth seek to work us woe;
His craft and power are great, and, armed with cruel hate,
On earth is not his equal.

Did we in our own strength confide, our striving would be
losing,
Were not the right Man on our side, the Man of God's
own choosing.
Dost ask who that may be? Christ Jesus, it is He;
Lord Sabaoth his name, from age to age the same,
And he must win the battle.

And though this world, with devils filled, should threaten to
undo us,
We will not fear, for God hath willed His truth to triumph
through us.
The prince of darkness grim — we tremble not for him;
His rage we can endure, for lo! his doom is sure;
One little word shall fell him.

That word above all earthly powers — no thanks to them —
abideth;
The Spirit and the gifts are ours through Him who with us
sideth.
Let goods and kindred go, this mortal life also;
The body they may kill; God's truth abideth still,
His kingdom is forever.

Martin Luther